BOMBS AWAY! Volume I

BOMBS AWAY!
Volume I

ANTHOLOGY OF B-24 AND B-17 BOMBING MISSIONS AND OTHER STORIES AND ILLUSTRATIONS RELATED TO THE LIFE, TIMES, PERSONNEL OF WORLD WAR II

RALPH WELSH, AUTHOR AND AGENT

Laura Joakimson, Editor

Contents

Book Review from the 8th AF News

June 2010 From Mark Copeland, editor of *8th AF News*, a publication of the 8th Air Force Historical Society

It seems like my reading time becomes more limited each day and that is why books like *WOW!—Anthology of B-24/8th Air Force/ World War II Stories* by Ralph Welsh are always appealing. This excellent collection spans many segments of the air during World War II. Packed with well over 160 short stories, this anthology collection is also well illustrated and is an excellent value.

Ralph Welsh is a World War II, 8th Air Force veteran that flew B-24s with the 448th Bomb Group at Seething, England. Mr. Welsh has compiled a fantastic collection of veteran accounts making the reader both laugh and cry. This book is a very entertaining read. It is one of the finest collections of first person veteran accounts this reviewer has ever seen. This book serves as an archival testament to the men who flew with the 8th Air Force during World War II. It is an outstanding work.

This reviewer congratulates Mr. Welsh for the effort, but even more so, thanks him for keeping the stories of the 'Mighty Eighth' alive for future generations. VERY HIGHLY RECOMMENDED.

Prologue

BOMBS AWAY! Volumes I and II are composed of wartime stories—many are aerial combat missions written by those who experienced them, several decades after the event. While the majority of stories are missions of the mighty Eighth, they include the experiences of an 18 year old foot soldier, from the Battle of the Bulge to meeting the Russians at the Elbe. I kept a diary of my 33 missions as pilot/commander of a B-24, recounted word-for-worried-word of a 24 year old experiencing deadly situations. There's a lot of World War II here written, not by historians, but by the actual participants. It's the number one raison d'etre of this effort. Should aerial and related war stories grab you, you'll love this book.

Many of the stories were gleaned with permission from the 2nd Air Division's *Journal* printed from 1960-2012.

The stories in this book were originally self-published and titled *WOW! An Anthology of B-24, 8th Air Force, & World War II Stories.* Industry professionals said to delete extraneous material and produce a history book of the mightiest air force ever and the individuals involved. Another reason for republishing is that I received laudatory notes and letters from scores of readers, male, female, young, old.

ON WITH THE STORIES!

GLOSSARY AND ABBREVIATIONS

Bn, battalion

CAVU, ceiling and visibility unlimited

CW, combat wing

DR, dead reckoning

FG, fighter group

IP, a point above ground from which a straight bomb run was made to a target

Mae West, life preserver

Mickey, radar

OLC, oak leaf cluster (subsequent earning of the same medal)

PFF, pathfinder radar

SQ, squadron

ZI, zone of interior, i.e., US

ack-ack guns – anti-aircraft guns

ball turret gunner – one of the most undesireable, dangerous positions. Under the aircraft. Checked to be sure bomb doors were closed and to verify the effectiveness of a bomb run.

bombsight – device for determining bombing target coordinates

buzz job – flying especially close to the ground

B-17 (Flying Fortress) (Fort) – American four-engine bomber

B-24 Liberator (Liberator) (Lib) – American WWII heavy bomber aircraft

B-26 (widow maker) – American medium two-engine bomber

Carpetbagger Operation – aerial supply of weapons et cetera to the French Resistance beginning January 4, 1944.

DFC – Distinguished Flying Cross Medal, an award for aerial heroism awarded to British and American flight personnel.

flak – anti-aircraft fire

Hawker – line of British WWII aircraft and successful bombers.

Horsa gliders – WWII British troop carrying glider.

Focke-Wulf Fw 190 (FW-190) – single engine WWII German fighter aircraft.

Knight's Cross – highest award in Nazi Germany for battlefield bravery.

LST – tank landing ship used when the shore was not secure.

Luftwaffe – aerial branch of Nazi German military.

Maquis – guerrilla bands of rural French resistance fighters. Known to assist downed American and RAF pilots.

Messerschmitt Bf 109 (ME-109) – WWII German aircraft that served as bomber escort, fighter bomber, ground level anti-aircraft et cetera.

Messerschmitt Me 262 Schwalbe/Sturmvogel –"Swallow" "Storm Bird" world's first operational jet-powered fighter aircraft.

"milk run" – an easy mission

MOS – Military Operation Specialty

Mosquito – British light bomber, fighter aircraft with two-man crew.

Nieuport 28 – French biplane fighter aircraft

nose gunner – front crewman operates machine gun turret in the "nose" of the plane, could have a dual role in navigation etc. and nose gun could be manned by pilots or copilots.

P-38 Lightning ("fork-tailed devil")– American airplane designed as a bombing interceptor and escort, also used for fighting and other purposes.

P-47 Thunderbolt – American heavy fighter aircraft, could carry half tonnage of a B-17 bomber, designed as an escort and fighter.

P-51 (mustang) – American single-seat fighter aircraft

Siegfried Line – WWI line of forts built by the Germans in northern France, built further during the 1930 opposite the French Maginot Line.

Sopwith Camel – British biplane fighter

Spitfire – British single-seat fighter aircraft, designed as an interceptor aircraft

strafing – shooting targets on the ground from low-flying aircraft, often but not necessarily accompanied by bombing.

Sutton harness – aviator's locking seatbelt, designed in WWI.

waist gunner – primary job to look for and fight enemy fighter planes. Danger of frostbite as the waist windows were open. At 200 mph, and fifty below zero the stream of air was dangerous.

The Roar That Gave

Them Hope

James M. Davis, 489th

Our duty as part of the Eighth Air Force during World War II was to drop bombs on German targets such as industry, airfields, transportation, communication facilities, and many other targets as well as to destroy the German Air Force. A terrific price was paid in men and planes.

It was forty-three years later that I discovered that we did much more than we were aware of at the time.

In 1987, my wife Jean and I attended the Second Air Division Association reunion in Norwich, England. After the reunion we flew to Switzerland to visit that country for a week. One day we took an all-day bus tour. About two o'clock in the afternoon we arrived at Bern. The tour director told us that we would have an hour of free time to do what we wanted to. There were about forty people on the bus. They were from all over the world, and I don't believe I heard English spoken. Jean and I decided that we would walk down the street and do some window shopping. We had walked about two blocks and were looking in a window when a gentleman approached and asked if we were on the same tour bus. I had seen him on the bus and told him we were.

He said, "I believe you are Americans." I told him that yes, we were from the United States. He said, "Pardon me, but I would like to visit with you," and suggested we go down the block to a sidewalk café where he would like to buy us a drink. We told him we would be happy to visit with him. We ordered our drinks and he asked what part of the United States we came from.

We told him we were from Texas, and he said he had always wanted to visit Texas because he had heard so much about it. He spoke good English with only a slight accent. He asked if we were tourists or on a business trip. We told him we were on vacation and had visited England for about a week to attend a reunion, and since we had never been to Switzerland we decided to make a visit before returning to the States.

During our conversation he asked what kind of a reunion we had attended in England. I told him I had been a member of the Eighth Air Force during World War II, and that we returned every four years or so to have a reunion. He asked me what I did during the war. I told him I had been a pilot of a B-24 and flew combat missions over Germany and the occupied countries of Western Europe. He paused for a moment before he arose from his chair, and with tears running down his cheeks, he put his arms around me and embraced me as I had never been embraced before. For a long time, he held me in his arms. Finally, with a broken voice he said, "Excuse me but I owe you so much. I owe you my life." He told me I was the first member of an aircrew that he had had the privilege to meet, and he felt so indebted to me and would like to explain why.

He was a young Jewish boy, sixteen years old, living with his family in Poland when the Germans invaded the country in September, 1939. He was taken prisoner and spent the rest of the war in various slave labor camps. He told me the only way they could survive from day to day was hearing the roar of the airplanes flying overhead. They had no knowledge of what was happening, but as long as they could hear the airplanes they had a ray of hope and it provided them the will to survive another day. The noise of the planes provided their only hope and communication from the free world.

After the war he returned to his home town in Poland. There was no home, no family, no kinfolks or friends. They had all been killed or destroyed during the war. He migrated to Israel and started a meat and sausage processing plant which was very successful. The reason he was in Switzerland was that he had gone to Frankfurt, Germany to attend a display of meat processing equipment by manufacturers from all over the world. He had debated for three years whether he could stand to go back to Germany, and at the last minute he decided to go, even though his family had begged him not to. When he arrived at Frankfurt and stepped off the plane into the terminal, he suddenly realized that he could not emotionally stand it, and rushed over to the airplane ticket desk and asked what was the next plane leaving Frankfurt. It happened to be a flight to Switzerland that was loading and had room. He had a day to lay over before he could get a flight home, so he decided to take the tour that we were on.

He asked us to go with him to Israel, where he had a lot of friends who would be just as happy to meet me. He showed us a picture of his daughter's wedding party. The party was made up of the highest government officials, including the leader of Israel, the defense minister and all of the cabinet members. He assured us that we would get royal treatment and be most welcomed guests. We explained that we could not go at this time because we had to get home, but that someday we planned on visiting his country. I am sure it would be a trip that we would always remember.

He was the most grateful and gracious person that I have ever met.

Somehow all the difficult times I experienced while flying my tour seemed to have a different meaning. Until I met this gentleman I never realized that just the sound of an airplane could give a person the will and courage to survive another day. I never regretted the effort and difficulty it took to survive a tour. Now it seems such a small effort compared to the untold millions who suffered so much in Europe during the war.

Ludwigshafen—A

Mission to

Remember

Major R. B. Seigh, USAF (Ret.) 389th

January 7, 1944 is a date I shall remember the rest of my life. I was a member of Capt. Jerome M. Kennedy's crew flying the right waist position. We joined the 389th Bomb Group in September of 1943 and were assigned to the 565th Bomb Squadron. On this particular mission our crew was flying deputy lead on the right wing of Capt. Willhite. The mission to the target was uneventful and without too much trouble. As we came off the target for the return to England, my pilot became concerned, as did Lt. Col. Jack Dieterle, who was flying as Command Pilot, about the route the Group Leader was taking. He elected to leave the main bomber stream and head toward Paris. The flight over France was without trouble until, approximately 26 miles from Paris, we were hit by fighters. Captain Willhite was hit almost immediately by a head-on attack. I saw the shells hit the right engines and set them on fire. Shells also hit the nose, cockpit area and waist area. Capt. Willhite's B-24 started a bank to the right. My pilot attempted to bank with him but the angle became too steep and we were forced to pull away and level off.

In the meantime, Willhite leveled off and flew directly over our aircraft, almost colliding with us. Willhite's plane did a steep turn, nosed down and about 5,000 feet below us the right wing came off and the B-24 cart wheeled toward the ground. Meanwhile, the steep bank had forced us away from the group. Seeing this, Capt. Kennedy increased his speed and took over the lead position of the 389th. At about this time a lone P-47 came by and kept some of the fighters from us but eventually he had to leave the fight and return to England because of a low fuel supply.

I have no idea where the 445th was, but I can tell you that they were not near the 389th. We lost eight or nine B-24s that day. A group of Spitfires picked us up near the French coast and escorted us to England. As a side note, only one man survived from Capt. Willhite's crew and that man was the top turret gunner and I believe his name was T/Sgt. Swetz. We were lucky that day and I guess the Good Lord was with us.

Author's note: This account wouldn't have been told if the group leader had done the sensible thing, and that is to follow the main bomber stream. There is strength in numbers! The larger the formation, less likelihood enemy fighters attack you. Maybe he thought it was a short cut, or maybe he wanted to see what Paris looked like. War casualties occur oftentimes because of a lack of common sense. I always had a beef with the military's rank consciousness. We would have a mission leader recently from stateside with little or no combat experience, only because of rank, and it would increase the risk. Higher rank didn't always mean better judgment. Experience in combat definitely increased one's odds. Aside from the chance of sheer luck in catching a flak burst in your bomber's belly which could happen on your first or your last mission, the newer the crew the more likely the casualty. This was more true of the ground soldier, where inadequately trained newcomers to the front lines had really high loss rates. Read some of Steven Ambrose's WWII recounts and you will realize that war breeds many mistakes and generals are not exempt.

Ploesti

Edwin C. Baker, 93rd BG

Orders came down from Command for the raid on Ploesti. August 1, 1943 was to be the day. The evening before we taxied all aircraft out on the field and parked them in a straight line, but cocked at 45 degrees. We were fueled and bomb-loaded from this position, so when we started the engines in the morning, no one would have to eat dust and sand. It would also prevent clogging of engine intakes and other sand related problems. We didn't want any aborts. We were loaded with incendiary bombs and some 500 pounders with delay action fuses from one hour to two days—the theory being it would prevent their fire crews from entering the area not knowing when another bomb would go off. The final preparation was to have all gas tanks topped off. We were going to need every drop of gas to make this round trip.

As operations officer, I went about assigning the crews and aircraft positions. Of course, I assigned myself as copilot/Plane Commander on my old crew and also assigned Little Lady to the left wing position of the first element of our squadron. In this position, I would fly the aircraft. The squadron and element lead ship (Tupelo Lass) was being flown by Maj. K.O. Dessert (Sqd. C.O.) and Capt. Jake Epting. Lt. Hoover, Wilkie's regular copilot, begged to go on the mission. Observers were OK'd, so I let him go as extra copilot and he stood between the seats throughout the flight. We had one other passenger (Observer) 1st Lt. Edward E. Mitchell. I can't remember why he rode with us, or what he did during the mission. I don't remember the positions I assigned for the rest of the aircraft in our squadron. The only reason I remember flying left wing off of Dessert and Epting is because I stared at them for almost six hours. I know that the 409th Squadron put up a full complement of ships—nine aircraft. On August 1, 1943 we had a short briefing at 0700 hours. Breakfast, for those who could eat, and we were in our aircraft awaiting flare signal from the tower for start engines and takeoff. The field was wide enough to permit us to takeoff in our elements of three at a time. This put our Group into the air in short order and we were formed on Colonel Addison Baker (Group C.O.)—no relation—way before other Groups. We finally moved into position behind the 376th Bomb Group and headed out across the Mediterranean toward first land fall—Corfu (on the Ionian Islands, off the coat of Greece). The target approach plan was to fly at treetop level, passing over two towns before reaching the IP. The towns were Pitesti, Targoviste, and then the IP, Floresti. Each of these towns was nestled in a valley surrounded by rolling hills. At the IP we would make a right turn, southeast, and string out into a single straight line, still in formation, wingtip to wingtip, attacking the refinery on the paths we were trained to follow. K.K. Compton (our 'ole 409th Squadron C.O.) was transferred to the 376th Bomb Group as their C.O. His group would be the lead into the target. We would follow him and be second over the target. The rest of the groups would follow in a stairstep fashion, each a little higher than the other. Shortly after we went out over the Mediterranean, one of the ships in the group ahead of us must have blown up. It went straight down into the sea. We didn't see any parachutes or survivors.

We hit Corfu on the money. Turning inland, we were confronted with high mountains, which were covered with cumulus
clouds that rose well above them. A cold chill went down my
spine. It was obvious we were going to have to fly through. We
loosened up the formation, spread out, noted the compass heading
and headed straight in, climbing. At 10,000 ft. we put on our oxygen masks. We finally broke through at about 15,000 ft. and leveled off. It was a great feeling to see the other ships around us and
in fairly good order. We quickly squeezed into our 'V' elements of
three ships as before and crossed the mountains. We felt sure we
had been detected now. The plan was to skim across the mountains
at a minimum altitude in the hopes of staying below the radar
beams. As we crossed the last range, we started a zigzag descent.
We leveled off low and continued pressing forward. We stayed at
treetop level, only climbing to get over hills and terrain. Still no
flak or fighters. Maybe we were actually going to get away with
a surprise. Before us lay a basin of beautiful farmland, green with
neat cross-hatched rows of planting, something we hadn't seen in
a long time. We began to see our first peasants. Women in gaily
colored dresses with upturned smiling faces waving handkerchiefs
at us.

Before long we came upon our first town— Pitesti. Then the
second town came into view—Targoviste. To our complete shock,
the group turned south. Hebert called on the intercom, "Where the
hell are you going? This isn't Floresti —you've turned too soon."
I answered, "I can't help that; we're sticking with the group." By
that time radio silence was broken and I could hear several calls
saying, "wrong turn; wrong turn." We moved out to our straight
line frontal attack position, wingtip to wingtip. As I looked at K.O.
in the lead plane, he shrugged his shoulders and made a motion,
indicating he didn't know what was going on. He, too, realized we
made a wrong turn. We pressed on. Still no fighters—where were

they? Suddenly, the flak started to come. It was bursting above us. Our reaction was to get lower and lower. Our waist gunners were now firing at gun emplacements. I could see men toppling over and doubling up as we passed over them. We came along side of an electrical substation. The gunners let a blast go into the transformers. The fireworks were spectacular. Colonel Baker broke away from the 376th and started a left turn. I had to pull off power. Since I was so close to the ground, I couldn't drop down. I kept pulling off more power. I was afraid I was going to run over K.O. from my momentum. Finally, we straightened out and I had to really pour the power to the ship in order to keep up. All hell was breaking loose. Anti-aircraft guns, ground fire and the pursuit ships had shown up. We came across a lake area with sunbathers laying around. Some were military and they jumped up and fired rifles at us. A burst from our gunners sent those left standing scurrying for cover. A machine gun turret on a tower in the area fired at us. The gunners raked the tower longer making short bursts; they were going almost steadily. We had to raise our left wing to clear a church steeple with a clock in it. The time was five minutes to three o'clock. We leveled off and opened our bomb bay doors. Straight ahead was a row of eucalyptus trees. From underneath anti-aircraft, guns started shooting point blank at us. You could hear the swish and feel the shells go by us. My God, we're sitting ducks! As fast as we were going, I had the feeling we were standing still. The roar of our engines, and noise of guns and flak was unbearable. Planes on both sides of us were being hit. Were we next?

We got two hits, almost simultaneously. One in our #3 engine on the right side and one under the belly of the ship. The hits gave us a feeling of being stopped cold in mid-air. K.O. and Eptings' ship shot ahead of us and out of sight. I never saw them again. Finally, we were at the eucalyptus trees and had to pull up to clear them.

Wilkie and I were both on the controls now trying to keep the ship straight and level. Our #3 engine was on fire and gas was pouring out of our belly tank from flak holes. Silverman opened the bomb bay doors as we came into the refinery area. This added to the drag and our airspeed started to drop. Hoover reached down and pulled the fire extinguisher on #3 and I feathered it. Silverman hollered "Bombs Away" and our ship made a lurch upward from the relief of the weight. The gas fumes were getting stronger and it was hard to breathe. Wilkie and I opened our windows for air. The fresh air felt good, but added to the noise.

The fire in #3 engine gradually went out after it was feathered and shut down. Why the fire stream from our #3 engine and raw gas from our belly tanks did not get together and blow us up, I'll never know. Everything was happening at once. I saw Colonel Addison Baker, our group C.O., take a direct hit. He pulled out his aircraft up and as it fell off on its right wing, two chutes opened, but they drifted right into the holocaust of fire as their ship went straight into the ground. They didn't have a chance. Silverman called out "bomb bay doors closed." I yelled for him to open the damn things; we were being flooded out with raw gas and fumes from the bomb bay tanks. A storage tank blew up in front of us and we flew just to the right of it. The plane on our left went right through it and I never saw him come out. As we passed the heat of the explosion, it felt like passing a hot iron close to your face. Silverman opened the bomb bay doors. The few seconds those doors were closed is when we passed beside the blown-up storage tank. I'm sure if our bomb bay doors had been opened the raw gas flowing out would have caught fire and blown up.

Luck was still with us. We had little fires all over the wings, apparently from gas leaks and debris. They went out on their own, fortunately, before any more serious damage was done.

We zigzagged through columns of black smoke and fire. We

still were not out of it yet. The other groups were coming in on their bomb runs above us. We were taking in the percussions of their bombs and the debris they blew up. Suddenly, we popped out of the hellhole of fire, flame and smoke into the clear sky and green fields beyond. We were clear and still flying, badly damaged, but not fatally. Wilkie and I looked at each other and smiled. As I relaxed my grip on the wheel, I realized and felt the pain of numbness in my hands and forearms. My knuckles were white from gripping the wheel. I took a deep breath, leaned back in my seat to relax. I felt as though I had held my breath through the entire bomb run. The thumping in my chest was so hard and fast that I thought my heart was going to pop out.

Hits on our ship not only blew out #3 engine, but damaged our control cables. Wilkie was fighting desperately to keep the ship in the air. I grabbed the wheel again and started helping. Over the intercom the gunners were calling off fighters again and their guns were blazing away. We reduced our power and Hoover periodically called off our airspeed. It was steadily going down, so I had to increase it well above normal. If we could keep this plane in the air, our next goal was to reach the prearranged rendezvous for crippled aircraft. I called Rolley (flight engineer) to come to the flight deck from the top turret. He said there were fighters around and he was fighting like mad and swinging the turret from one side to another. I told him to get out of the turret and let Kimtantas (radio operator) take over and do something about the gas in the bomb bay. Rolley switched us over to using the gas from the "Tokyo" tanks, which seemed to reduce the flowing from the flak holes. We headed westward and were all alone, easy meat for the pursuit fighters in the area.

We were so close to the ground, coupled with our gunners still firing, that the fighters didn't press too close. Out of nowhere a ship from one of the other bomb groups pulled up alongside of us and flew formation. The combined firepower of our planes completely discouraged the pursuit planes and they left us for easier pickings. Our companion ship was not damaged and he was finding it difficult to stay with us at such a slow speed. We were indicating about 150, just staying airborne. We reached the rendezvous point and started to circle, waiting for the others. None showed up. Finally, the companion ship called on the radio and said he could no longer stay with us. I thanked him and told him to go on his way; we were fairly safe now.

Rolley came on the flight deck and reported that we lost almost all of the gas in our "Tokyo" tanks and couldn't possibly get back to our base. We called Hebert and asked him for the nearest friendly airfield. He responded with "Our first alternate is a small airfield in Turkey near the town of Edirne, just across the Turkish border. Or possibly the British held island of Cypress, in the Mediterranean, off the coast of Turkey." O.K., that's it—he gave us the heading.

Every time we pulled the nose up in a bid for altitude the airspeed would drop off dangerously close to stalling. We were still having control problems and running on three engines. We kept stairstepping, but we were nowhere near the required altitude to go over the Balkan mountain range. We were at 1500 feet when the mountain range loomed in front of us. Now we had real problems. We didn't have enough altitude to go over them and we were committed too far south to turn back. Damn, after all we had just been through, and now we were hemmed in. As we approached the mountains, we saw a large valley and headed for it. We were about to play the greatest game of chance in our lives. We forged on in.

As we entered the valley, an anti-aircraft gun emplacement was spotted on a mountaintop above us. They must have heard us coming and were looking up. When they spotted us below, they couldn't get their guns down to fire at us. They waited until we were well into the valley and then fired. They didn't come close enough to do us any harm. Suddenly, the valley split into a 'Y'.

We went left. The next time we came upon a split, we went right, trying to keep in the general direction and heading Hebert gave us. Each valley produced another 'Y' and another choice. We came into some narrow places where our wingtips just cleared sheer walls. We expected to come upon a dead end every time we made the choice of valleys. We must have picked the only route through those mountains. Finally, to our relief, we broke out into the open country.

Beautiful green trees and some farmland. The pressure was now on Hebert to determine where we had come out. Wilkie cautiously asked Hebert for a new heading. "Hell, I don't know where we are with all that zigzagging through those mountains. Give me a couple minutes to find something to orientate us. Do you see any towns or railroads?" Folley cut in on the intercom and said we had less than an hour's worth of gas left. Wilkie insisted that we try for Cypress. We discussed our options if we ran out of gas trying to make Cypress. A crash landing at sea or at best on a sandy beach on the coast of Turkey. No way! Hebert said we could make the small airport in Turkey and gave us a heading to try. As we crossed the border into Turkey, one last attempt by anti-aircraft was made to shoot us down. Again, we survived. I prayed our luck would hold out a little longer.

We finally spotted the airfield and headed for it. We made a circle to survey the field and soon realized that it was for pursuit ships and the runways were very short. We could see other B24s on the field. If they made it, we could. We picked out the runway that looked longest and Wilkie started his landing approach. We were still having control cable problems. It was hard to get the ship to respond. I told Wilkie we had only one chance to make it; there would be no going around.

We had no electrical power for lowering the gear and flaps. I went to work hand pumping our landing gear down. The wheels finally came down, but our waist gunners couldn't confirm if they were in locked position. With our landing gear in the air stream, our airspeed started to drop rapidly. Hoover was calling it off for Wilkie. My arm felt like it would break as I pumped harder and faster. Wilkie was hollering for flaps. Wheels down or not, I had to give Wilkie some flaps. I switched the selector and pumped like mad. Wilkie pulled off all power to the remaining three engines.

When I looked up, we were coming in too steep and too fast. I grabbed the wheel and we both pulled with all our strength back, back as far as the column would go and tight against our chest, literally standing on the rudder pedals. We hit nose wheel first, and then the main gear with such force that we ricocheted back into the air. We held the wheel tight to our bellies, as we mushed back onto the runway again with a bang and the sound of scraping metal. The landing gear held together, but there were no brakes. I let go of the wheel and hit all switches to 'OFF.' We rolled off the end of the runway into a dirt field and up a small hill before we came to a sliding halt. Gas fumes, dirt and dust were everywhere. I hollered, "Get out before she blows up." I went out my side window head first. I got hung up a little, but made it. Scrambling, half crawling and running, I headed up the hill until I felt I was far enough away to be safe. The others quickly joined me. We all sat there in complete exhaustion staring at Little Lady. She never caught fire or blew up.

We all sat there in silence and transfixed awe at the ship that brought us through Ploesti unharmed. I thought to myself—My God, what we had been through today and this magnificent aircraft stayed airborne and even held together throughout the most abusive landing I have ever seen or experienced. As the dust settled, I could see the holes in her. It was unbelievable. She looked like a sieve, yet not a man on board was even scratched. The landing gear cracked and slowly lowered the belly of the ship to the ground as the left wing buckled at the fuselage and sagged until its wingtip dug into the soft earth.

Little Lady was dying and never would fly again. I almost expected her to make a final flutter of her wings. I started to choke up and shake inside not knowing whether it was finally realizing I was still alive or that I was seeing an airplane that we had cared for and babied all these months, slowly die.

Nazis Kill 491st BG

Crewmen

Reprinted from "Briefing," Fall 1987

The Liberator was named "Wham! Bam! Thank You, Ma'am." It was from the 491st Bomb Group. On 24 August 1944, 8th Air Force Bomber Command attacked many targets in Germany. As "Wham! Bam!" dropped its bombs on an airfield north of Hanover, the aircraft was hit by flak and dropped out of formation.

This was the beginning of what was to be one of the most gruesome, nightmare-like incidents to befall a bomber crew in WWII, as reported in a 20-page lead article in *After the Battle*, published in England.

As the crippled B-24, #42-110107, neared the ground near Greven, some ninety miles southwest of Hanover, the pilot, 2nd Lt. Norman J. Rogers, Jr. gave the order to bail out. First to jump was Sgt. William A. Dumont, ball turret gunner, who injured his ankle on landing. Next was Sgt. Thomas D. Williams, radioman; followed by William M. Adams, nose gunner, who was wounded in the arm; Sgt. Sidney E. Brown, tail gunner; Flight Officer Haigus Tufenkjian, navigator; Sgt. Wilmore J. Austin, waist gunner; and Staff Sgt. Forrest M. Brininstool, engineer, who had a flak wound to his stomach. Last out were 2nd Lt. John N. Sekul, copilot, and Lt. Rogers.

All the crew were taken from Greven to a railway station where they traveled to a Luftwaffe airfield where they were interrogated by German officers. "They treated us decently and asked about our wounds," a crewman related.

Adams and the engineer were taken to a field hospital where Brininstool was operated on to remove a piece of shrapnel from his stomach, after which he was taken to a hospital in Munster. Adams returned to the others.

Next morning the crew was taken by train to Dulag Luft aircrew interrogation center at Oberursel, north of Frankfurt. On the 26th, the train arrived at Russelsheim, fifteen miles southwest of Frankfurt. Here the RAF had hit the town with over 400 Lancasters to knock out the Opel factory, which killed 179 of the residents.

The deaths "did not auger well for the American crewmen who arrived in the aftermath of the attack. The mood in Russelsheim that morning was ugly, and tempers against the 'terror-fliers' were running high," the article relates.

The article describes what followed:

As the railway line was blocked, the eight Americans, escorted by their three Luftwaffe guards, dismounted from the train. For a while it seems that the guards were unsure of what to do next, for the senior man left the group and they never saw him again. The other two guards then started to move the group off the station and across the Bahnhofplatz on the northern side of the tracks. Sgt. Dumont with his injured ankle was having difficulty walking and was being helped along by the other crewmen.

The American airmen soon attracted a hostile audience which very quickly grew to a crowd of 'between 250 and 300 people.' It still appeared that the two Luftwaffe guards had no idea of where they were supposed to be going, and when people began throwing stones, they made no attempt to intervene or try to take the party back to the station.

Reaching Frankfurter Strasse, someone in the crowd threw a piece of iron, hitting Lt. Rogers on the head. This appeared to be the sign for a free-for-all to begin, and a hail of missiles began to bombard the men. As they proceeded east along the road, they passed the Park Hotel where three women came out of their shop shouting to those in the crowd to kill the airmen. The women joined in the general tumult and, and as the Americans stumbled along, they were subjected to a continual rain of blows from bricks, broomsticks, shovels, or whatever came easily to hand.

Sgt. Brown later described how "we were attempting to help Dumont, who had a broken ankle, along as best we could in the crowd, but as we moved on he soon fell to the ground; he was the first to fall, and the people pounced on him and beat him to death right there in the street."

The article goes on to describe the vicious, continual beating the crew received. After they were beaten to the ground they received additional poundings, then the crowd began to disperse.

A wagon was then used to pick up the bodies of the crew, with Brown and copilot Sekul still alive but pretending to be dead.

Brown testified later, "I saw some person, whom I can't describe, with a club in his hand, come over to the wagon—apparently to finish us off. Sekul's hand was on my shoulder and I could feel him wince as this person beat him on the head. I felt his hand slide from my shoulder as he died. Thomas Williams was also next to me, and I heard him make a sound as he was finished off. I thought that all of the crew had been killed by this time. I could see that the flight officer had his brains beaten out and the pilot, Rogers, had his head beat in on one side..."

The so-called "death-march at Russelsheim" became one of the first war crimes to be investigated after the war. Those townspeople who could be identified with the incident were either hung or jailed.

15th Air Force

Mission to Brenner

Pass

from Bomber Legends, *as told by the tail gunner*

December 27, 1944, 1100 hours. We were flying lead for the group, trying once again to destroy the German supply and escape route in the Brenner Pass, northern Italy. We had turned on the IP and started the bomb run. The flak was heavy, intense, and accurate. I saw Dalrymples' plane take a direct hit and explode in a ball of fire. I watched MacGrath's plane fly through that inferno of flaming gasoline and debris and come out with his Liberator completely on fire, one end to the other.

We unloaded our bombs and got the hell out of there.

The following day, Brenner Pass again! Evidently we hadn't hit the tunnel but had started an avalanche that blocked one end of it. I was cursing and praying at the same time when we started the bomb run. I heard and felt a big explosion, and the plane nosed over into a dive with the pilots fighting the controls to get leveled off. As we were going down, I heard the "prepare to bail out" signal, and opened the hatch just in time to see three men bailing out. I didn't know which crew members they were, it could have been the pilot and copilot. The ship was still plummeting to earth. As I started to jump, someone behind me held me back. I told him they were bailing out up front. He just looked me in the eye and kept shaking his head "no." All of a sudden the plane started to level off. Somehow the pilots managed to get back in level flight. We had lost two navigators and the bombardier, the men I had seen bail out. Now we had to find our own way back. We were in bad shape, a flying wreck. One engine gone, flak holes everywhere, hydraulics shot out and gasoline leaking and dripping all over. One spark and we would be an inferno. Our plane, "Lady in the Dark," was struggling toward friendly territory. We were losing altitude and gasoline. Spotting an airfield, we were going to try to land, friendly or not. But the wheels would not come down hydraulically or manually. We couldn't make a belly landing. Sparks would set off the gasoline.

Suddenly the engines quit. No more gas; time to bail out. Clear of the ship, I pulled the d-ring. Nothing happened. Pulled it again, still, nothing. I pulled up the flap in front of the chute and dug out the little cable that released the chute. The pilot chute popped out, filled with air and dragged the main chute out. What a relief!

I landed on top of a small mountain. The other guys who had bailed out ahead of me were still in the air, drifting toward friendly territory, passing over me. I was just sitting there and heard someone walking toward me. It was an Italian soldier in full uniform and a holstered pistol on his belt. I figured I was a "goner," but he asked me for cigarettes. I gave him a pack of Chesterfields. He said "Grazie" and some other words I didn't understand, and walked away. A few minutes later I heard someone speaking Italian, asking if I was English. It was a young girl, fifteen or sixteen. She was hanging back but when I said "Americano" she helped me get on my feet. She took me further up the mountain to an old farmhouse, and the two women and an old man gave me a glass of wine. I gulped it down, and did the same with another. They gave me some kind of soup. They seemed very poor. They had some haystacks to feed the goats, and showed me one with a hole, where the dog slept. They apparently wanted me to hide in case some Germans came around. I crawled in, and slept overnight.

Going back to the farmhouse, they fed me again. I gave them about half of my parachute, the chocolate in my escape kit, and my sheepskin pants to the old man, who thanked me endlessly. I found the British, and they took me back to the American Fifth Army lines. The infantrymen asked me a lot of questions about anti-aircraft fire, fighters, types of targets, and what it was like to go deep in enemy territory. They kept me awake half the night. They took me to an airfield where a C-47 took me back to my base. I then learned the rest of the crew got out of the plane. Frank Visciglia, the engineer, practically rode the plane down before he jumped. He always told me he was deathly afraid of parachuting and wouldn't be able to do it. He apparently pulled his ripcord before he got out of the plane. His chute opened but got on the tailskid, with no time or way to get free. He rode the bomber down knowing he would die on impact.

The three who had bailed out first were taken POW. We were sent to the Isle of Capri to rest up and try to forget what we'd been through. I had to fly ten more missions to complete my fifty. Somehow I managed to live through them and was sent back to the good old USA.

"The Poor 100th"

Kenneth Kinney

Reprinted from the American Legion Magazine, *June 1947*

When ex-Army Air Force men get together and talk for more than five minutes at a time, the conversation invariably gets around to the various outfits that flew and fought from England, Italy and points west.

From there the talk will turn to reminiscences of big raids, flak and enemy fighters. Then let one of the former buzz-boys say he was in the 100th Bomb Group, and the respect for this man will fairly permeate the air. For the rest of the men realize that they are conversing with a museum piece—an ex-pilot, bombardier, navigator or gunner who flew a tour with the 100th and lived to tell about it.

When the 100th, a B-17 outfit, joined the Eighth Air Force in England in May 1943, it became just another in the rising tide of groups helping flatten Germany from the air. But it wasn't long before the 100th gained quite a reputation and earned the ingratitude of Goering's fighter pilots.

In October 1943, the 100th was responsible for a stunt, seemingly insignificant at the time, which snowballed into something all out of proportion to its origin.

Nobody seems to know where or how it began, but the word got around that if an American bomber lowered its wheels over German territory, it was a sign that the ship was going to crash-land. Thereupon, enemy fighters would close in, unmolested and unmolesting, to escort the crippled ship down.

It seems that one enterprising pilot of the 100th Bomb Group thought of a way to get a feather in his cap and at the same time give his gunners some good practice. Undoubtedly self-preservation was a major factor too, for this pilot was flying his B-17 back over France after hitting a target in Germany. His ship was shot up some, enough that he'd had to drop out of formation.

Two FW-190s spotted the crippled '17 and closed in. The pilot lowered his wheels and the German fighters came in, one on each wing tip, to escort the big plane down. Whereupon the '17's gunners opened fire, and being in a position where they couldn't miss, quickly downed the two '190s.

The story later got out. The B-17 was crippled and losing precious altitude, so the pilot ordered the crew out, and out they bailed. Most of the crew later reached England with the help of the French underground. The pilot just managed to reach England's shores before he crash-landed safely.

But it seems the Luftwaffe got wind of the incident, too, for almost immediately the German fighters, trying to intercept American formations, began to single out the planes of the 100th for special attention, identifying them by the "Square D" insignia on their tails. One gunner, a member of a group in the same wing as the 100th, has related how the FW-109s and ME-109s would barrel perilously through his formation without firing a burst to get at the ships of the 100th.

It certainly wasn't coincidence that caused the 100th to have

100 percent losses in the short space of two days. On October 10, a short time after the incident, the group sent 20 planes, full strength for the group, into the air. Eight of the 20 were shot down. The next day, 12 out of the 13 that left England failed to come back, making a loss of 20 in two days.

Then during the following February something else happened that amplified the losses of the 100th. The target was "Big B" (Berlin) for the first time.

It was an all-out attack involving the whole Eighth Air Force. Bad weather, however, forced all but a few groups to turn back before reaching the target. The 100th was one that persisted. Thus it gained the distinction of being one of the first outfits to hit Berlin.

It probably would have waived that distinction, though, for right after that raid the 100th was given more special atten- tion—Luftwaffe style. The "Square D" group lost 82 planes during February and March 1944, eighteen of them, almost an entire com- plement, being downed in one day.

So if the guy tells you he flew with the 100th, be nice to him. He deserves it!

Author's note: It's said this story has been debunked.

It's interesting, true or not.

Memories of an

Interlude in England

in 1944

Russell M. Barnes

Reprinted from Gannett Westchester Newspapers, June 6, 1990

Soon it won't mean a thing...

The sleepy hamlet of Hurn, tucked neatly away in southern England and just a few miles from the English Channel won't mean a thing to you, but then why should it. For most parts of the year it doesn't mean much to me and Hurn is only a few miles from where I live.

But once a year I visit. Every June I make the journey, preparing myself, as I drive over the narrow humpback bridge and under that line of tall trees, for that tiny lump to arrive in my throat—and it never fails.

You see, in June 1944 I was a teenager. The German army was on the other side of the Channel, which meant they were only 80 miles away—or just 20 minutes as the Heinkel 111K bomber flies—and you tried not to think about that.

Me and the other kids had eagerly watched the "dog fights" up in the blue summer skies of 1940 when Spitfire battled it out with Messerschmitt. We tried to sleep under kitchen tables as German heavy bombers overhead made their journeys in black winter nights across the very heart of England to obliterate the centers of Birmingham and Coventry.

But soon the Russians, who by then had lost six million people, were at last getting the better of the huge German land forces which had torn their countryside apart and the British "Tommy" was doing OK in North Africa...but little did we know that soon our world would be turned upside down! The GIs were about to invade. Laughing and singing, truckloads of them winding their way down narrow Dorset lanes, winking and grinning at the girls who giggled and thrilled in their delightful embarrassment.

On Sunday the village green had echoed with the sounds of English cricket as young men swung bats against a hard ball and proud parents gently clapped and murmured "bravo." Now it was "yippee," and words we dare not mention, as a softball struck by baseball bat sped so unbelievably fast across neat gardens and out of sight.

Yes, the Yanks arrived. They shared a drink in our pub and shared a hymn book in our church. Some even shared Sunday lunch with us and sat around our fireside at Christmas. And to some of those fresh-faced lads our mums became their moms.

In the spring of 1944 the lanes and fields of southern England were choked with American, Canadian and British forces and their equipment. It wasn't difficult to see that plans were underway for the Normandy landings—and Dorset was very much in the front line.

On that first day of June 1944 as I walked across that lane and over the humpbacked bridge, I saw a sea of blue or khaki uniforms. Groups of GIs laughing and talking. Some played cards. And others, alone with their thoughts, sat quietly writing letters home—or some perhaps their last letters home.

Within a week it was the Omaha and Utah beachheads. For all it was a nightmare journey to hell and back. And sadly for many—far too many—the soft and gentle down lands of Dorset would be the last thing felt under foot.

Throughout the weeks that followed, aircraft and ships brought the wounded back to Dorset—young men made older. In the market town of Blandford, the 22nd U.S. Military Hospital, with a devoted staff working day and night, tended wounds and mended bones.

A mile away, a Dorset mum carefully placed a GI's personal belongings in a tin box and reverently buried them deep in her garden. He wasn't her son, but he was somebody's son. Only two weeks before he'd been around her home for a cup of tea and a chat. He left a neat assortment of personal things on her table, asking that she look after them and saying, "I'll be back for them when it's all over." He shut the wooden gate behind him and turned to look at her for a second...and was gone.

She had been told that he wouldn't be calling back.

That kind soul, with kids of her own, didn't bury his photograph. Without fail, each June she took it from the drawer and placed it on view. And she did that every year until she died. Now someone else performs that simple but dedicated token of annual remembrance.

When at long last it was all over, GI Joe went back to Los Angeles or Long Island. Tommy Atkins to Liverpool or London. Now there is nothing more across the soft down lands or along the winding lanes of Dorset to tell the generations to come what happened here a lifetime ago. Nothing which even begins to record in history the sacrifice and courage of people, who it seems, may already be forgotten.

Only memories in the minds of those who lived through it all.

The sad fact is that one day—when nobody cares—it won't mean a thing.

B-24 Bashing—The End

Edward J. Reilly, 93rd

Murray Grainger, you and Bob Chapin may not be in as much disagreement as your three letters would suggest.

Much of what Grainger says is undeniable fact. Our casualties were 30 percent higher than our brother Fort crews in the Eighth. Aside from combat losses, the old Lib was more prone to fatal accidents. I can personally recall two fatal accidents of Libs on takeoff that took twenty lives, one of whom was a dear friend. Experienced flight engineers kept the bomb bay open a crack to reduce risk from fumes of gas leaks. Her glide angle—like a brick. Ditching the bird was almost certain suicide. 17s did it like ducks.

To most of us in our early twenties safety didn't seem to be of much concern. Personally, I was disappointed when I wasn't assigned to B-26s, and their safety record was worse than ours. On that score I could have no beef with being assigned to 24s.

I was trained in 17s and knew what they were. They were tough, reliable, sleek, and beautiful. And they came home more often. But if you could stand away from one's feelings and look at facts, the B-24 was a better bomber. It could outrun the 17 by at least 20 knots, carry a ton more bombs 800 miles further and hit targets 400 miles deeper into enemy territory. Her four electric turrets were the ultimate state of the art. Her ten guns were more effective, in my judgment, than the 17's thirteen. But our formations were not as tight as the Forts because of the Libs inherent sloppiness above 18,000 feet. Our optimum altitude was between three and five thousand feet below theirs, making us more vulnerable to flak. Her Pratt and Whitney engines were the most reliable of any built for any aircraft during the war.

I recently heard a leading German fighter ace tell a group of American bomber crews that they would always pass Forts by, seeking out and attack Libs, because they were easier to kill. It was not fire power that failed. The Lib just could not survive the same level of battle damage as the Fort. And the enemy well knew it. Flak or fighters, in combination, knocked off only seven Forts for every ten Libs.

But only the Lib could have hit Ploesti. And it took eight Forts and 80 men to drop the same tonnage of bombs as it took six Libs and 60 men mounted in Libs.

The B-24 Liberator was a great old bird. Those of us who flew her loved and hated her. We would fight with 17 crews whenever her name was sullied. But deep in our hearts, we know that the 17 was built for crews and the 24 for the Air Force. If I were underwriting life insurance to bomber crews instead of flying with one, I'd be looking for the Fort crews. If shopping for the weapon that could do the most damage at the lowest cost, I'd be pushing Libs.

The Libs were not as bad as Grainger felt they were. I'm glad he wrote the article. I'm glad Chapin responded as any good loyal Lib crewman should. For most of us who flew Libs and Forts, feelings ae deep and facts mean different things to different people. None of us are likely to change feelings that run as deeply as we all feel about an argument that can never be settled... (I think the B-24 bashing has run its course and the above article puts it in proper perspective. Thanks—Editor, *2nd Air Division Journal*)

Dedicated Control Tower Personnel

Much has been written about the exploits of the Fighter Aces and Combat Crew Heroes, however very little has been written about their friends in the Control Tower who "Kept 'em flying"!

Ours was not a glamorous job, and at times, it was a long, hard grind under conditions that were less than ideal. There were times, too, when it was touch and go, and no two situations were alike. We did just what we had to do, and I'm quite sure most of us would not have traded places with the Air Crews.

Nevertheless, it seems appropriate after all these years to give some recognition to the dedicated men in the Control Tower who were always ready to help and DID help!

We were down at the runway talking them in when our fickle English weather decided to play tricks on us. Always on the look-out for red flares letting us know there were wounded aboard. Giving priority landing to aircraft in distress. Landing 'em with wheels up, out of fuel, shot up and other various and sundry conditions which required delicate handling. We maintained the

Airfield with regard to the safety of the planes, examining the runways after a mission and before takeoff to make sure there were no cracks or potholes. Getting the Engineers to make quick repairs. Making sure that all the lights were working properly. Removing obstructions from the runways.

Getting to crashed aircraft with ambulance and fire-fighting equipment. Many times we were called upon to make split-second decisions (and pray that hopefully they were the right ones). We had to contend with rain, cold, fog, sleet and snow, in addition to our planes being shot up when trying to land.

We were on duty 24 hours a day to assist RAF planes diverted to our field after night missions. We arranged transport, billeting and mess for those crews who remained overnight. We answered Darky Calls and Mayday Calls. Well, sometimes it was just one darn thing after another!

(No author listed)

Marine Pilots Flew Medium-Bomber Missions

Robert F. Dorr

"WWII unit faced setbacks on, off field" Marine Corps Times,
Aug. 23, 2004

When the United States geared up for World War II, the Marine Corps began for the first time to operate large aircraft with two pilots and a crew. Former Capt. Bill Parks, 82, of San Jose, California, had an advantage over some Marine aviators. On the eve of U.S. entry into the war, he earned a pilot's license in a government-sponsored civilian program. He knew that when you fly a big aircraft you usually start out in the right seat as a copilot and build your experience before switching to the left seat. "But the Marine Corps didn't have anyone with multi-engine experience to put in the left seat," Parks said. "Those of us who'd received the most training started out as left seat pilots." From his first day as an aviator in a combat squadron, Parks commanded his aircraft and crew. It was a big responsibility, and it grew bigger when Parks arrived in the South Pacific to fly missions against Japanese island bases.

Born in 1922 in North Carolina, Parks "enlisted in the Navy in summer 1942 under a program that would allow me to fly," he said. "I was just a country boy from the mountains. I didn't even know the Marines had aviators."

At Pensacola, Florida, Parks was among cadets who received a pep talk from a Marine major who wanted them in his service. The major told the trainees, "The Marines have row upon row of P-38 Lightnings at Cherry Point, N.C., and no pilots to fly them." The P-38 was the plane that captivated every youngster of the era. After earning his wings and Marine commission in March 1943, Parks was dismayed to learn the recruiting pitch wasn't true. The Marines didn't possess a single P-38. Instead, Parks became a pilot of the PBJ, the Marines' version of the twin-engine B-25 Mitchell medium bomber. It was the plane Army Lt. Col. James "Jimmy" Doolittle had flown on his famous raid on Japan in April, 1942.

Parks flew with Marine Bomber Squadron 433, the "Fork Tailed Devils," first at Green Island and then at Emirau Island in the South Pacific. "My logbook shows that our first mission from Green was July 21, 1944," Parks said. "It was a full squadron strength daytime raid on Rabaul." By July 1944, the Pacific war was moving to the northwest. Bloody battles for the Solomon Island chain had ended. Some Japanese troops remained on Guadalcanal, Munda, and Bougainville. The Japanese base and airfields at Rabaul, New Britain, were less active than previously. Yet 200,000 Japanese troops remained on New Britain and New Ireland and were occasionally reinforced. The job of the four Mitchell squadrons on Emirau, including Parks, was to prevent these forces from impeding the Allied island-hopping advance toward Japan.

Parks' squadron suffered both of its combat losses in September 1944. On Sept. 2, a PBJ piloted by 1st Lt. Charles Ingals took off on a night mission—and vanished. All six aboard died and were accounted for only after the war. On Sept 11, 1st Lt. Eric E. Terry, Jr., and another Marine were among the lost after being hit by Japanese gunfire. Parks said that a typical mission involved carrying fourteen 100-pound bombs 250 miles from Emirau to Rabaul. That took two to three hours, including about 15 minutes of vulnerability to Japanese fighters and heavy anti-aircraft fire. Parks completed 50 missions and never saw a Japanese fighter but was fired on from the ground often.

A clarification: Parks and other VMB-433 veterans, who held a reunion in Nashville, in October, say that for most of its 25 months in the combat zone the squadron had excellent leadership. They believe a story in this newspaper placed too much emphasis on the squadron's "hard luck" status, which, they say, describes only a brief period in 1945.

Big-B by Day

Glenn R. Matson (458th)

It was our third mission and at briefing we were told our target was Berlin, Germany, the capital city of the Third Reich. The date was 6 March 1944 and the Eighth Air Force was about to penetrate the heart of Germany for the first full-scale daylight raid on Berlin. The 458th Bomb Group scheduled thirty-three B-24 bombers, thirteen of them aborted or failed to make the mission. The remaining twenty bombers joined up with the 14th and 96th Bomb Wing to form a composite Wing of the 2nd Air Division. The 2nd Bomb Wing would lead with the 14th and 96th composite to follow six miles behind. The 20th Bomb Wing would follow six miles behind them, bringing up the rear of the three Bomb Divisions of the B-17s and B-24s to make a bomber stream of over ninety miles long.

The bomber force consisted of 243 B-24s and 567 B-17s. Originally our target was to be the Heinkel Aircraft Factory at Oranienburg, North of Berlin. It was feared that we would have to fly through the heaviest of flak over Berlin to reach our target, so they switched our target Genshagen to hit the Daimler-Benz Motor Works. Bombers had to fly over 1000 miles to the target and back.

Temperatures at altitude were near 60 below zero Fahrenheit.

We were to stay below 21,000 feet to prevent contrails and make it harder for the German fighters to spot us. At Horsham St. Faith at takeoff, visibility was below 1,800 feet and patches of fog, with complete cloud cover between 3,000 and 6,000 feet.

About 10:30 we departed England and headed for the North Sea and across Holland. We picked up our first fighter escort, the 56th Fighter Group, somewhere over Holland. We were following the 3rd Division B-17s when they got off course between Enschede and Osnabruck. The B-24s and part of the B-17s saw the error and stayed on the planned route.

Our Bomb Group took a course Southeast after passing between Brandenburg and Magdeburg to the IP, then swung north into the wind to the target. The worst flak hit us as we approached Oranienburg. There may have been kids firing those 88mm flak guns, but they were good. It was bad enough riding that flak road in and out of Berlin, but as we arrived at the IP (Initial Point to start bomb run), we were on a collision course with a B-17 Group on their bomb run. Our group leader who was a Lt. Col. had to abort our bomb run, change course and close our bomb bay doors to set up for another run. Again we were off our target and he turned us 360 over Berlin instead of away from it. That put us in almost constant flak for over thirty minutes. He wasn't satisfied with our other two runs, he wanted to hit the rail station and yards, not just Big-B.

We were flying in the lower left three plane element in the position of Purple Heart corner. The guy leading our element took us under the main group's formation. By now our bomb bay doors were open again and we were in a very precarious situation. We didn't like looking up at those open-loaded bomb bays directly above us. Our pilot, 2nd Lt. Charles A. Melton decided to leave the element and slid back up in the formation where we belonged. Our element leader and the other wing man were two of our five losses that day. We feared at the time that our own group's bombs fell on them. It was on this third bomb run that our navigator, 2nd Lt. Charles C. Weinum stuck his head up in the navigator's dome in front of the pilots and thumbed his nose at them. He noticed a dog fight and got down inside to get a better view through the side window. After he had left, a chunk of flak made a hole through the dome about the size of a fist. If his head had been there, Pow! No head. He stuck his head up there again, saw a flak hole and got the surprise of his life.

We had to divert to an alternate target. By then we had heavy cloud cover and ended up dropping our bombs near Potsdam. With the target no longer visible, we had to resort to PFF (Pathfinder Forces Radar) and the results were very poor.

Shortly after leaving the target area, we were attacked by two FW-190s. Our group had been badly shot up by flak, one aircraft lost over the target. This was 2nd Lt. G. Clifford's crew on B-24 42-52515. It crashed West of Berlin; eight men were killed, two bailed out when the plane exploded. Three men of our badly shot up B-24s made it to Holland.

The next to go down was Captain J. Bogusch's crew on 41-29286. Four men were killed and six survived the crash and were taken prisoner. Then 2nd Lt. T. Hopkins' crew on 41-29299 crashed. All ten men survived and were taken prisoner. Next to crash was Crew #52 of 2nd Lt. Beverly Ballard's on 42-52450. Three were killed and nine men taken prisoner. The Ball Turret Gunner, Sgt. Victor W. Kruger evaded capture for fourteen months when the Dutch Resistance found him and hid him out until the British troops rescued him in April 1945. Second Lt. J. McMain's crew was shot down by a ME-110 and crashed near Uelzen, Germany. Two were killed and eight taken prisoner.

As for our crew #67 on the B-24 41-28719Q *Paddlefoot* experienced a bit of flak damage, but no one on the crew was injured and our return to England was uneventful.

This was a very costly mission for the Eighth Air Force as well as the 458th Bomb Group, which alone lost five bombers and three returned with minor battle damage—the most ever for one mission throughout the remainder of the war.

Of the 702 bombers and 832 fighters that reached enemy territory, 69 heavy bombers and crews were lost. Eleven of the 832 fighters were lost to enemy flak or fighters. Of the 69 bombers lost, 53 were B-17s and 16 were B-24s that failed to return. 701 men were lost in action of which 229 were killed or missing. Three hundred and forty-five German civilians were killed or wounded and 36 German Airmen were killed and 25 wounded, with a loss of 66 aircraft. Approximately one out of every ten bombers were lost on this mission, the greatest on any separate mission for the Eighth Air Force. We knew we had been on a big one. Yes, it was a big one— "BIG B."

The First Time I Saw

Paris, June 2, 1944

John W. Crowe, 491st

We hadn't flown the "Renegade" since May 23, 1944. The weather began to improve and we were briefed for a practice mission early in the morning of June 2 and told to stand by. Just before noon the practice mission was canceled and we were told to report to the briefing room again. This time it was the real thing, our first mission. The briefing officer, Lt. Col. Goldenberg, told us our target was an enemy airfield just south of Paris. The map showed our flight path in to France, to the target, and the route out, carefully plotted to avoid the many red dots which were known locations of enemy flak guns. The area around Paris looked like the face of a kid with the measles, nothing but red pockmarks. We were assured that the target, some eighteen miles to the south, was out of range of the Paris flak guns and the mission, as planned, ought to be a "milk run"—no problem at all!

Thirty-six planes from the 491st and forty-one from the 489th. The 489th would lead with the 491st following. The 489th had been in England a short time and had flown their first mission on May 30. They were leading the 95th Combat Wing into battle. It would be a very interesting afternoon with the blind leading the blind.

Our escorts were P-51s and P-38 fighters. The "Renegade", as the other planes of the 491st, had her belly full of five hundred pound bombs.

With a briefing for a real mission and a reloading of the planes with bombs, it must have been 1730 or 1800 hours before we taxied out, like thirty-six pregnant elephants, one behind the other, waiting to take off.

Lt. Col. Merrel, group leader, was the first to take off, followed by the other 491st planes at thirty-second intervals. We climbed at five hundred feet per minute, some forty minutes later we reached the forming altitude of 20,000 feet. Twenty minutes later the group was formed. It was 1930 before we departed the English coast at Selsey Bill. We arrived over enemy territory just after eight o'clock and continued southeast to the IP some six miles southwest of Paris. We had some inaccurate, sporadic flak but the "milk run" mission was going as advertised. At eight-thirty we crossed the IP and headed for the target at Bretigny. Then all hell broke loose and the sky around us suddenly turned black with intense accurate flak from enemy flak guns below, thick enough to walk on and close enough to hear the muffled explosion with the familiar R-U-M-M-M-P-H sound that we were soon to know so well.

We didn't know it at the time, but the 489th had failed to take a short zigzag left turn off the IP to the north, then back to the right toward the target. In doing so, we were directly over the heavy concentration of flak guns just to the south of the target. The sky was filled with the black mushroom explosions of 88mm shells.

We continued straight for the target. Lt. Getz, nineteen-year-old pilot of the "Renegade," with instructions from the bombardier,

Chuck Voyles, prepared for bombs away. Everything except the exploding flak looked normal and then in the blink of an eye it happened. The plane slightly ahead and to our left, Lt. Bill Evans' crew, close enough that I could have hit him with a rock, one of the two engines on the right wing simply disappeared. There was only jagged metal, twisted pipes, and a gaping hole where the engine had been only a minute before. The right wing dropped gently downward and the wounded plane began to drift over and down to the right directly toward the "Renegade." It seemed like an eternity but it probably was no more than two or three seconds. I hit the control wheel with both hands, forcing the yoke all the way forward. The "Renegade" responded, her nose went down, and everything not fastened down went up. I had not taken my eyes off Evans' plane, headed toward us on a collision course, and in response to Lt. Getz's silent stare, I pointed above us with my left thumb. As Getz looked up, Evans' burning plane slid gently across the top of the "Renegade," just above the Plexiglas canopy covering our heads. It couldn't have cleared us by more than a few feet and that may be a conservative opinion. Sgt. Turnipseed (TTG), who was closer than most, said, "I looked up and it was right on top of me. I let out a scream because I was sure it was my last." It was over as quick as it happened. Lt. Getz pulled back into the formation and continued our bomb run toward Bretigny.

Things continued to deteriorate as the 489th approached the target and they found it largely covered by clouds. Only one squadron of the 489th managed to drop on Bretigny, thus a decision was made to go for the secondary target at Creil. The 489th plowed straight north, via the Eiffel Tower and Paris. The 491st lead bombardier managed to see the target at Bretigny and unloaded there, but unwisely the 491st followed the 489th over Paris.

The evening and the land below had given way to the late

darkness of the long summer day. The view below was spectacular as we crossed Paris, with the hundreds of bright flashes from the muzzles of flak guns surrounding the blacked-out city. It looked like the Fourth of July on the ground and in the sky around us, which was now blackened with intense flak. It lasted all the way to Creil and beyond.

If the 489th had tried they couldn't have flown the route to be avoided any better. We exited Paris and took the most direct and dangerous route home. It was well after ten o'clock and we landed at Metfield and to add insult to injury, the engines of the "Renegade" began sputtering and cut out as we taxied to our hardstand. We were no longer virgins; the "Renegade" had a great number of holes in her fuselage and wings, all reparable.

The 95th Combat Wing had paid a high price for the mistakes in navigation from the route as briefed. Of the seventy-seven B-24s dispatched on the June 2 mission, five were lost, three crash landed in England, fifty-eight suffered reparable flak damage and one had major damage.

The next day I came to the conclusion that if this was a "milk run" then there was no way short of a miracle that we could survive thirty missions with the 8th Air Force. I therefore decided from that day forward that I was living on borrowed time and that it would be prudent to enjoy to the fullest extent whatever time I had remaining. I never asked others how they wrestled with the problem of survival; perhaps they, too, came to the same conclusion. The first time I saw Paris had been one hell of an experience, never to be forgotten.

Two months later, in early August 1944, Bill Evans showed up back at Metfield, a little lean and haggard but none the worse for being shot down over Paris. He told me that his plane had taken a direct hit in one of the engines in the right wing. The debris from the explosion shattered the cockpit canopy, throwing slivers of Plexiglas into his and the copilot's faces. Neither Bill nor his copilot could see enough to fly or control their wounded plane. He was unaware of his plane's near mid-air collision with the "Renegade." After more flak and more hits, he lost another engine. Realizing the hopelessness of the situation, he ordered the crew to bail out. All exited the plane safely but were subjected to enemy ground fire—rifles and machine guns. The tail gunner, Pvt. Le-May, was cut in half in his chute before he came to earth. The navigator, Lt. Blue, was killed when tracer bullets from machine gun fire ignited his chute and he plunged to earth. Four other members of Evans' crew were taken prisoner. Evans and three others were picked up by the French Underground. He told of working on several night sabotage missions with them.

His benefactors decided the safest place to hide him during the days he was in France would be in the numerous houses of prostitution. Thus Evans was gradually moved from one whore house to another, town to town, between Paris and the English Channel. He smiled when he told me he literally "worked" his way out of occupied Europe to freedom. What a way to fight a war! For Evans the war was over after just one fateful mission. Evaders were not allowed to return to combat duty.

Jinx Ship

John White - 448th BG

In the summer of 1944 John White was a 448th airplane commander whose crew by June 22 had put thirteen missions of their mandatory number behind them. Now one of the dreads of any crew seasoned in combat was to be assigned an aircraft with a "jinx" reputation. B-24 (last three numbers 758) was one such machine and the following account by John displays how she lived up to that reputation:

We had an experience these last two days, June 22-24, that I shall never forget to my dying day. It was extremely interesting and terrifying at the same time. We were briefed for an afternoon raid on one of the airfields south of Paris, and the ship we were assigned to fly was #758, one of the "jinx" ships Today a couple of the boys remarked how glad they were we got rid of it!

There was a good deal of flak at the target but we managed to drop the bombs OK after having a great deal of trouble with the #1 and #4 superchargers. I don't think we received many hits at all over Paris from the flak. About five minutes after we left the targets we really hit it; we flew over some batteries and they opened up with perfect tracking fire. The fellows in the crew later said they counted 10-12 bursts that hit right under us. We could hear them very plainly and feel them rocking the ship.

I knew right away that we must have suffered some severe battle damage, so I called the boys to look her over. In the waist and tail they reported holes torn all over the thing, while Paladino said the engines were hit. Bush said that the tail looked like a sieve and that a piece had hit him on the foot. Part of the interphone was shot out and we had what Vic said amounted to about 50 holes in the bomb bay. He also told me gas was leaking in there, so I had him open the doors and when I looked around, I just about fainted—gas was just pouring from the wing-tanks into the bomb bay and waist. About this time our control cables broke and I had to set up the A-5 to fly the aircraft. The servo-units in the tail had been hit as well so the A-5 wasn't working very well. Dick knew we were in deep trouble, so he gave me a heading to the beachhead, our original intentions being to land there on an ALG. However, fire broke out in #1, and we had very poor control of the ship, so I decided it was time to leave it. It was just a question of whether we should bail out over enemy territory or wait and take a chance on making the beachhead. There was not any question in my mind that she was going to blow. Looms gave me a position so I called some P-47s who came over and gave us excellent cover all through the experience. I called all the turrets out of their positions and told the entire crew to stand by to bail out. Bob was flying and working his head off to keep the plane on an even keel. Everybody was anxious to leave, but I was amazed at how calm they were—our training had obviously stood us in good stead.

All this time gas was pouring out, so Vic took a big piece of cloth, walked out onto the catwalk and tried to plug the hole. We were at 21,000 feet and despite this, he went out there without gloves or oxygen! He froze his hands, which did not do him any good whatsoever. It took a lot of guts to do that and I recommended him for a decoration for that. We started losing height and we were just about to bail out when more 'Ack Ack' opened up on us. We found out later that it was British but at the time thought it might be Jerries, so we went on a little further. Only when we were sure we were over our own lines did I tell the boys to leave. Dick said he would let me know when the last man left the ship and then he would go; he duly did so and jumped, and then I told Bob to go. We shook hands and I witnessed his safe departure. Just before I jumped, I headed the ship out to sea and then pulled the A-5 release, thinking that the ship would nose down and hit it in the channel. However, it blew up a few minutes after I jumped and struck the ground about 200 yards from where some 9th Air Force Engineers were cutting out a landing strip for their fighters. (The next day, a medical Capt. took us around to the spot and the ship was really a mess, all we saw being very small pieces. We could not identify wings, engines, fuselage or anything.)

I delayed my jump for a few seconds—possibly as long as a minute—and found the sensation of falling was very pleasant. I tried to control my body, but it was quite hard. When I finally pulled the ripcord, the chute opened with a severe jolt and the first thing I remember is looking up and seeing the canopy. A few seconds later I noticed that I still had the ripcord and I was very surprised at that. I remember thinking how I would razz the boys who dropped theirs.

Another thing that surprised me was how clearly my mind functioned through the ordeal. It seemed to work perfectly with absolutely no excitement or fear; it must be the training that does it. After the chute opened, it seemed as if I would never reach the ground. The only way I knew I was falling was the fact that I had to keep clearing my ears. I also noticed it was very quiet all the way down. In fact, it was the most intense lack of noise that I had ever experienced, and was very pleasant and delightful.

As I neared the ground I heard rifle and machine-gun fire and later on I found out it was directed at me and the crew! I hit the ground with a severe jolt while facing the wrong direction: my head contacted the ground and I was knocked out cold. In fact, I hit so hard that I could still feel the effects two days later. I hadn't any idea how long I was out, but when I woke up I was bleeding and surrounded by American soldiers. I do remember my first words were, "Thank God you're Yanks." We hit within four miles of the front line, and I was afraid the Jerries would get me. The fellows who picked me up were from an artillery outfit and it so happened that some of them were at Camp Shelby at the same time I was two years before. They sent me up to a Clearing unit of the Medical Corps and there I met Bob and Bush. The former said he had counted ten chutes, which was a tremendous load off my mind. I had heard a few minutes before that one of the officers had sprained his ankle, and I'm pretty sure now that it was Looms. We tried to find out where he was taken, but so far without success. Everybody treated us wonderfully. When Bob and I met, there was a newsreel camera-man there to take our picture and I can assure everybody that the smiles on our faces were genuine.

The Medics were from the 104th Medic Bn attached to the 29th Division, and acted as a clearing unit while operating near the front line. The Division had seen fighting since D-Day and these boys had been through hell. The Bn is commanded by Lt. Col. Arthur N. Erickson and they treated us as if we were kings; they have the highest respect for the boys in the Air Forces.

Of course everybody wanted to hear our story and we had hundreds of questions to ask them in turn. They were in a good position to give us a clear picture of the fighting, and seemed awfully eager to tell it to us. They've treated a lot of Germans, Poles, Czechs, Russians, and even Japs! I was surprised by the fact that the Germans have so many other nationalities fighting for them. They told the Russian boys that Russia had surrendered, and the way they made them fight was to stand over them with a gun and make them.

The next day one of the Captains took us on a tour of the beachhead and it was a tremendously impressive sight. I could never hope to put into words what we saw. How the boys landed is to me a miracle. We saw the flooded fields, hills with tremendous pillboxes and tunnels with catacombs all through them. The captain said they were a mile deep. We saw boats sunk on the beach, and graves of men killed on the landings. We saw landing strips literally hewn out of the woods, roads being cut where there had been nothing but trees and rocks. To see how completely organized the entire operation seemed to be gave one a feeling of absolute confidence in our Army, for a change.

In contrast, we saw the beautiful French countryside with its large hedge rows along every road and highway and large herds of dairy cattle grazing in the fields as if there was no war. The expression on the French people's faces as we drove by seemed that of a liberated population. Overall it was an impressive sight, one which I will never forget.

We took a C-47 back to England and there was an NBC broadcaster at the field. When he found out who we were he had us talk over the radio a bit. It seems everybody on the beach had seen us fall out, and in fact one person made a broadcast of it as we left the ship: this had been heard back at Seething. This is very crudely put, but expressing the facts of the story, is what will probably be my most unforgettable experience.

Nazi Hell Under My
Blue Heaven
Nathaniel "Bud" Glickman, 93rd and 44th

Twenty-four of my thirty lead or deputy-lead missions resulted in flak damage to the aircraft I flew in.

The first target I was to bomb as a member of the 93rd BG on April 8, 1944 was the ME-110 aircraft plant at Brunswick, Germany. The mission would take us over Dummer Lake, "Flak Alley" en route to the target. In addition, the largest number of enemy air bases protected Brunswick. Our group following the 44th watched as enemy fighters hit them repeatedly. Within minutes I counted five bombers spinning in and then saw one ship take a direct flak hit in a bomb bay and explode in a bright red flash.

After dropping my bombs and turning off the target, we were again under attack. Another 44th bomber was hit and we counted ten chutes getting out. That day our 2nd Division lost 34 bombers and 24 fighters. My first mission was over, but I would return to Brunswick two more times.

Upon completing my seventh mission with the 93rd, I was assigned to a "mickey" crew and transferred to the 66th Squadron of the 44th BG. My first mission with them was to Brunswick, recalling memories of my first flight. As we approached the target we were jumped by FW-190s and I was lucky enough to shoot one down as he made a pass at us.

The morning of June 5, the day before the invasion of Europe, my crew was to lead a three-plane javelin formation to bomb a rocket site in the Pas de Calais area. This would be my eleventh mission and was referred to as a "milk run." I lost my first roommate on his 35th mission on a "milk run," and so failed to find this amusing. The two bombers we would lead were from the 489th BG, whose deputy C.O. was Lt. Col. Leon Vance Jr., who would fly with us as the command pilot. He missed the briefing and arrived at our plane with takeoff being delayed awaiting his appearance. I now believe he was aware of D-Day and our flight was a diversionary tactic to draw attention to the Pas de Calais area. Our pilot informed him of the briefing instructions, including the fact that we were to make one run on the target. If there was a mishap the bombs were to be dropped in the Channel. After his acknowledgment we took off on the mission. I flew as the pilotage navigator in the nose turret with a series of photographs to aid the bombardier in spotting the target.

The only danger was the flak batteries situated on the French coast. The mickey crew consisted of Capt. Lou Mazure, the pilot; Lt. Earl Carper, copilot; Col. Vance, command pilot; a navigator, a radio operator, a bombardier, a bombardier/navigator, a radio man, an engineer, and three gunners.

As we crossed the English coast it was evident that the invasion of Europe was imminent, and that every harbor along the coast was filled with boats and landing craft.

We climbed to our bombing altitude and headed towards the target. Approaching the IP, the aircraft was turned over to the bombardier. Light flak arose off to our right. I indicated the target and the bomb bays were opened. The bombardier called out

"Bombs Away." Nothing happened. Every bomb was still hanging in the bays. Either there had been a malfunction in the bombsight or the arming release switch in the bombardier's panel had not been activated.

We turned off the target and I notified Mazure to head over the Channel and jettison the bomb loads according to the briefing instructions. Colonel Vance countermanded my request and ordered a second run, informing us that he was in command of the flight. We turned south of the target at the same altitude and speed, flying parallel to the coastline and giving the enemy gunners an opportunity to zero in on us. We were sitting ducks.

The second run became hell. The first flak burst exploded off our port wing, killing the pilot. The copilot then took over the controls as we continued the bomb run.

Colonel Vance was standing between the pilots when the next blast hit and tore through the flight deck, hitting him. Flak had raked his right foot so that it hung by a shred. At the same time my nose turret took a series of bursts that shattered the plexiglass and cut open my forehead, and ricocheting, hit the base of my spine. Meanwhile the radar operator applied a tourniquet to the Colonel's shattered leg. Flak continued to explode as we continued on the bomb run. My immediate concern was having the bomb bays hit before the bombs were released. The starboard outer engine shaft was snapped with the blade drooping downwards. The top turret was shattered plus part of the right rudder and elevator had been hit. Nearing the previous release point, I called out that I would drop the bombs using my turret toggle switch. This would bypass the bombardier's and release the bombs. After the release my turret took another hit, cutting my left hand and blasting off the remaining plexiglass, leaving me sitting in open air.

Checking my pilotage map, I advised the copilot of our position and gave him the return heading to England, since the radar operator was working on the Colonel's leg and the navigator in checking found his maps and table damaged. The radio room had been hit, with the radio operator sustaining wounds. As we headed towards England the plane was hit again, cutting the gas lines and forcing the copilot to cut the switches to prevent a fire, which also stopped the power to the three remaining engines as well as my turret controls.

We started gliding towards England without a prop turning over, when I heard "Bail out!" Then the bail out bell rang. My turret was turned half around to the port side, with me being buffeted by the air currents. I could feel my hand bleeding in my glove as well as seeing my flight suit stained from the blood dripping down from my forehead. With no power to turn the turret, I called on my throat mike that I was trapped, and as I turned to try to force the turret around, my throat mike wires which had been frayed, separated.

Turning in my seat I watched the bombardier snapping on his chute. Waving to him to turn my turret so that I could fall out into the well was an exercise in frustration and futility. He looked at me, turned and crept through the wheel tunnel toward the bomb bays to bail out. Perhaps he believed my waving had another meaning. Wiping the blood from my face, I tore all my connecting wires free and tried to turn the turret manually without success. It was impossible to get my fingers into the space between the turret opening and my present position. I then disengaged one of the 50-calibre machine gun charge handles, inserted it in the opening and using it as a lever, turned the turret and fell out into the well where my chest chute was lying and I snapped it onto the harness.

Discovering I was paralyzed struck home as I inched towards the bomb bays while we were still dropping in altitude. Leaving the tunnel and unable to stand, all I could see was the dead pilot and what I believed to be another body next to his seat. I continued crawling to the bomb bay and noticed a 500-pound bomb hanging in the forward port bay. Standing on the catwalk was one of the crew, evidently frozen with fear, holding onto a metal strut blocking my exit to bail out. I shoved him out and then rolled off the catwalk, hoping that I wouldn't hit anything as I left the plane.

The ripcord being on the right side of the chute allowed me to use my good hand. After my chute opened, I spotted an RAF air-sea rescue launch circling under me, which gave me some comfort since I couldn't swim at the time. With the blood running into my eyes, trying to see was a problem. I still worried that when I hit the water the chute canopy would drift over me and I would drown.

Meanwhile the wind was blowing me towards shore, and somewhere over the cliffs of Dover I blacked out. Fortunately, I hit the ground in a relaxed state to find that I had landed on the lawn of the Royal Marine Hospital at Deal. Standing over me was a Marine in battle dress, with a rifle pointed at me and asking if I was a Jerry. My response was less than polite, at which time he replied that I was too fresh and must be a Yank.

Believing I was the last man alive to leave the plane, I later learned Colonel Vance had stayed to pilot the bomber into the Channel, at which time the 500-pound bomb exploded, blowing him clear of the cockpit. He was rescued by the RAF launch.

There were more injuries as a result of bailing out. The radio operator was not only wounded by flak but also shattered his ankle on landing. The engineer broke his ankle on landing, and I was to learn that the navigator breaking his leg in two places as he landed probably saved his life. He had put down in a British mine field and was unable to move. The pilot, Captain Louis Mazure, is resting at the bottom of the English Channel.

Visiting Col. Vance at his hospital, I learned that he believed the radio operator had been trapped, not knowing two gunners had freed him.

Colonel Vance was evacuated to the States via a medivac plane that disappeared in the North Atlantic. He received the Medal of Honor posthumously. The airfield at Enid, Oklahoma was named in his honor.

On July 6 I returned to flying combat. The target was the submarine pens at Kiel and I would be the lead bombardier on a PFF bomber. It would be my twelfth mission and a long way to my final mission, No. 30.

North Sea Bailout—May 29, 1944

Charles M. Trout, 492nd

We were doing fine until we ran into flak over the target. We were hit pretty bad. The copilot was hit, but his flak suit prevented injury.

The #4 engine started throwing oil at about two gallons per minute. The engine was still putting out power, when the oil pressure reached 20 PSI it was feathered by the copilot. I checked the gasoline and it was very low. I transferred the remaining fuel from #4 tank and we were still low on fuel. We thought we could make it to the English coast, but we weren't sure.

The radio operator started to send S.O.S. signals as we knew we were lower on fuel and couldn't make it. We started throwing out everything that was loose or that could be loosened. While we were doing that, two of the planes from our squadron stayed with us but we were flying too slow for them to stay behind, so they left. The radio operator was still sending S.O.S. signals but couldn't tell if he was being heard, for his receiver was shot out as was the trailing wire, the antenna had been knocked off by flak. Then two P-38's started circling us and stayed with us til they saw there was no hope for us and left.

We knew we would have to ditch or bail out, for our fuel was awful low—about three minutes. The crew decided to bail instead of crash. Water was rough with big breakers. Then the pilot heard "Boat in area" when he called "Mayday—Mayday." The rescue boat was below us. We all said a prayer, and I was first to jump. I tried two ways to jump but neither was satisfactory, so I stood up and dove out like I was diving into a pool.

When the propeller and slip stream hit me it took my breath and threw me around pretty rough. When I was down low enough for clearance and everything got so quiet, I pulled the ripcord but nothing happened. The chute didn't open. I reached in and pulled the pilot chute out. Everything came out of the pack and I stopped with a sudden jerk, looked up and was very pleased to see that nice white parachute above me. Looking around and saw more chutes, but didn't count them.

Then I saw the plane circle, which gave me a funny feeling for I thought it was going to spin down among us. But the pilot was just getting closer to the rescue boat before leaving the plane and he was the last man out. The plane started to descend slowly on a straight course and #2 went out when the pilot left.

I looked down and seemed to be about 100 feet above water but hit very quickly, a second or two. Don't know how far I went under but came up immediately. When the cold water got through my clothes it took my breath. I struggled for about ten minutes before I finally got enough breath but breathing was almost impossible due to breaking waves right over the top of me. I unbuckled my chute harness and thought I was rid of it until it started pulling me under. I said another prayer and something made me think of a knife I had in my pocket. I cut everything I could get free, but could not get down far enough to cut it off my feet as my strength was gone. I gave up hope when I couldn't see the rescue boat, but it came to me in about 35 or more minutes. Boy, was I glad to see the boat! They threw me a rope and I hung on and was pulled into a rope ladder. Three Air Sea Rescue men tried to pull me up but couldn't; they had to use a hoist. The rescue team told me to save my strength as I didn't have much left, laid me on deck and told me to go below. I had to crawl so they carried me, cut my clothes off and gave me dry ones, but they had to dress me. I couldn't help myself at all; I was shaking like a leaf in a hailstorm. I was given a hearty welcome by the survivors already picked up. One handed me a cigarette, which took the salt water taste out of my mouth. When everybody was picked up that could be found, they gave us hot tea and brandy to drink so we would get warmed up, and later hot soup and bread and butter. It sure tasted good. We hadn't eaten for a long time. Headed for shore and when we got there we were led in prayer for the missing crewman by the chaplain. We felt bad about losing him, for he was a great guy.

We stayed there for a few days and were treated like kings. When we finally got back to our home base, most of the clothes were gone, divided out, but we got them all back. The best news was that we would all get a week's rest at a Red Cross sponsored rehab center. I thank God I am alive today.

P.S. A great big thanks to the British Air-Sea rescue. They deserve a lot of credit. This story was written two weeks after bailout and had to be censored. That is the reason for no names.

Bedtime Ramblings

Jacob T. Elias, 44th BG

Why? I often wonder why. It is now over thirty-eight years since I left Shipdham-in-the-Mud, and yet, in those half-real moments before I fall asleep, my mind flies over the sea to that place I was happy to leave. A potpourri of memories slowly floats through my consciousness. People, places, smells, violent scenes, rain, hoarfrost on overhead wires, muddy tires on a bicycle.

Transfer to the 14th Combat Wing at Shipdham. The bustle of organizing the Wing, the excitement as word came of Leon Johnson's promotion to Brig. General, the impossible attempts to make the long cold brick barracks livable. Cold. Summer, I was told, had lasted several weeks this year instead of the usual three days. A tiny stove in the center of a long, high-ceilinged room with concrete floor and brick sides, totally inadequate for heating anything but a few inches of air directly above it. Our ration of two buckets of coke was fireproof anyway. We fled to the Red Cross building when we could, basking in the warmth of that fireplace. Mud everywhere, sticky, cold, mocking.

I found a bicycle for two dollars, one of the best investments I ever made. American style coaster brake, too, instead of the handle levers, probably the only one on the base. Rides through narrow roads, over gentle hills, past high hedgerows, mist and fine rain. A stop at a tea shop in the village, and hot aromatic tea with heavy cake or scones. They were Spartan confections – would never be allowed within a hundred yards of a 'patisserie,' but they were full of the good stuff that enable the Briton to withstand the soggy winter.

Typing letters and filing reports was not my idea of winning the war and getting the Congressional Medal of Honor pinned on my chest by the President of the USA himself. My attitude was probably noted by – (I'll be charitable and not mention his name). My request for transfer to a combat crew was quickly approved and I moved to the 68th Squadron area. A month later I found myself listed on the alert sheet for my first mission as waist gunner.

Shaking with fear as we rose in the half-night and assembled in the blueing sky, headed for the Channel. Tension and fear as I looked at the Dutch coastline. "Clear the guns" came the order, and the shaking gun in my hands told me this was no bad dream, but reality. A terrible fever raged through me as I realized the ground underneath was hostile.

Coming in over the target on the Pas-de-Calais, black blossoms with red centers appeared miraculously around us. Pretty, I thought. What are they? A few blossomed closer, thuds shook the plane. Then it struck me – this was FLAK! More evil blossoms flowered all around us and then we swung away as the bombs were released, the shuddering stopped as the bomb bay doors closed and we headed back for home. How welcome was the sight of the Channel, more welcome the sight of Lowestoft and the friendly fields of Suffolk and Norfolk. That first step on solid ground, how good it felt!

A couple of days later and over to Abbeville. The flak was heavy, the ship bounced and shook as we went in. Bombs away, bomb bay doors closed, a swing west, then I felt it, like a hammer hitting my leg. What was that? I asked myself, then felt something wet rolling down inside the heavy clothes. The bombardier came back and powdered the wound with sulfa, wrapped a bandage around it. The ambulance was waiting as soon as we stopped on the revetment, a fast trip to the base medic, and then a longer trip to Wymondham where the nickel sized piece was removed, the smaller pieces left in my leg for souvenirs.

A month there, living in a warm room, clean white sheets, food served on dishes, attentive nurses. Like a vacation, except for feeling hemmed in, useless. Restlessness grew as the tension before D-Day grew in the British Isles. I persuaded the doctor to let me go back to Shipdham earlier than he wanted.

Back at the 68th I was assigned to the "Flak Magnet", Joy Smith in charge. What a pilot! Cool, efficient as a computer, a rock of strength, knowing his job. Also, Kenny Sprowl, "Sparks", Gene DeWaters, Flight Engineer, Johnny Shelton at the waist window across from me. Several missions to France and Germany, then D-Day. One engine knocked out, we flew alone on the return, but we made it OK. Another time Johnny got a piece of flak in the neck and the bombardier and I were frantic in our efforts to stem the blood. He made it in spite of us. Bastogne and bombing by radar, praying the bombs didn't drop on our own troops – a good friend of mine was down there with the 82nd Airborne.

My thirty missions were finished just a few days past New Year of 1944. What a relief! Yet it was hard to part with all those guys on the crew and in my Nissen hut. As I packed and readied myself, the radio with the cracked case up on the shelf faithfully sings out with "Take The 'A' Train", "One O'clock Jump", "Deep Purple", "I Walk Alone". I looked at the guys, stretched out on their bunks, reading, or sitting on the edge, writing a letter. Van Rogers was heating water for tea, dropping an extra piece of wood down the insatiable throat of that little stove to hurry up the heat. Harry Ricketts was sewing a button on his jacket, almost as though he knew what he was doing. Elvin Scheetz was writing a letter. How I hated to leave them, much as I wanted to go home! What a wrench to go from them. That scene made a mark on my consciousness that has faded but never gone.

In 1955 I went back to Norfolk to visit my friends in Wroxham. Monica dropped me off at "The King's Head" one day, where the road goes into the airbase from the Shipdham-Dereham road. I refused her offer to drive me into the base. "I'll Walk Alone", as Lily Ann Carroll used to sing in 1944.

The day was one of those normal ones, low gray clouds fleeing ahead of the cold wind though it was August again, the same month I'd come in 1943. The barman in "The King's Head" assured me I was at the right place. Then he gave me the name of another man who'd stopped a few weeks before, a professor at Syracuse University in New York, who wanted to hear from anyone who followed.

I walked slowly along the road, sad. Why was I sad? I couldn't understand. The runway that ended on this road came into sight, seams in the concrete sprouting weeds. In the distance stood the control tower, silent, like a mourning sentinel in the bleak landscape. Not a soul in sight. Ghostly and unreal. Around the corner and there was the grove of tall trees where "Southern Comfort" used to sit. A little further and I found the 14th Combat Wing Buildings. The brick buildings were battered and broken, shattered ruins, but the Nissen huts were intact, used for sheltering and feeding cattle. Windows were broken, brambles growing through the frames.

Up in the recreation area I found the pond where General Johnson was dunked during the 200 mission party. The Red Cross Building and Library were gone, across the way was no sign of the

68th Squadron Area. Down at the mess hall and theatre, shells of buildings, concrete floors the only remains of some buildings. Out on the main runway stood an abandoned farm machine. Up in the control tower broken glass covered the floor, a door swung eerily in the breeze, rust ate at all the frame.

I stood looking out at the world that seemed deserted by humans. And my mind saw once again the slow moving lines of lumbering bombers, one by one stopping at the end of the runway to gun their engines, gently start to move and then roar in a mighty effort to lift their bomb-heavy bodies from the clinging ground. And I saw the trucks and jeeps busily going to and fro, the ground crews watching warily as their ships made their run and lifted off, worrying and praying.

I walked back toward the Dereham road again and faces flitted through my mind, faces of men – boys, really, but men ahead of their time. Faces I had come to look forward to seeing in the morning, faces of men I had come to think beautiful no matter what the shape of nose or chin or color of eye, faces of men I had come to love for their smiles, their teasing, their sadness in unguarded moments, for their courage in facing death though the fear in their hearts was deep as in mine.

My heart was verily sad as I trod with heavy heart toward Dereham. Where were they, those wonderful kids? Those great-hearted kids with smooth cheeks, a few stray hairs on their upper lip, kids who did not speak of patriotism, love of country, fear of death, but who went out and did the best they could, clumsily at times, perfectly some times, but always the best their only human minds and bodies could do. All the time they were trying, they were wondering if they would ever again see their loved ones in Pennsylvania, in Texas or Georgia, Brooklyn or L.A. As I remembered those faces a corrosive sadness spread through my veins. I shivered with the cold sadness. And though I have been back to Norfolk four or five times since, I have never returned to Shipdham. I just could not go back.

Yet many and many a time, in those moments before I fell asleep, I do return to that Nissen hut. Again we are making tea on that little stove, and there is teasing and laughing, faces smiling at me, and the radio is playing again. "One O'clock Jump," "Begin The Beguine," "Deep Purple," " Frenesí," "Green Eyes," "Chattanooga Choo-Choo," and Lily Ann Carroll singing blue, "I'll Walk Alone."

I don't want my sons to experience war. But I wish they could experience that complete camaraderie that I had at Shipdham-in-the-Mud. A friend to ride his bike beside yours through the beauty of the country, a friend to drink some hot tea beside the comforting fire after a walk in cold rain, a friend with you when the going is tough, a friend beside you when trouble gets almost too much for one person to handle. I had those friends at Shipdham. That is why my mind often goes back to Shipdham, finds comfort in going back to Shipdham, and most likely will keep going back to that barracks full of love.

A Bit of Trouble
Over Norwich
Fred Becchetti, 445th

July 31, 1944, and the 445th Bomb Group is headed for Ludwigshafen, our B-24 bomb bays loaded with unarmed fragmentation bombs.

Pilot Keith Palmer lifts off from Tibenham at 9 a.m. and takes her over the 500 ft. ceiling for the assembly of the group formation over the Wash.

At 16,000 ft. and climbing, our No. 4 prop runs away. Palmer feathers it, calls in an aborted mission and reports an altitude loss of 300 feet per minute.

There's no returning to base with the unarmed fragmentation bombs, so I give Palmer a heading to a point over the Channel where we are to jettison the frags.

We dump the bombs, but the ship continues to lose altitude. Then a second engine begins to act up, and our rate of altitude loss increases.

To lighten the ship, Palmer gives the order to toss out everything that is loose. We wrestle with guns, ammo, flak suits and even the generator and send them whistling through the 500 ft.

layer of clouds to whatever lies below. At one point, I jokingly grabbed waist gunner McGovern by the leg as though to toss him out. Lots of laughs later about that!

At 2000 ft. and still losing altitude at a dangerous rate, Palmer polls the crew and we vote to bail out in the hopes of saving the ship by lightening it even more.

Over the Norfolk region but unable to see the land because of the clouds, we line up at the rear hatch and bail out one at a time into the unknown beneath the cloud cover: first, waist gunner Gregory McGovern (who fractured his leg on landing); then tail gunner Robert Sherrick; waist gunner Lawrence Sladovnik (who broke his leg); ball turret gunner John M. Smith (who sprained an ankle landing in a British WAAF base, where the women took care of him splendidly); radio gunner Carl McHenry (who sprained an ankle); engineer Bernard Goldstein; and finally myself.

Bailing out at about 1000 ft., I count quickly to three and yank the ripcord, while the noisy B-24 flies off, leaving me in the dead silence of the sky as I drift downward through the clouds into who knows what. I whistle to myself to break the eerie silence.

In the clouds I begin to hear sounds from below. People talking, vehicles. I burst through the cloud cover. I am coming down in a residential area of Norwich. There is only the slightest wind, so I am coming straight down with a little lateral movement.

To my right, a large tree and a house. To my left, a row of small trees and a house. And directly in front of me, there is a small, newly-spaded garden, an eight ft. high hedge and beyond the hedge, a house.

Delicately, I maneuver toward the center of the garden. I land without a roll, both feet together and falling forward comfortably, with my face slightly pushed into the soft soil of the garden.

Slightly dazed, I lie there and monitor my body, feeling a

slight twinge in my left ankle, but otherwise feeling good and thankful, though somewhat reluctant to move.

I hear a rustle of branches in the hedge in front of me. The hedge parts and a ruddy-faced man peeks through, catches my eye and with a twinkle and a smile asks me, "Having a bit of trouble, Yank?"

And I laugh, reviewing in my mind all that has happened since 9:00 in the morning.

Mr. Morris pushes through the hedge while I unhook the harness of my chute entangled in the tree. He helps me into the house and serves me a scotch and soda. After a while, two Bobbies pedal up, eye my Italian name with some suspicion, until the MPs show up to take me back to the base, where I learn that pilot Palmer and copilot Cliff Bolton were able to land the ship after the bailout.

As for my parachute entangled in the tree, we never found it.

They say that several little girls in the neighborhood had new dresses for school the next year.

Tondelayo's Last Mission—Target: Politz

Jim Blanco, 392nd

(My 14th, and I failed to write it up upon returning, and after going to Berlin the next day, didn't remember much of this tough mission)

Lt. C.L. Bell was last seen heading...

That partial sentence covers nine different experiences which could add pages in terms of experiences. As a member of Bell's crew I remember quite vividly the experience of *that* day.

The mission started about 2300 hours of 19 June, when the C.Q. came to roust us out of our sacks with the usual info of breakfast and briefing times. After the breakfast briefing, I still recall the feeling in the pit of my stomach, because the excess trace line of our route in and out of the target area was not visible on the floor. This meant a long haul. The first two missions, or maybe five, it's still an adventurous experience. After that you start to sober. This was our twenty-fifth. After briefing it was the usual jokes and horseplay to buoy up our spirits as we made our way to the locker room to don our heated suits.

After dressing I locked my locker and discovered I had not put my sidearm away. At that time AAF Regs ordered no sidearms to be taken on missions. Being a little late, I decided to check it in to Tech Supply. I told the Sarge, "I'll pick it up, *if* I come back." The Sarge remarked, "Don't worry. Bell's crew always comes back." At day's end it was certain that a seer he was not.

As we rode to the dispersal area, I felt apprehensive. This was my first mission without Joe Knight. He was grounded with a bad cold. Group superstition was when one man stayed down, the odds were the crew doesn't return, or the man doesn't on a make-up mission.

Joe and I had a ritual we did before take-off. We ate our caramels from the high carbohydrates box because we didn't want the Luftwaffe to get them, and chewed gum. As we prepared for take-off, we'd stick our gum wads on the tail fin of a bomb and say, "Remember when you're up there your soul belongs to God, your heart belongs to the girl back home, and your a– is strictly the Luftwaffe's."

Takeoff and forming were normal and I prepared my duties transferring gas from the wingtip tanks to the main tanks and leveling the tanks. Then the tensions started with the call, "Enemy coast ahead." Somewhere over Denmark our first fighter escorts dropped off and there was the usual wait of five to ten minutes before the next pick-up. Sometimes these minutes seemed like an eternity. This was one of those times.

Flying on, and always on the alert for enemy fighters, I noted and alerted the crew of a group of forty to fifty fighters flying level and at five o'clock. Someone remarked that it was the second group of our escorts. I was reluctant to accept it, and kept watching them. They were too bunched up to be our escorts. As they approached three o'clock, they were a mile and a half to two miles from our formation. One fighter did a slip maneuver. I noted tail booms—P38?—hardly! How long I watched I do not know. The 492nd was leading the Wing and was starting to turn on the IP I thought they were spreading out too wide. It was then when the fighters hit. They definitely were not our escorts! I was fascinated, appalled and scared stiff as the fighters took their toll.

As we turned on the IP, they turned on us. I can still remember rocket streamers and the machine gun fire. Fortunately, I think they had used their Sunday punch earlier, but what was left was still terrifying. We sustained some minor damage. After they broke the attack, I had the impression those fighter pilots must have been totally without experience or training. The couple that had pressed their attack on us were a JU 88 and an ME 210. They attacked us flying with the formation. The JU 88 started the attack at five o'clock and about two hundred feet above us. I saw the stitch marks my fifties were making on his fuselage before he broke away. The ME 210 came in at the same height from six o'clock, and I put the same stitches in his wing.

As we approached the target area someone remarked on the intercom, "Those flak-boys are really checked out." I turned my turret to twelve o'clock to check. I will affirm they certainly were "checked out." It seems they were shooting in a perfect rectangular pattern of about 400 X 600 feet. What seemed worse was, our line of flight would put us right through the center of the barrage. I observed the element leader moving ever so slightly to the left, and mentally I was telling Bell to move it over, out of center.

My next actions are burned deeply in memory. I looked at the flak and knew we would not see any enemy fighters; so I started to think of other targets with heavy flak—Berlin, Brunswick and Friedrichshafen. I didn't recall flak coming either from the pilot's compartment or the bomb bay. I did experience it coming from the sides. My turret had one-half inch armor in front and I had put flak vests at the back and under the jewels. My sides were unprotected. I rotated the turret to nine o'clock so that my right side was toward the cockpit and my left to the bomb bay. Next I thought of the plexiglass dome. Shrapnel can and does pierce and shatter if a burst comes close to it. So I reached down and put my helmet on. At this point my guns were elevated, so for added protection, I lowered the guns so that the receivers were on each side of my head. In this cocoon I went I went into the "Valley of Death" with a prayer to the Almighty and the usual promises to reform. I was scared! Not caring to lift my head to see anything that wasn't in my line of sight, I watched the blossoms of flak and felt several bumps indicating hits in the aircraft. Then came the relieving signal: "Bombs away, let's get the hell out of here."

After leaving the flak field, I climbed down from the turret to survey battle damage. Up front, flak had hit our radio and it was a mess. There were numerous holes in the skin, letting in daylight, and one piece of flak severed a run of wires—some of which were for the #3 and #4 engine instruments.

I started to go aft and I will attest to the fact that the combination of rubber flight boots and hydraulic oil make very slippery catwalks. Fortunately, the bomb bay doors were closed when the flak hit the hydraulic system. As I entered the waist section, gunners Asch and Seymour were doing a jig trying to avoid being hit by pistol flares set off by a piece of flak.

Returning to flight deck, I was surprised to see we had left the formation. The #3 and #4 engines were running smoothly, but without a tachometer and manifold pressure gauges we did not know how much power to pull back or advance. It was decided to leave the settings as they were for a while and use #1 and #2 for flight changes. By this time, we had hit the deck. Time had lost its magnitude as I busied myself leveling gas tanks and watching #3 and #4 engines for the slightest malfunction.

Decision time came when Bell announced we had three options:

1. Land in Germany
2. Ditch in the North or Baltic Sea
3. Land in Sweden

Personally, I did not like the idea of being a POW, nor did I care to ditch. As for Sweden, it was an unknown, and I thought it the best of what was available. It must have been, in spite of the last few hours, my lucky day. We headed for Sweden.

What confronted me on landing was that I would have to crank the gear down and kick-out the nose wheel. Not knowing the field in which we would set down, I was more than concerned because we had only enough hydraulic pressure for one application of brakes. With the gear cranked down and locked, the nose wheel kicked-out. Our landing pattern was normal. As we turned in for our final approach, another wounded B-24 cut us out. Luck was with us as we applied power to #3 and #4 engines and they responded. We nursed our angel around again to the base leg. The B-24 that cut us off had touched down, ground looped and burst into flames.For Bell's crew it was a very long haul that lasted for five months. Bell and I stayed behind for a total of ten months. Through all the years and future years I always say, "Tack a mika for Sverige"—literally translated, "Thanks a million for Sweden!"

Under the conditions we had flown, our landing was normal. As we passed the burning B-24, the ammo aboard was exploding. Then came our moment of truth. Our one application of brakes brought us within three feet of the end of the runway. Later, after conversations with Swedish friends, we learned that on that day the Swedes thought the entire 8th Air Force was going to land there. Twenty bombers had landed. I never could verify it, but my

Swedish friends say the plane that blew up on landing was the 13th to land.

We limped along nursing that "gawky angel" every mile to Malmo, Sweden. As we approached Sweden, two fighters appeared high at seven o'clock. I turned my turret to meet them and thought, "Here we go again." For some unknown reason we all held our fire. This was unusual because we were all pretty jumpy. The planes were unusual. They did not have the lines of either the FW'S or ME's. Someone identified them as Italian. As they approached closer, we were all tense waiting for them to flash their recognition lights (guns), but none flashed. They were fighters from the Swedish Air Force coming to escort us to Malmo.

What confronted me on landing was that I would have to crank the gear down and kick-out the nose wheel. Not knowing the field in which we would set down, I was more than concerned because we had only enough hydraulic pressure for one application of brakes. With the gear cranked down and locked, the nose wheel kicked-out. Our landing pattern was normal. As we turned in for our final approach, another wounded B-24 cut us out. Luck was with us as we applied power to #3 and #4 engines and they responded. We nursed our angel around again to the base leg. The B-24 that cut us off had touched down, ground looped and burst into flames.

Under the conditions we had flown, our landing was normal. As we passed the burning B-24, the ammo aboard was exploding. Then came our moment of truth. Our one application of brakes brought us within three feet of the end of the runway. Later, after conversations with Swedish friends, we learned that on that day the Swedes thought the entire 8th Air Force was going to land there. Twenty bombers had landed. I never could verify it, but my Swedish friends say the plane that blew up on landing was the 13th to land.

For Bell's crew it was a very long haul that lasted for five months. Bell and I stayed behind for a total of ten months. Through all the years and future years I always say, "Tack a mika for Sverige"—literally translated, "Thanks a million for Sweden!"

Wings of Memory

Mary Lou Wilson

Reprinted from the Vacaville Reporter, July 22, 1991
Submitted by W.H. "Bill" Beasley, 492nd

Navigator Berl Robinson grabbed frantically at the maps blowing about the bullet-riddled turret of the B-24 Liberator. Flames were streaming from the plane's No. 4 engines, hit by flak just after bombardier Jesse Briggs dropped his load of bombs on the Stettin Oil Refinery in Politz, Germany.

There were gas leaks everywhere. The fuel gauges in the cockpit were broken and the bomb bay was full of fuel mist. No one knew how much gas was left or which tank it was in.

Certain that the crippled bomber was doomed, one crewman had already bailed out through the nose wheel door. Eleven of the planes flying with them had dropped into the Baltic Sea, but pilot Joe Harris decided there was a chance the "Silver Witch" could reach neutral Sweden.

It was up to Robinson to set the course to safety. He corralled the maps and directed the pilot to a small airfield at Malmo on the Swedish coast.

That day—June 20, 1944—is a part of World War II history, the time when "the air war over Western Europe reached a new peak of fury," the International News Service reported.

That day was also the reason for a quiet reunion in a Davis restaurant a few weeks ago when Robinson, now 78, and Briggs, 72, saw each other for the first time since their internment in Sweden.

Forty-seven years had passed, but in memory they were still the snappy looking captain and lieutenant who shared that heart-stopping flight across the Baltic.

"It's great, we can't describe it," said Robinson when a friend asked how it felt to be together again.

Robinson has lived in Vacaville since 1949; unknown to him, Briggs has been in Rancho Cordova for 25 years. They got in touch by phone after each received a letter forwarded by the Veterans Administration from tail gunner Willis Beasley who was trying to contact all crew members of the "Silver Witch." It took a while to set up a reunion. But finally—joined by a few relatives and friends, including Robinson's wife, Adele, and Briggs' wife, Christine—the two met again.

They had already caught up on the years that followed that mission. Robinson left the service in 1945, was recalled in 1948 and sent to Japan to replace personnel flying the Berlin Airlift. From Japan, he returned to the then Fairfield-Suisun Air Force Base and became a public information officer for Brig. Gen. Robert Falligant Travis for whom Travis Air Force Base was named. Out of the service, he earned his teaching credential and taught at Vacaville Union High School for several years. After that, he owned a toy and hobby shop in Vacaville called Robby Hobby and later operated Vaca Welcome, a greeting service. He also worked in real estate.

Briggs was recalled by the Air Force in both the Korean and Vietnam wars. After serving in Vietnam, he stayed in. His last assignment was at Mather Air Force Base where he retired in 1970 as a lieutenant colonel.

But those were years spent apart. What they wanted to talk about was the harrowing flight and the four months together in Sweden.

Their memories fit together like pieces of a jigsaw puzzle. One would start a story, the other would finish it; when "Robby" Robinson hesitated over a name, "Snuffy" Briggs supplied it.

Briggs had a few precious snapshots with him. Another member of the group had newsletters from the 492nd Bomb Group which had sent 35 bombers, including the "Silver Witch," on the June 20 run. The newsletter noted that there were 3,500 to 4,000 planes in the air that day—at the time it was the greatest concentration of American heavy bombers ever sent into action.

Robinson and Briggs said they could still picture the chaos: smoke filling the plane; the nose turret being punctured by their own machine gun bullets set off by anti-aircraft fire; crew members inching through the unpressurized plane wearing heated suits and shoes and oxygen masks.

As they headed for Sweden, Briggs jettisoned the ultra-secret Norden bombsight into the sea. When they entered Swedish air space, they found German planes, flown by Swedes, on their wingtips.

They were directed to a grassy field where they landed. They learned later that 21 planes from the 8th Air Force had found their way to Malmo that same day.

"It was lucky the 'Silver Witch' made it," said Robinson. "Despite the maps, I was guessing at where I had been and where I was going. I just told the pilot to head in the general direction of Sweden."

The Swedes treated the internees well, agreed Robinson and

Briggs. When given passes, they could bicycle about, visit Stockholm and enjoy the beaches.

But they were anxious to get home. In October, under cover of bad weather, Robinson flew to England with 100 other men in a converted B-24 bomber. Briggs followed in November. So both were back in the States with their families.

On the June 20, 1944 mission to Politz, Colonel Gerry Mason (448th CO) and Major Chester B. Hackett, Jr. (CO of the 715th Squadron) flew with 389th Pathfinder crews. Col. Mason was Command Pilot leading the 20th Combat Wing, while Major Hackett flew as his deputy off his right wing.

Major Hackett Remembers the Mission: Politz - 448th BG

"Just before midnight on the evening before my 24th mission, Col. Mason and I were driven to Hethel airfield to fly with 389th crews on a mission to bomb the oil fields at Politz.

The mission was uneventful en route to the target with the usual flak and German fighters. We had escort fighters for the entire trip to Stettin and over the target. The weather was clearing as we proceeded across Germany and by the time we changed course just north of Stettin the sky was absolutely clear.

We could look over to the south and watch each twelve-ship formation make their bomb runs on Politz. We were flying at 30,000 feet and the anti-aircraft fire over the target was heavy. Before turning south to the IP, I called Col. Mason and asked him to consider changing our altitude to avoid some of the flak. This was my 24th mission and Col. Mason had only recently joined our Group. He called me back having decided that we would not change altitude. So we made our run at the same altitude as the formations ahead of us.

Just after we dropped our bombs the aircraft seemed to stop in mid-air. We had taken flak hits in the nose section, bomb bay, fuel tanks and waist compartment.

Dropping out of formation, I called Col. Mason and told him I was going to try to reach Sweden.

Power on all four engines was about nil, so I called the crew and directed them to bail out. As it turned out ten men jumped, one of the waist gunners called and informed me that Lt. Rose had been hit and was hurt badly. I instructed him to attach a static line to Rose's parachute, help him out of the waist window and pull his ripcord for him.

After this, I unbuckled as a faint odor of smoke began filling the cockpit. I was about to jump out the open bomb bay when I saw Capt. East walking back from the rear of the plane up the catwalk into the bomb bay. I asked him why he had not jumped. He told me he had no parachute. He was wearing a harness but no parachute pack. The bombardier uses a chest-type parachute. He just keeps the harness on and places his chest pack in back of him. This enables him to operate the bombsight. A piece of flak had hit a walk-around oxygen bottle which had exploded, ripping his chest pack.

He had gone back to the rear of the aircraft looking for another chute. There was none to be found and he said Lt. Rose was dead in the waist section. He also stated that fuel was running all over the rear bomb bay.

With Capt. East missing his parachute and Lt. Rose dead, I really had only one course of action. I told East to climb into the copilot's seat and I got back into the pilot's seat.

East and I proceeded to shut down everything—all power and electrical equipment to lessen the chance of a fire. After everything was shut down the smoke in the cockpit subsided.

All this took only a few minutes and I told him I intended to crash land. He said for me to go ahead and bail out, he would take the aircraft down. There was no way I would allow this, so we proceeded to descend. Our altitude was now down to about 15,000 feet. As we continued our glide, two ME-109s attacked us from left side. The only thing I could think to do was dive, pick up speed and turn into them closing the distance between us as quickly as possible. That was the last I saw of the fighters until we were about to land in a grain field. When we got down to about 2,000 feet I started looking for a field and circled the one I had picked out.

There was very little wind at about 300 feet. We lined up on the field and lowered the landing gear. However, I touched down too fast. After rolling about 2,000 feet we hit a ditch and snapped the nose wheel. The aircraft came up on its nose, but did not flip over. As the plane slowed, the tail section settled back down and we slowly came to a stop. Capt. East immediately went down into the bombardier's compartment and detonated the explosives on the Norden bombsight and H2S radar system, destroying them both.

During the landing approach, I had seen a ME-109 crash a short distance away. When East and I got out of the aircraft, two P-51 Mustangs flew over, turned and climbed for their flight back to England. It was a great feeling to witness the dedication and bravery of our fighter friends.

We had crashed a few miles northwest of Stettin and were immediately surrounded by the German populace. They had watched our approach and landing, converging on us very quickly. They took us to the local village and eventually turned us over to the Luftwaffe. After being interrogated, we were sent to Stalag Luft 3 near Sagan, Germany."

Lt. Col. Hackett was a POW until May 1945 when they were liberated from Moosburg by General Patton and remained in the USAF until 1962.

From Al Ciurzack's Diary

"September 11, 1943: Took off at 8 o'clock for Paramushiro. Trip was uneventful on the way out, but after the bombs dropped on the target our flight was attacked by a flock of Zeros. We all headed for the deck, and when we got there we stayed at about 50 feet. Major Gash's ship on our right wing crashed in the water not over a hundred feet from us due to enemy fighter action. It sure was a shock to see them hit the water, for I knew the crew well since I flew with them on prior missions, especially Walter Feuer, the photographer, who I have known since I first joined the Army. The Zeros kept coming. We got hit above the bomb bays. All our radios were knocked out and another shell put a big hole in our deicer tanks and hydraulic system, it's lucky we didn't blow up. I went up to the flight deck to tell Lambe (our engineer) about the deicer tanks. Just as I stuck my head in the door, two 20 mm shells hit the top hatch and went off when they hit the armor plate of the top turret. The place was filled with smoke.

When it cleared a bit I climbed in to talk to Lambe, who was standing behind the pilot and copilot. Just then a shell hit the front windshield, hitting the copilot in the face. Lambe and I got the copilot out of his seat, sat him in the corner and Lambe got into the copilot seat. I took care of the copilot. He was bleeding like a stuck pig. I ripped open all the first aid kits I could find and put on all the bandages, but the blood kept coming. I then ripped off my winter underwear for it was the cleanest thing I could think of and wrapped it around his head and face leaving an opening near his mouth so he could breathe. The blood slowed up so I gave him some sulfanilamide tablets. He was sure taking it well, didn't squawk one bit, even when I gave him a shot of morphine in the leg to ease the pain. A shell hit alongside me, just above the radio table and the felt lining of the plane caught fire. I put it out by pulling the felt loose. The Zeros finally left and was I glad, so was the rest of the crew, especially the pilot for it was a hard job flying the plane with one hand (the shell that came through the front windshield had also hit him in the right arm.) It's a good thing Lambe, our engineer, knew a lot about flying and he really helped the pilot. When we were sure the Zeros had gone for good, Lt. Lemons, our bombardier, came up to the flight deck and we cleared the empty shells from the top turret and made a place for the copilot to lie down. We had a few blankets and bed rolls in the plane so we wrapped them around him to keep him warm.

"Then I left the flight deck and went to the back of the ship where the gunners were talking about the Zeros they had shot down. Rodd, the top turret gunner, found a hole made by a 30 caliber bullet in the bill off his hat (he wore it with the bill turned up.) There were lots of happy gunners, four Zeros to the ship's credit. (Top turret—one; fixed nose guns—one; tail gunner—one; left waist gun—one.) Our happy spell didn't last long for when the engineer tried to transfer fuel from the bomb bay tank to the wing tanks, he found that the pump wouldn't work. That meant that we had about one chance in ten of making it back to Attu. The pilot gave the order to toss everything out of the plane that was loose. Everything went out the bottom hatch; machine guns, cameras, radio equipment, and we even chopped the armor plate out alongside the gunner's position and tossed that out the bottom hatch. We all put on our life vests and went up forward so the ship would fly better.

I don't know about the others, but that's when I started to pray and think. I guess this was the hardest I ever prayed in my life. The thought that kept running through my mind was not being able to see Kitty, my wife, again. The engineer and I climbed into the bomb bay and tried to fix the fuel pump. No use, we didn't have the tools. All we could do was pray. According to the gas gauge, we had enough fuel left in our wing tanks to fly until six o'clock. The navigator told us we would hit land at 5:55. I relaxed a little for I knew if the weather was clear we could find the field. At 5:15 we were told to go to the back and prepare for a crash landing. We packed our sleeping bags against the rear bulkhead. While this was going on the radio operator was helping the pilot fly the ship. We all stuck our noses to the windows to look for signs of land. At 5:55 we spotted land and our hopes went up. Fog was rolling in, no sign of the airstrip. The ship banked sharply and headed away from shore. We didn't know what was going on but found out later that the pilot couldn't find the Attu landing strip and headed for Shemya, sixteen miles away.

It was six o'clock and our gas gauges read empty. We were flying on borrowed time. Landing gear went down. We heard the wheels hit the end of the strip and we all jumped out and hailed a jeep, sending the driver for an ambulance. We all helped the copilot out of the ship and waited for the ambulance. The mission was over. Looking the ship over later, we found it was full of holes and it's a wonder it didn't fall apart."

"I'll always remember the copilot as we helped him out of the ship at the end of the flight. His head was covered with my bloody underwear. He was standing and he wanted to pee. Someone said, 'Pee in your pants.' He said, 'Are you kidding?' The ambulance came after he relieved himself near the nose wheel and climbed on the stretcher. They slid him in and away they went. Although I had tossed out the cameras when we got the word to lighten the load, I kept the exposed film magazines and headed to the base photo lab. Great pictures. Wasn't able to keep a set— 'Classified.'

"I will always remember September 11, 1943."

Retired U. S. Air Force Captain Al Ciurczak received two DFC's during his Aleutian Island tour.

Who Packs Your Parachute?

Jim H. Reeves, Group Relations Committee

I recently read an interesting article written by Charles Plumb entitled "Who Packs Your Parachute?" Many, many 2nd Air Division personnel wore parachutes while on active duty. This article can reflect upon our active duty days as well as our daily lives since that age and time. The message is simple, yet very thought-provoking. In his article, Charles Plumb tells about his experiences. As a U.S. Naval Academy graduate and a jet fighter pilot in Vietnam, he flew 75 successful combat missions before being shot down by a surface-to-air missile. He spent the next six years in a Communist prison. He survives and now lectures about his experiences.

One day Plumb and his wife were sitting in a restaurant when a man approached him saying "I know you. You're Plumb! You flew from the carrier Kitty Hawk! You were shot down!"

"How in the world do you know that?" asked Plumb.

"I packed your parachute. I guess it worked," the man replied.

Plumb relates that he didn't sleep much that night. He thought about the man who spent hours in the bowels of a ship carefully folding the silks of the chutes. He wondered what the man might have looked like in uniform. Had he seen him? Had he ever noticed him? He wondered how many times he had not offered a smile nor said good morning, for you see, he was an officer and a fighter pilot, and this man was just a sailor.

We all have our parachutes—our physical parachutes, our mental parachutes, our emotional parachutes, and our spiritual parachutes. It's important for us to realize that we don't weather storms by ourselves.

There are others—some we know, some we don't—who help us survive.

Mission to Zwickau

After a number of missions, and a ten-day rest period, I was assigned on return as tail gunner on a newly formed crew. The following is an account of my first mission with this crew.

April 14, 1944: The much dreaded sound of the Jeep halting at our Quonset hut; the hut door opened, and the driver calls out our new pilot's name. Before we knew it, we were eating chow and off to briefing prior to takeoff time. After briefing, we made our usual preparations: checking out personal equipment; preflight preparations, start engines, and taxi out. We took off one at a time and slowly gained altitude. We joined formation in our assigned rear slot spot, and we were on our way to Zwickau, Germany.

As soon as we crossed the Channel and were over Belgium, all hell broke loose. Flack hit our far left engine and black smoke started pouring out of it. A hole the size of a basketball opened up at the feet of our waist gunner. Another direct hit in the waist ripped open the floor. As we gathered our wits and resumed our gun positions we were informed over the intercom that the nose also was badly hit. Bullets began ricocheting around my tail turret; a ME-109 was coming in at eye level. I opened up fire when I felt he was in proper range, and was rewarded by the Messerschmitt disintegrating in a ball of fire, almost hitting the tail turret as it exploded. By now the ship was too crippled, and we lost altitude and dropped out of formation, becoming a "sitting duck" for the rest of the enemy fighters. We tried to keep our guns firing to discourage the fighters from getting in close enough for a clean kill. But the handwriting was on the wall by this time. The intercom ceased to function; then a crew member from up front crawled back to tell us to bail out. Bail out! Those were words we gunners heard in training lectures, saw demonstrated in training films; but to each of us it was always going to happen to "the other guy," not to me! I quickly put out the fire (luckily it was superficial) and put on the chute. There were four of us in the rear section by this time; S/Sgt. Wayne Luce, badly wounded by our first blast; S/Sgt. Pete Clark; our radio operator "Chet"; and myself. We got Luce's chute on, carried him into the waist window and released him, pulling his ripcord at the last possible minute. The chute opened clear of the plane and we looked at each other and smiled. The rest of us decided to jump out the camera hatch as our exhausted condition and the urgency made any other exit impossible. I gave a last look down, jumped, pulled the cord, and looked up to see the ship moving away. Everything then became a blur until I hit terra firma; the stinging pain ran from my ankles up to my head as I buckled over and passed out.

I opened my eyes some time later, to see German soldiers looking down at me and mumbling, and civilians in the background gawking at me. I was carried to what looked like our American-type police wagon, driven through the city to a school hall, stayed there overnight, and then by bus (with three of our crew members who also had survived) to a ward in a walled-in hospital in Brussels. There we stayed for two weeks. The patients were wounded Luftwaffe, plus about five American flyers. I was treated for splintered ankles, and a gashing forehead wound from a fragment that hit me just prior to when I jumped. All during this time we were forbidden to speak or in any way communicate with the others; in fact, our own policy was to act as if we were complete strangers to each other, to minimize security leaks. Every morning a Luftwaffe Colonel doctor would enter our ward, a German nurse would shout "Achtung" and, regardless of our physical condition and pain, we were expected to come to a rigid attention, and say "Good morning, doctor."

April 20 came, and I remember it especially because the guards and hospital staff celebrated with much champagne and booze, as it was Hitler's birthday.

After a week of recuperating, I was allowed to go out into the walled courtyard and sit in the sun and watch our bombers and fighters fly over. It was an odd feeling to look up and realize they were free, even though in enemy skies, while I was so close to them, yet captive.

It didn't seem logical in the least. Many times I would wait anxiously for their return flights and take note of the formation pattern to see if they had had a rough mission.

One morning, the nurse came in, re-bandaged and re-splinted both ankles, and issued me a pair of wooden shoes, pants too big for my small frame, and an old shirt. Then struggling, I was escorted by two Gestapo agents to a rail station and a train headed for Germany. I was warned not to talk to anyone for they didn't want to provoke trouble as they were responsible for my safe arrival at Dalag Luft, my next stop.

The Frankfurt Station was the rail terminus, and I must say the 8th AAF had done a beautiful job of destruction. The station and the city was just rubble piled on rubble. Everyone wore black, and death was all around us. As we were herded to a trolley for our short trip to Dalag Luft, civilians shook their fists at us, spat on us, and made threatening gestures and remarks.

Dalag Luft was comprised of long, wide hallways and appeared to have been built during World War I. Hallways were flanked with endless doors that opened up into 5 x 7 rooms for prisoners. Each room had a small glass window near the ceiling, a cut-out section at the bottom of the door to slide food plates through, and it was furnished with a cot and improvised urinal. There was no sink, other plumbing, nor electricity. The prisoners consisted of flight crews: some British, but mostly American. Every day a Gestapo agent with a satchel and a large dog would visit me in my cell. He would open the satchel and bring out all sorts of forms for me to read and confirm. Most had to do with military installations in England and the United States (PS: He knew lots more than I did!) He would then bring out American cigarettes, light one and let the smoke drift my way. Then he would try to con me into denouncing America and embracing Nazism, and give him Allied information. He would start out very friendly, offering me a smoke, and chatting. But when he would offer me a pen to sign his forms, and all I would respond with was my name, rank, and serial number, he would become very angry, slap me across the face, gather up his items and leave the room. This procedure went on for ten days, but instead of offering cigarettes, he would try different offers to get me to cooperate, such as the promise of good living quarters, fine food, women, etc.

Eventually I was released and joined hundreds of airmen ready to be transferred to Stalag 17. We were put in closed box cars which proved to be a nightmare all the way to the Stalag 17 area near Krems, Austria. We were overcrowded and with very little food. We could not see out, and how horrifying it was when the train would stop suddenly, ack-ack guns would fire nearby, and the cars would shake from the vibration of nearby exploding bombs. I heard much cussing and banging on the sides of the cars just because of terrible fright. A steady diet of this would crack a person up in a very short time.

How happy we were to arrive at our destination and imprisonment. You have no idea how great a feeling it is to be let out into an unrestricted atmosphere from a totally restricted one. Then, you walk through the main gate of the prison camp, and you begin to feel different and wonder if you'll ever walk back out free again. The first building we entered was a large washroom and resembled something that was used 50 years before. We all were deloused and our heads shaven clean. Then, with large searchlights on watchtowers lighting our way through the dead of night, and with barbed wire and guard towers ringing our periphery, we walked into the first barrack building, and got our first view of how it was going to be for us for a long time. The boys were sleeping two together set up in three tiers and attached one to another. The tiers were about two feet apart.

The guards began the talk of awakening the men and telling them to make room for "your new comrades." New P.O.W.'s meant up-to-date news on how the war was progressing. No one slept the remainder of that night as question after question was asked.

Stalag 17's living quarters consisted of long wooden barracks with a washroom separating the next. The lighting was very dim, and the floorboards thin and drafty. Mattresses were made of burlap filled with straw about 2" thick. The springs were wooden slats about 3" apart. We were each issued one thin blanket. Occasionally, odd noises would come from the mattresses, which upon investigation would reveal a new nest of mice or other vermin. While you were sleeping, it was common for large mice to run across your body during the night. Our diet consisted of hot water to make coffee for breakfast. For lunch we had hot water, dehydrated cabbage, or boiled carrots, and a piece of black bread which contained sawdust to give it body. Supper was hot water, boiled beets, potatoes, and what looked like horse meat. (Hell, what more would one expect of P.O.W. food when all of Europe was hard up for food?!).

In accordance with the Geneva Convention, all P.O.W.'s of convention member nations were to be assured of food quantity of at least six percent above starvation level. This was barely met by the Germans and so the U. S. government, via the Red Cross in Geneva, had food parcels made up of a can of beef, powdered coffee "D" bar, blades, and five packs of cigarettes. These parcels were to be rationed out two a month, but unfortunately the Germans handed them out according to how they felt and how we behaved. Many times they would tell us that our bombers destroyed the train load of parcels, etc. There were times we wouldn't see a parcel for as long as two months.

When the camp Commandant was upset about something, he would order us out of the barracks about 5 a.m. and line us up for roll call. We then had to greet him with a loud "Gut morgen Herr Commandant," followed by a "Heil Hitler." (The latter never occurred). He kept us standing for hours and dismissed us when he pleased.

When the RAF was in the area, their chandeliers would light up the valley in yellow, and then they would unload their bombs. Punishment for us would invariably follow the next day: elimination of rations, "roll calls" for hours on end, etc.

The 5th USAAF came over with their medium bombers many times to bomb the huge fuel tank storage facilities just down the valley from us. To hit the tanks, the bombers had to release the bombs just before flying over the camp, and by heck you would see the bombs dropping right at you. In seconds the bombs were falling right past you with the odd sound bombs make when falling. Then the explosions, the black smoke, the earth shaking. Of course, all this was preceded by the camp air raid alarm, shouts of "Achtung! Achtung! Flieger alarm! North American bombers approaching!" We would all make a wild dash for the trenches, body on top of body. Then the all clear, and we would drag back to the barracks in silence, and all contemplating the ordeal of punishment that would face us shortly in retaliation.

I certainly will never forget about the endless attempts at tunneling and what great efforts were made to keep them a secret. Just about the time the diggers were ready to break through to the top, the guards would be waiting with spotlights on the breakthrough spot. It was always a surprise how accurate they were in picking the spot; but it soon dawned on us that the Germans had planted a few of their own men in each compound unknown to us to monitor our actions. I recall that from time to time a few were suspected, but we were helpless to do anything about it.

We experienced other incidents during our imprisonment brought on by our attempts to aid escape attempts or to resist cooperating with bizarre German directives. Two prisoners escaped on one occasion, but were recaptured soon after. Although none of us were aware of the attempt, punishment, as usual, was meted out to all. In another incident, an American prisoner escaped from another prison camp, was unable to make contact with the underground, and was in desperate condition without food, etc. Our camp prisoners were able to smuggle him into camp, hide him and care for him, and finally deliver him to the underground for safe passage. In almost every incident, the German guards would eventually dig out the story of our disobediences, and punishment in the form of cut-off food or heating supplies, and/or roll call formations in which we stood for hours at attention in the rain and cold, etc. were meted out.

Dead of winter was now upon us and snow covered the valley. The days grew shorter and more time was spent indoors. To fight the devastating cold, many days were spent huddled up in the sack just to keep warm and alive. Coal rations became less and less and we resorted to tearing out the guts of the barracks for fuel to keep warm, only to realize we had thereby created even more drafts and cold. Morale worsened, and our bellies were empty. Our clothes were tattered rags from constant wear. The only good thing we looked forward to was a War news report which was brought around verbally on a frequent basis by a US flyer from Chicago; how he got the up-to-date news (which proved to be very accurate and complete) is still a mystery to us. He would circulate from barracks to barracks, under stiff security cover by his fellow prisoners, letting everyone in on the latest information. He was never caught, to my knowledge.

Soon, spring was near at hand, and the war news began to come alive with action. The guards were becoming less tolerant as the Air Force was turning Germany into a heap of rubble. Rumors of Allied breakthrough all along the Front was indeed promising and liberation was now becoming more real. A rumor swept the camp in March, 1945, that we were all going on a forced march heading westward because the Russians were just east of Vienna. It was all true, as we could hear big guns going off in the east, and the nights brought pink glows in the Vienna area. And sure enough, on April 1, 1945, we prisoners all began to be herded in a westerly direction and into what was to prove to be a frightful travel experience. Our days consisted of marching a good nine hours, with ten minute breaks every two hours. We were out about five days when the rations started to run out. Now, the guards found it too much of a problem to allow us to get water, and so we suffered continually of thirst and dehydration. Two weeks out, and many were now without shoes; more and more were depending on their comrades' shoulders to hang on for dear life. Others, too tired and starving, were falling to the ground, causing many behind them to fall on each other. Many were left to die on the road. It was a sad sight indeed; it has left an indelible memory of how a mass of humans can be made to look undignified by the hands of man.

Into our third week American fighter planes began appearing daily to keep tabs on the P.O.W.'s. The German guards ran scared for cover as the planes came down to buzz us and dip their wings to reassure us. You have no idea how happy it made us feel.

Bombing was taking place just ahead of us at Linz, Austria, causing us to halt for a few hours. Then we resumed our march, and passed through the small town of Braunau am Inn, Hitler's birthplace. It was a quaint town, with very narrow sidewalks and streets; stucco houses and iron gates covering the very low first floor windows. I clearly recall the guards pointing to a yellow/beige stucco house and telling us it was the house that Hitler was born in.

Our forced march came to an end on April 29 in the woods of Braunau. We couldn't go further because the G.I.s were about 15 miles beyond. Orders were to settle down and wait to see what happened. Some of the wagon horses were slaughtered and the meat cooked and eaten. We then cut pine branches to make makeshift beds and overhead cover, for by now it was raining. All sorts of rumors were now sweeping the group. Some had it that the Germans had started a heavy offensive. Others had the Germans surrendering unconditionally.

The following day many of us scattered independently to nearby farmhouses to get food. Rifle and machine gun fire by this time were close at hand, so we knew the Front was very close, and liberation near. That night no one slept because of the very increasing roar of guns. Next morning German troops were seen in full retreat; our guards were to be seen no more. Very shortly we began to hear the rumbling of tanks coming up the dirt road, and in a few minutes we saw an American tank come in view. Boy!

What a thrilling sight to behold! An officer standing half out of the tank hatch waved at us. G.I.s were now appearing in the area in pursuit of the retreating Germans. We all yelled with maddening joy as more US tanks appeared, and we mobbed them.

We now settled down for the night with smiles on our faces and happiness in our hearts, and all agreed that General Patton's Third Army, 15th Armored Division, was the best fighting unit in the world.

To finish with a happy ending: the next few days brought arrangements to evacuate us first to Stuttgart, then Metz, France, where we were debriefed, got medical assistance, clothes, and etc. Then to Dieppe, and by troop shipped to Hoboken, New Jersey, and the good old USA!!

The Hard Luck
492nd

Robin C. Janton (From "Bomber Legends")

It was not the "Bloody 100"; nor was it any one of the scores of bomber groups stationed in England, Italy, or the Pacific, which were decimated; it was the "Hard Luck 492nd" at North Pickenham, England, that lost more men and planes in a shorter period of time than any other bombardment group in the history of the US Air Force. This is their story.

The 492nd was one of seven Heavy Bombardment Groups—488th through 494th —activated in the fall of 1943. These were to be the last AAF heavy bomb groups of WWII. The 492nd, on a hurry-up schedule, beat all the others into combat.

In personnel, if not in official lineage, the 492nd could trace its origin to 1920 when the Flying Club of Baltimore was organized for reserve officers of that city. This club became part of the Maryland National Guard on the 104th Observation Squadron. At the outset of WWII, the 104th became part of the Anti-Submarine Patrol used along the East Coast, operating out of the Atlantic City Municipal Airport. On 17 Oct. 1942 the unit's planes and personnel were transferred to the newly formed 517th Bombardment

Squadron, which a month later became the 12th Anti-submarine Squadron under the command of Major Joshua Rome, one of the original Baltimoreans. The Squadron, now based at Langley Field, continued their anti-sub patrols until the fall of 1943 when the Navy took over the anti-sub role from the AAF. (By this time the "sub menace" had basically passed.)

On 24 September 1943 the Squadron was transferred to Blythe Army Air Field and became the 859th Bombardment Squadron. It was designated as the cadre source for the new 492nd Bombardment Group that was to be formed at Alamogordo, New Mexico. The other 492nd squadrons were the 856th, 857th, and 858th.

In early March 1944, an Operational Readiness Inspection proved that 32 crews were "not sufficiently advanced" to fit in with the rest of the group. The CO, Lt. Col. Snavely was then able to arrange that they be exchanged for a like number of crews from Biggs Field, Texas. These replacement crews had pilots who had been instructors in the B-24 transitional training schools. They were Captains and 1st Lts. with many hundreds of hours flying B-24s. Together with the original cadre pilots, who had built up similar B-24 flight time in the anti-sub squadrons, the 492nd was able to complete its training ahead of schedule and fly the southern route to England without serious incident or loss (a record).

The 492nd was based at a newly constructed airfield near North Pickenham, with the required 6000 ft. runway. Experienced ground crews, drawn from other groups already in England, were assigned to the 492nd. Practice missions were conducted on May 4, 7, and 8 and a full dress rehearsal on May 10 that assembled 40 aircraft. Now it was time for the real thing.

The first operational mission was flown the next day against the marshalling yards at Mulhouse, France. Due to a target recognition problem, they made multiple runs over the area and never did drop, for fear of hitting French, or worse yet, Swiss civilians. As a result of this excessive time-over-target, two B-24s ran out of fuel and were written off in crash landings. It was not an auspicious start for the group. However, the next three missions went well and were without loss.

Then came the mission to Brunswick on May 19. Nearing the target, German fighters fell on the 14th Wing with a vengeance, bringing down three of the 392nd's B-24s. But it was the 492nd that paid more of the bill, losing eight ships—five of them from the 858th Squadron. War was real; the wreckage and remains of one of the group's planes was not discovered and identified until 1998.

During the first week of June the 492nd attacked airfields and V-weapon launching sites in France. On D-Day, they bombed coastal defenses in Normandy, and continued attacking bridges, railroads, and other interdiction targets in France until the middle of the month. By June 19 a total of 33 group missions had been flown to strategic targets in France and Germany.

It must also be noted that beginning in June 1944 and for every month thereafter until VE Day flak, rather than fighters, was the number one enemy of the heavy bombers over Europe. While the 492nd lost its share to anti-aircraft fire, it was the Luftwaffe fighter pilots who remained the Group's chief nemesis. This was the case on 20 June when the 8th Air Force attacked oil installations at Pölitz. In thirty minutes of concentrated attacks, mostly by Bf410 twin-engine fighters, fourteen of the group's B-24s were shot out of the sky. (Some of them managed to make it to nearby Sweden.) Every plane and crew in the 856th Squadron that participated in the mission was lost. When the following day's mission was announced, it was a maximum effort to Berlin! The force the 492nd was finally able to put up was pitifully small—only eleven aircraft. But they went, of course, including three crews that had flown the Politz mission the day before.

Author's note: my mission notes show that my crew also flew these two very tough missions.

Each month seemed to bring another 'black day.' On July 7 when the 14th Wing attacked Bernburg, the 492nd could put up only 23 planes, so the third squadron of their formation was provided by the 392nd Group. The 492nd lost twelve, and the 392nd, five, all to fighters. This time it was the 859th Squadron that was wiped out, losing every plane on the mission, nine total.

By the first week of August, mission losses had reached 58 Liberators and 578 airmen, (KIA, MIA, POW, interned or returned.)

During the first week of August sweeping changes were made by the 8th Air Force. The 492nd would take over the Carpetbagger Operation, the dropping of agents and supplies behind enemy lines, at night. The 491st was chosen as the group that would continue to bomb Germany. The 489th was scheduled for redeployment to the U.S. to be equipped with B-29s for the Pacific Campaign

There is much speculation as to the cause of the 492nd terrible losses. No paint silver airplanes—loose formations—lousy position—vendetta for their former anti-sub activities through the 859th Squadron—bad luck; whatever it was, as a comparison, the US Marines in WWII lost a total of 29 per thousand combatants. The 492nd lost 442 per 1000!

Author's note: I believe that if you took Marine losses at two or three of the Pacific Islands, you would find losses considerably in excess of the 29 mentioned in this article.

Second Time Around—August 16, 1944

Charles M. Trout, 492nd

After 22 combat missions we were shot down again over the North Sea by friendly fire or so we were told. We were supposed to have a high officer (General) fly with our crew and we were to fly high in back of formation, filling in the diamond so he could see how the group looked on a mission. Why over the North Sea? No bombs on board and no targets to shoot at but the orders were changed at the last minute.

I was sitting in the top turret when I heard a thud and the plane shuddered. I looked all around and saw no other planes as they were all below us. Then I smelled rubber burning and no voices on intercom, so I got down on the flight deck, looked in to the bomb bay, and it was full of swirling fire. I tried to use the fire extinguisher, but only a short burst and it was empty. Then there was an explosion and fire flew all over, burning everything it struck, even me.

I went up on the flight deck and told the pilot we had to aban-

don the plane immediately. I told the copilot and radio man, Ed
Foss, as I went by them. I had trouble getting my chute harness
hooked with my back to the fire. It was awful hot and I had to go. I
opened the bomb bay doors and there was a plane right under us,
60-70 yards, so I had to wait a while for it to move out of the way.
The fire extinguisher fell when the doors opened and just missed
#3 and #4 engines on that plane. I couldn't wait any longer, so I
jumped and passed out from the heat but the plane moved enough
that I cleared it. Bob Mattson had the same problem.

On the way down, after I came to and pulled the ripcord,
everything was quiet but pieces of the plane were falling close to
me. I heard a noise and here comes a P-47 right at me. This scared
me almost to death. He made a few passes and dropped one-man
life rafts for us to get into, but most of them burst when they hit
the water and I saw two crewmen in the water approximately a
mile away so I finally reached them in an hour or so. Two men
were in the raft and I hung on. The water was warmer than the
first time. The fog had started to move in just before dark. The
chance of getting picked up wasn't too good, but I looked up over
at Ed Foss and there was the Air-Sea Rescue boat. A man extended
his hand. He looked at me and said, "I know you. I picked you up
a few months ago. You cut my finger the other time." We had a
reunion right there. I'd like to see him again.

We headed for shore and the rescue boys worked on us,
bringing us clean clothes, hot drinks, soup, and I suppose dope to
stop the pain from burns. Ed Foss was the worst off. When we
landed on shore our C.O. met us. That showed us he really cared
about the fighting men in his unit. We went to a makeshift hospital for a week to rest and start healing. In about three weeks we
were on our way home. My final trip to the U.S.A. was with a boat
load of German prisoners—all officers. We stood guard night and

day with riot guns—12 gauge 00 buck shot. Ten days later I saw the Statue of Liberty. What a feeling to be home on our own soil!

To sum it all up at the end of my tour of duty, I say this: Would not have missed it for anything; I'm sorry for the crews and men who lost their lives. I forgive those who made mistakes, and I thank God it's over. I will never get in the Hall of Fame or be nominated for an Oscar, but my name is pasted to a brick on a wall someplace.

The Thirteenth

Mission

Wesley Sheffield, 492nd

It was August 1, 1944, and we were set to fly our thirteenth mission. We were a Liberator crew—four-engine heavy bombers—attached to the 857th Squadron, 492nd Bomb Group, Eighth Air Force. Before this day was over we would find an engine afire from a flak hit, ourselves out of gas and still over enemy-occupied France, losing three engines over the English Channel, getting them back only to lose two on the final approach.

The target was Anizy, about 50 miles northeast of Paris, and we were to bomb from 26,000 feet, each carrying a maximum bomb load of 8,000 pounds.

August 1 was a hot summer day—a surprise for England!—and our two Lib crews parked on adjoining hardstands were whiling away the few minutes prior to takeoff by casually ribbing one another about the coming mission. Bill Foster, pilot of Pregnant Angel, kept reminding me that this was my thirteenth mission and that old, battered Sweat Box probably wouldn't make it. I wasn't superstitious then, so I took his digs with good humor, telling him that my crew could come through anything. We took some snapshots of both crews, looked at our watches and climbed aboard our respective ships. In a few minutes, we were airborne.

As the formation approached the enemy coast, it soon became evident that bad weather ahead was either going to seriously hamper the mission or going to cause us to turn back entirely. Then came my first stroke of bad luck, and Bill's words began to take on an ominous sound in my ears. A burst of flak hit my number 4 engine as we crossed the coast. Smoke poured out.

I called to Evan Jones, my copilot, to feather the engine—but it wouldn't feather. It ran away and could only be controlled by the throttle. If I cut off its gas supply, it would act like a huge airbrake and I couldn't keep up with the formation. If I didn't, it might well blow us sky high any second. I opted to keep it running, keep up with the formation and hope for the best. That meant I was forced to pull extra power on the three good engines, thus burning extra gas. It was always possible to abort, but I decided to stick it out.

True enough, the weather got worse and worse, and though the formation strained higher and higher, it was no good. We had to turn back—still carrying full bomb loads.

When the coastline again hove into sight, I called "Butch" Carlson, my engineer, on interphone and asked him to check the gas supply. I knew that, due to the bad engine, I had been burning a lot of fuel. Carlson wasn't long answering. "We'd better get the hell out of here, because we're out of gas!" When you check B-24 gas gauges, first you get air bubbles and then a tube filled—or partly filled—with gas. Now, nothing.

My mind raced. Carlson could be wrong. It was just about the same distance to England as it was to the Cherbourg peninsula—where our troops had a widening beachhead and where a crippled bomber could crash land, under an extreme emergency. Number four was now smoking in a steady black stream. I felt as though we were sitting inside a bomb about ready to go off. Stubbornly I didn't want to bail out, yet the thought of ditching a 24 in the Channel was enough to make me turn very, very pale.

I told the crew we were going to try to make England, giving the choice of bailing out over water or ditching if Carlson was right about the gas. We now moved fast. I left the formation, salvoed my bombs in water beneath, throttled back as far as I could, called Harry Abrams, my navigator, for a heading to the nearest air field in England.

When I left the formation, Bill Foster did too and flew off my wing for a few minutes as if to say, "I'm sorry for being such a wise guy." I was too busy to do anything except fly my plane. I couldn't talk to Bill, or anyone else for that matter, since our radio had been knocked out by flak.

New trouble soon developed. Harry had no good maps of air bases in southern England, and I couldn't contact any other ship without our radio. Our luck hadn't run out altogether, however. A lone P-47 spotted us by the trail of smoke pouring out of the bad engine, came up alongside and motioned with his hands that he would guide us to the nearest field.

The worst was yet to come. At 10,000 feet, Sweat Box abruptly nosed down and headed for the chill waters below. The three good engines had cooled off during the long descent, probably developed carburetor ice and conked out before I could move to cover up my error. I frantically pushed turbos, props, throttles full forward—to no avail. Meanwhile I had to crank in full trim to hold the controls against engine number 4 which was still roaring away. And I pushed the "abandon ship" bell. I later learned that the only reason I didn't lose my crew into the Channel was because they were back at the waist gunner windows, arguing over who was going to jump first.

At six thousand feet, I made the last possible move—I pulled the mixture controls back into emergency rich. And I remembered the old adage about no atheists in foxholes and took time to mutter to myself, "No praying around here!" Never before or since have I felt so impotent in face of impending disaster—when I found out that that last move did it! Engines roared anew and the ship promptly went into a steep turning climb—because all the trim was set against number 4 engine. For the one and only time in combat, I yelled for help. "Jonesy, get on that rudder!" We got the plane under control and back on course for England. We were safe, at least for the moment.

England now came into sight, but a low cloud cover prevented me from spotting a field from a safe altitude. The P-47 ducked down through the clouds and I could do little but follow, expecting my engines to quit at any moment. We had now been airborne for almost six hours and for the last hour of flight the gas gauges had been bone dry.

Hurrah, it's a field! The P-47 swooped low over it, then hovered above as I made a straight-in approach for landing. With only a few hundred feet to go, engines 1 and 4 quit—out of gas—but by hitting the other two throttles to the wide open position, I made the end of the runway with number 4 still streaming black smoke. We had made it!

All the way in, while taxiing, I urged Jonesy to keep trying to start the dead engines. I just couldn't comprehend what a close call that had been.

When the ground made their check, they found that we had landed with about 50 gallons (we took off with 2800 gallons) in the tanks of 2 and 3, and just enough oil in number 4 to wet the end of a stick. The flak had hit an oil line, which then dripped oil on the hot engine all the way home.

Unlucky thirteen had almost found its mark. And the ten men riding in Sweat Box that day have been religiously superstitious ever since. A later ground check indicated that the oil filters on all four engines were badly clogged, which had led to unusually high fuel consumption aside from the flak damage. A certain crew chief, nameless, got a great chewing out and not a few demerits for that kind of maintenance.

A postscript. When we landed, I congratulated myself for keeping cool through that long ride. Somehow, though, I guess I wasn't so cool. About an hour after landing, I found myself in the tower of that Polish fighter base, wondering where all my gear was. I took a jeep back to the plane—and found all my personal gear strewn haphazardly beneath the plane. I obviously got out in a hurry.

Author's note: After WWII, Sheffield went on to become 1) a tabloid news editor, 2) a minister, 3) a college president, 4) a fundraising consultant. He and his wife, Luise, live at Beebe Lake in Vermont.

The "Unforgettable Second"—That Was a Rough Mission!

George A. Heropoulos, 448th

On December 31, 1943 we were to attack a German air base at La Rochelle, France near the Spanish border. After a long haul, our formation of B-24s finally reached our target. As our bomb bays opened, we caught holy hell. I don't know why, but I had to toggle our bomb load from my nose turret. Fighters and heavy flak hit us. A burst of flak exploded in front of the nose of our B-24. The flak wounded Lt. Harmon, our bombardier, and me. The lieutenant lost an eye. We were banking to the right when our wingman received a direct hit to the gas tanks. It blew up like a big puff of smoke. I knew no one survived the explosion. My friends from Ohio, Sgt. Holesa and Sgt. Ball, from Canton, my hometown, and Sgt. Indorf from Massillon, were members of that crew.

Messerschmitts jumped us as we hit the target. We had to get out of there fast. On our way home we were forced to land at a Royal Air Force base in Southern England. We had been in the air for nine hours and forty-five minutes and had to refuel. We spent the night there, and the next day, New Year's Day, we had dinner at a U.S. Army base. Although we had been wearing the same clothes for two days, they treated us royally. After refueling we flew back to our base.

After finishing my thirtieth mission on June 22, 1944, we went home. I immediately went back to Canton. After a few days, Sgt. Holesa's sister called and asked me to stop by the house. I hesitated about going, but knew I had to go. I knocked on the door. When his sister opened the door, Mrs. Holesa burst into tears. I froze.

His sister took her mother to another room. We sat and talked. She told me that the War Department sent them a telegram—her brother was missing in action. I was speechless and didn't know what to do. Should I tell her what really happened? I knew I had to tell her the truth, that there was no way he or his crewmates could have survived that blast. I told her I was very sorry. Miss Holesa thanked me for telling her what happened. Our crew was lucky—we came home. More than fifty years later I still remember that second mission.

The Second Time

Was a Charm!

Luther S. Bird, 93rd

The 93rd Bomb Group completed its formation and headed across the North Sea for Norway.

There was a low lead section and a high section on the right of the lead. I was the pilot of "El Toro," and we were the co-lead ship in the high section. As I recall, our route and bombing altitude was 12,000 feet. It was extremely cold with the cockpit centigrade thermometer registering below minus 50. Periodically the group had to pass through scattered clouds and on these occasions some ships left the formation to return to base. About halfway to Norway, we passed through clouds, and more ships, including the lead, aborted. At this point, the remaining ships formed on "El Toro," and we became the group lead. Except for seeing a Stuka dive bomber off towards Denmark, the flight to the IP was uneventful. But then our problems began.

My Form five listed the November 18, 1943 target as Oslo and nine-and-one-half hours flying time. According to Roger Freeman's *Mighty Eighth War Diary* (page 139) the 93rd's November 18 target was Oslo–Kjeller with twenty planes dispatched, fifteen bombing and one with ten men MIA. According to Cal Stewart (*Ted's Traveling Circus*, page 258), on the November 18, 1943 mission to Kjeller repair base "the Circus made two bomb runs, commencing at 11:43." Mention of the two bomb runs stimulated me to write this account.

At the IP we turned on the bomb run. Immediately the bombardier (we had a substitute that day) called notifying us that the bombsight was frozen—a disturbing message meaning we were useless in contributing to a successful mission. There wasn't time for the radio or flares. I rocked the wing tips a few times and went into a left turn to circle and return to the bomb run. About halfway around, another ship cut inside and took the lead. All ships formed on the new lead and the run from the IP to the target continued. No flak or fighters were encountered in the target area. The new lead bombardier did a good job and all ships released on his bomb drop. The men in the back reported that the bombs were all on target. The target, a hangar, literally disappeared from the earth! A mission that could have been a failure became very outstanding for the Circus. (Regrettably I cannot recall the ship or crew that made the day for the 93rd!).

After leaving the target area and heading for the North Sea, our armorer-gunner called with the news that we had a bomb hanging by one latch in the right rear compartment. The decision was made to leave the bomb alone until we were over the North Sea. However, the bomb didn't wait as it dropped knocking the right rear bomb bay door off its tracks. The door was hanging down for the flight back. This did not interfere with the flight characteristics of the plane, flopping in the breeze. But we were concerned about our "stray" hitting civilians.

Despite our flapping bomb bay door, we made a successful landing, and when we reported to interrogation, the Norwegian underground had already reported the success of the mission. The report indicated that high level Germans were involved in a military review and an open house ceremony, and that our aircraft overhead were thought to be a part of the review! Needless to say, we surprised them at a very opportune moment.

The Norwegians did report that some stray bombs caused some minor damage to their civilians. We immediately reviewed and estimated that our stray bomb would have hit in unpopulated country. It was good to be back at the home base with the warm feeling that another successful mission was completed, even though this time we had to make two bomb runs!

Jane Windham, Flight Engineer, Killed in Crash

Jim Russel

Reprinted from Stars and Stripes, 4/2/45,

PFC Jane B. Windham, who considered flying for Air Transport Command as a flight engineer no more dangerous than crossing the street, was killed in a crash at a U.K. base on March 31, 1945, the first WAC to lose her life on flying duty in a theater of war. PFC Windham, who was 23, was one of a crew of three aboard a B-17 which collided with a C-47 while attempting to land. None of the crew of either ship survived the crash.

Jane Windham's background was strictly flying. She studied aeronautical engineering at the University of California and could fly anything from a Piper Cub to a B-17. She was a licensed pilot, and taught women to fly before joining the WAC 18 months ago.

She came into the army with the MOS of an aircraft maintenance technician and at a Montana ATC base from which she shipped to the ETO five months ago. She earned her wings crewing bombers ferried by ATC to bases in the states and Alaska. On dozens of trips she took over the controls of the big ships, "just to keep her hand in," as she put it.

With ATC's Air Inspector in the ATO, Jane's flight duties were modified by administrative work. She might have stuck to a desk and lived, but she settled this with: "I didn't come overseas to fly a desk."

She was too enthusiastic about flying to be content on the ground. But nothing vexed her more than someone idealizing her for doing a "man's job."

Most reporters, though, had a penchant for plugging this "man's job," a tendency that made her shy about publicity. It promoted too many embarrassing situations. A note scribbled about a "control cable" might not be legible to the reporter come deadline, and most reporters not being flight engineers, the transcription might result in Jane doing something awfully silly with a control tower.

It was the sincerity of this blonde, blue-eyed girl from San Antonio that made her most attractive.

Something she said three months ago, haunting and ironic today, summed up her attitude. 'I can't say that I envy those men who fly combat," she said. "They put their lives out on a limb every time they go up." Then she added: "The flying I do is like walking down the street."

Yanks in Britain

Cpl. Edmund Antrobus

Reprinted from Wartime "Yank" The Army Weekly

On January 16, 1945, First Lt. Albert J. Novik of Tarrytown, N.Y., dived from the flight deck of his fuel-less Liberator headfirst through the bomb bay and saved his life. His leap gave him enough speed to clear the plane while it was still gliding.

On February 16, a month later to the day, he had to bail out again and tried to maneuver a second time. But the plane nose-dived before he could make it, throwing him up against the ceiling, where he stuck, looking down at a fire sweeping through the fuselage and thinking that at any moment he would be dead.

This was the climax of four and a half bad hours for Lt. Novik. He had been flying with a squadron in the 392nd Bomb Group when, a few seconds after dropping his bombs, another Liberator in a higher formation had moved in on top to obtain a more compact bomb pattern. It came too close and dropped six bombs through Novik's left rudder.

Minus a huge chunk of its tail assembly, Novik's Liberator dropped 500 feet, becoming so nose-heavy that it took all of Novik's strength at the wheel to keep it from diving.

Novik, however, decided to continue over the target so that he could stay with the formation as protection against enemy fighters. In this way he managed to struggle back to England, but was unable to land because clouds had closed in over the home base and emergency landing fields. Together with the rest of his group, Novik was ordered to go back and land in France. Realizing that his ship would never make it, he decided to land in England if he could.

It was getting harder and harder to hold the ship in the air. Novik was under a tremendous strain, and the back of his neck was ridged like a weight-lifters. "It was a good thing," says the navigator, F/O Wade Hampton of Toronto, Ontario, "that we had a strong, as well as a good, pilot."

For two hours they looked for a suitable field but all were fogged in, and at last they decided to head towards The Wash and bail out.

It was a painful decision. The ship had flown 70 missions without an abort. Everyone knew it was in fine mechanical condition; the fact that it could fly without a left rudder was proof of that. Someone recalled that the crew chief, S/Sgt. Eugene S. Goldsby of Los Angeles, was up for an award for the way he'd taken care of his ship.

The gunners bailed out first, then the navigator, radio operator and engineer.

After that, Novik climbed out of his seat while the copilot, 1st Lt. Jack H. Graves of Birmingham, Ala., hung on the controls. Then, standing, Novik took over, holding the plane steady while Graves jumped. The elevator trim tabs, which normally keep the plane in level flight, were not working, and the automatic pilot could not be used because the slight shake it would cause when it went into control would probably be enough to crash the plane.

Novik found that even a ten-degree turn made the ship shudder as if its tail was breaking.

When the copilot hit the silk, Novik gave him thirty seconds to clear the ship and then prepared to jump from the flight deck through the bomb bay, as he had done a month previously. But the second he let go of the wheel, the plane dived like a Thunderbolt. Novik was thrown against the ceiling and pinned there while the plane dived 7,000 feet.

"My first impulse," Novik said, "was to try and beat my way out through the fuselage. I thumped with the sides of my fists, but the air pressure was so strong it was an effort even to move my arms. It was the sensation you have in a dream when you are running from something and your feet get bogged down in quicksand."

Dying did not occur to him—just then. "And yet," he says, "just about this time a guy gets very religious. You start praying to something super-human because you know nothing human can help you."

It was fire that made Novik give up hope. Spread-eagled against the ceiling, he saw flames sucked in from a burning engine, spread through the fuselage, and fan up towards him as if he were on a spit, being grilled alive. At that moment he lost his fear because he no longer thought he was going to live. He smelled his hair being singed. He felt, as he now put it, "eccentric and carefree." He was not delirious or suffering pain.

Then, suddenly, he was dropped from the ceiling, as a wing, or something, came off, changing the direction of the plane. He began to claw his way through the fire up to the bomb bay. He says he didn't feel that he was escaping from death, but from death in a particularly violent form.

Somehow he dragged himself to the bomb bay and fell through, and just as he cleared the bomber it exploded over his head. He pulled his ripcord but only two feet of chute came out. He pulled again, this time with both hands, and the chute opened. He was now about 700 feet from the ground.

Looking up, Novik saw burning pieces of the plane floating down like enormous flaming leaves. He put a hand to one eye and when he took it away it was covered with blood. He thought he had lost the eye, but that did not seem important. All around him burning debris was falling, great chunks of it catching up with him and passing within a few feet of his parachute. But, looking down, Novik saw that the real danger was on the ground, for parts of the burning plane had landed on the spot he was headed for. Only by luck he landed in a tree, which saved him being roasted in the wreckage of the plane.

Men have been hurt more turning over in bed than Novik was during his seemingly interminable brush with death. His face had been burned and his hair singed, and it was the hand he put to his eye, and not the eye itself, that had been cut. As a matter of fact, his fingers hurt more than anything else; they were numb for three days from straining on the wheel during the four and a half hours he had struggled to keep his plane in the air.

All in all, it had been a happier landing than the one Novik had made a month before. On that occasion, two of his men had jumped through the nose-wheel hatch, hit something, and been killed. This time they all landed safely and were in good condition to stand by when the colonel presented Novik with the DFC.

"Drama Over Cologne," 14 October 1944

Scott Nelson, Florida 58th BG

On 14 October 1944, B-24J, S/N 42-50864, "JOLLY ROGER," with a crew of ten was the lead plane of the 458th Bomb Group, 755th Squadron, to bomb the marshalling yards at Cologne, Germany. Immediately after bombs away, "Jolly Roger" was hit by three bursts of flak, knocking out the number three engine and injuring several crew members; the most severe was MC Miller who was struck by shrapnel in the head and face. Lt. Robert Ferrel and Lt. Ernest Sands pulled Lt. Miller from the nose turret and administered first aid. The "Jolly Roger" was on fire and going down. Pilot Lt. William Klusmeyer ordered everyone to bail out. Sands attached a line to Miller's parachute ripcord and pushed him out the camera hatch, immediately followed by S/Sgt. Joseph Pohler.

Lt. Sands left the ship via the nose wheel doors and pulled his ripcord after passing through several cloud layers. After landing, Lt. Sands hid himself in a depression till after dark, and then started walking west. The nine other crew members had been captured by German soldiers. Lt. Sands evaded capture for seven days but was caught and beaten by German civilians as he was trying to cross a river to get to Belgium. Sands ended up in Stalag Luft III, and on January 27, 1945, was marched west during a blizzard, eventually ending up in Stalag VIIA at Moosburg in the spring of 1945.

On April 29, 1945, an American tank burst through the front gate at Moosburg with a force led by General Patton. It was one day before Sands' 24th birthday.

Ernie Sands always wondered what had happened to MC Miller. The last he had seen him was when he had parachuted from the plane. Had he survived? Many years later, after the war, Ernie received a phone call—it was MC Miller. He had tracked Ernie down to thank him for helping save his life. Miller had survived after being treated by German doctors and had fully recovered in a POW camp.

Ernest Sands served as North Dakota's Lieutenant Governor from 1981 to 1984.

"Drama Over Cologne" Part 2

Scott Nelson, Florida 58th BG

While doing the story about Ernie Sands ("Drama Over Cologne," Vol. 46, No. 3, Summer 2007 *Journal*) and his being shot down over Germany, I was able to contact MC Miller and get his side of the story.

MC Miller (Millard C. Miller) was chosen to be pilotage navigator with the Klusmeyer crew on October 14, 1944. Target was the marshalling yards at Cologne. MC was the second navigator because the Klusmeyer plane was flying deputy lead and needed another navigator. As it turned out, the lead plane had to be turned back due to mechanical difficulty, so the Klusmeyer plane had to take the lead and Ernie Sands reluctantly became lead bombardier.

As the Klusmeyer plane left the target after bombs away, it was hit by several bursts of flak, the first shattering the nose turret in which MC was sitting. MC was stunned and noticed a lot of blood coming from a wound on the right side of his face and he could barely see. Someone grabbed him under the armpits and pulled him from the turret, and the next thing he remembered was the bombardier (Sands) giving him first aid. MC remembered being dragged back through the bomb bay and remembered seeing the bomb bay doors still partly open (they never got completely closed when they were hit but were not open far enough to bail out through). MC remembered being pulled back to the camera hatch, then being pushed out, and then a terrific jerk! MC doesn't remember much about his ride down (he probably passed out).

The next thing MC remembered is being on the ground with one of the other crew members next to him. As luck would have it, the other crew member was Staff Sergeant Joseph G. Pohler. Pohler was a German-born American and was fluent in Deutsche. Sands had sent him out right behind MC in the hope that Pohler could quickly get medical attention for MC. Well, it worked—Pohler called to the German civilians in the area and quickly got him the medical attention he needed. The aid kit that Sands had stuck in MC's jacket was used for his immediate care. Pohler even passed himself off as an officer, thus this also helped get MC quick attention. The Germans respected rank, even from the enemy!! The initial capture report from the German records lists Pohler as an officer! The Luftwaffe medical service took responsibility for MC's care and he ended up in a Luftwaffe hospital in Frankfurt.

MC was in rough shape with his injuries and his eyeball out of its socket. His eye was scheduled to be removed, but a Luftwaffe surgeon with the rank of Lt. Colonel examined MC and thought he could save the eye.

The doctor sewed MC's eye back in the socket and bandaged him up. After a time, the bandages were taken off but MC could not see out of his injured eye. The doctor said "let's try something" and they gave MC treatments of short frequency radio waves directed at his eye. After several days of this treatment, MC's eyesight started coming back and he regained it in full.

Miller remembered the doctor was from Hess and his last name was the Germanized form of Miller. He said he and the doctor could have been distant cousins because Miller's family was from Hess, a state outside Munich.

After his recovery at the Frankfurt Hospital, MC was sent to Stalag Luft 3 to spend the rest of the war as a POW.

Another interesting item about the Klusmeyer crew: The waist gunner on this crew was Jewish and was named Raymond Silverstein. To protect himself in case of being shot down and captured, Silverstein changed his name to Sills to throw off the Germans. Raymond's brother belonged to the 82nd Airborne and participated in Operation Market Garden and was wounded at Nijmegen, Holland. He had been sent to a hospital in England. Sills asked the squadron commander if he could stand down on the Cologne mission in order to visit his wounded brother. The Klusmeyer plane flew without one waist gunner that day and the act of visiting his brother saved Sills from being shot down over Germany. The fact that Sills changed his name did not guarantee that the Germans would not have found him out. Visiting his brother could well have saved his life!

My 33 Missions

the author

Mission #1, May 19, 1944 (my mother's birthday) Target: plane engine factory, Brunswick. Support: P-38s and 47s. Opposition: Thousands of fighters! Acres of flak! Load: 12 500 lb. M-17 incendiaries (hell to carry).

Took off at 0900 as copilot with an experienced copilot as pilot-commander. As we crossed the enemy coast I had a funny feeling. At last, I'm in the war, dammit! Went over the Zuiderzee. Germany was pretty. Had a few flak bursts on the way to the target. Not many friendly fighters about, it seemed. As we got closer to the target we spotted swarms of enemy fighters. Made one kind of think. Then came the flak! We had about 30 flak holes when we got back. The ship took a week to fix. Flak went into one of the fuel cells, and it had to be replaced. Part of our oxygen system was knocked out. Our rudder and waist were full of holes. One of the waist windows had a hole in it. Luckily, no one was hit in our plane. Fighters give you a hell of a scare when they start coming in, nose toward you, spouting cannon and machine gun fire.

Our gunners saw four enemy fighters go down. Our group lost one plane, by a Me-109. He was in the bucket of our four-plane element. Too close! ... We go at it again tomorrow. Now, 29 to go.

(Experienced crews say this was one of the tougher missions, if not the toughest, and they wouldn't expect to live in five missions like that, so we had a good initiation. Having nothing to compare it to, didn't know if it was normal, or not.)

May 20: Mission scrubbed. Aroused at 0230 for a 0400 briefing, and were briefed on two targets. Ground haze kept us from taking off. We were called back at 0900, only to find out it was again scrubbed.

A few minutes ago, when I went to shave, three Lts. came up and asked if I knew anything about their friend, Silver, who was shot down yesterday. They were from another group and came over to see him tonight. And the crew chief reported we had 38 holes from our Brunswick raid.

May 21: Mission scrubbed.

May 22, Mission #2: St. Pol, France, rocket installation and synthetic factory. 8 1000 lb GPs (general purpose).

Took off, a supercharger was out, but being an easy Nobal target, decided to go. When at 8,000′ #3 caught fire, so we feathered it and came back and landed with a full load (after the mission, the Sqdn. CO told us what a good landing it was). Anyway, we got another ship quick-quick and caught the formation half way to the target. As we did, #4 supercharger went out but on we went. Came out between Ostend and Dunkirk. No losses, only four flak bursts. Got some Link time, p.m.

May 23: A rest. Censored mail, Link (Link trainers, simulated instrument flying), screwed around.

May 24, #3: Airfield and 2, 400′ long hangars, five miles SE of Paris. Lots of inaccurate flak, only one hole, went through glass by bombsight and missed the navigator—good! 58 100 lb M47 jelly/gasoline bombs, no fun! Wiped out the target. Earlier GP bombs left nothing but girders, and our fire bombs burned out the wreckage. Saw Paris—darn good-looking city. France very pretty, farms look good, patches of woods here and there. Airfields and woods where there were guns and installations are darn well wrecked. Our fighters shot up 303 trains the last couple of days. (Not in notes, but we were getting ready for D-Day.)

May 25, #4: 12 500 lb. GPs. Nobal, Fecamp, France, on coast. Mission # 1 for Phil Goplen, our bombardier. Over enemy territory five minutes, no flak, fighter support didn't show up, no matter.

May 27, #5: 12 500 pounders—Marshalling yards, Trier, Germany. Good hits, blew to hell. No close flak, no enemy fighters, had 38s, 47s, and 51s escort. Long mission, at 23,000' for a while. Our #4 shook so badly across the channel we were afraid we might have to turn back, kept on, it got better. Yesterday I met a Tom Skeffington from Spokane, who used to come to Wallace and knows Herman Brass, Hoban, Doc Fitzgerald, Jim McCarthy, the Murphy boys, and Joe and Donny Codd. Damn nice to talk to him. He went to Gonzaga and U of Wisconsin, and sang with the Bob Crosby band.

May 28: Sunday, day of rest, went to church and communion, and went for a pleasure ride in a 24 to another field, and logged one hr. 20 minutes flying time.

May 29, #6: Air Medal day FW 190 assembly plant, Tutow, Germany. 52 100 lb M47s, (jelly/gasoline) No enemy fighters, some flak, quite thick, though missed us. Entered Germany near Kiel, and came way up near Denmark on the way home. Grounded tomorrow. Hooray!

June 5: Five easy missions gone to the devil: didn't fly all week (not scheduled). Calibrated airspeed yesterday and buzzed a P-51 and a Mosquito base and hedge-hopped home. Tonight at 2000 we went to a pre-briefing. Know what's going to happen tomorrow—this is it! Read a field order on it. Of course it's all very secret at this hour... Frank Gibson (Hoot to us, from Long Beach, CA) finished his missions today. He'll miss the big show. Sport (his copilot) is through, but Little Olo and Connole (bomb. and nav.) aren't through yet. Gotta hit the sack. Briefing is at 2300 and have to eat, so little sleep, if any, tonight.

June 6: at 1710 hrs. June 6 #6 and #7. First, to the invasion coast of France near Caen, pre-dawn takeoff at 0300. Flew around England in the dark along with a couple thousand more aircraft in a big mess, finally got in a formation and bombed the coast minutes before the troops landed. We were repeatedly warned not to drop our bombs on our troops. Couldn't see the coast, flying at 16,000', above a complete overcast. Before reaching the coast we could see ships shelling the coast. Our heavies were the only ones above the clouds. Had a little flak over the Channel Islands—Jersey and Guernsey, since then taken by allies. Got to sleep a couple of hours—first time in over 36—and went out again amid all the clouds, and bombed a bridge inland, visually. Ducked under the clouds before hitting England and saw a lot of ships, and made a 4th of July celebration out of it by firing the colors of the day, quite often, and the ships would answer. Came over Portsmouth, which was pretty with the sun shining through the clouds at different angles and hitting the ship-studded water.

Came back in formation, getting dark, the ceiling barely 500 feet, arriving at field all the ships dove into the funnel. Luckily, no collisions. Flew 12:45 hrs. yesterday. Bad weather keeping us down.

June 8, 2045: Did not fly today, but almost took off three times, and had two briefings. Weather, terrible. Ceiling from 1000' to over 25000', with icing, so we hoped the missions would be scrubbed. Sqd. CO, Major Glassel S. Stringfellow, got up in the soup, recalled, when salvoed the fragmentation bombs a couple went off in the bomb bay, knocking out hydraulics and wounding the tail gunner. Landed on one wheel, wrecked the plane.

June 10, #9: Evreux, France, airfield. Formed at 26,000', dense contrails at 24,000', undercast below that. Lucky no collisions, had a number of close calls. Big mess trying to form. Tired—had to do almost all of the weather flying today, though Al (Bacon, copilot, Ceres, CA), changed seats (we were flying off a right wing) after we got out of enemy territory. Lost one ship today—Tooles, a lead crew. A couple of bombs collided as they were released and the plane caught fire. Our tail gunner saw eight chutes, and from four to ten were reported. The plane broke in two just after one fellow jumped right at station six, just aft of the bomb bays. Those who saw it said it was the darndest sight and not pleasant to see, so my restricted visibility from the cockpit spared me from the sight. Had a burst we could feel and hear under the fuselage, but no holes.

Unexplainable, maybe it was a rocket, a shell, or something else.

June 11: Recalled on a mission to Redon, France. Used 57″ Hg. on takeoff and used all but 75′ of runway (ship had reputation as a bad one) and got off with good speed. Hit some prop wash soon after our wheels were off and I thought we'd lost an engine and I hollered to Al to fix it. All he could do was help push in the rudder. Lots of clouds. Flew over London on way back. Went to church. Am really tired, and hope we don't fly tomorrow.

June 13, 2130: Just got back from pass in London. Very good city. Couple of little air raids. Guns make a lot of noise, and shoot fast. By accident met friend Van Hersett and he showed me around, stage show, dance at Hammersmith, Piccadilly Commandos, St. Paul's, #10 Downing, Buckingham Palace, The Admiralty, House of Parliament, etc. Returned and heard that Bailey, in ship #710, didn't come back from a raid Sunday. Hope they're okay, but it sounds bad as they don't know much if anything about it.

NOTE—October 9, 1944: After 53 days in France, waiting for the army to come up, Bailey did come out. He lost one or two of his crew. Saw him back here a couple of months ago.

June 14, #10: 52 100 lb GPs—(actually, 130 lb) Airfield ten miles northwest of Orleans, France. Really hit the target today. There were a lot of rack malfunctions today, single bombs being kicked out all the way home. No enemy or friendly fighters. Quite a few ships had bad flak hits, but no one in our group went down.

June 15, #11: 12 500 lb GPs Railroad bridge ten miles west of Tours, France. Moderate, accurate flak on the way out. No fighters, but a fellow who aborted got jumped by four fighters, but 38s came in at the opportune moment and saved him... Think we bombed the wrong bridge... (We did, but the lead section got the right one.)

June 16, #12: 10 500 lb GPs Nobal—Rocket plane supply depot five mi. ESE St. Omer, France. Flew up through clouds and formed at 20,000'. No flak or fighters, made instrument letdown.

June 18, #13: 52 100 lb M47 gasoline/jelly. Hamburg. More and closer flak than I have seen before, and again, I hope. Four ships lost in group. Beckman, from our barracks was one, and we ghouled (okay if you save personal items for them, later, or relatives). The flak was thicker than air, and it was damn close. We could hear it go BANG, not just puff, and see the flashes of light as it burst. The air was thick with smoke from the bursts, and we were in light clouds and contrails. Good fighter support from 51s and 38s. We could have been murdered by fighters over the target as we were spread out and confusion was high, not bombing the proper target, a nice mission to have behind you.

Author's note—The history of my group was assembled by Jeffrey E. Brett in The 448th Bomb Group (H). Information on the purchase of this complete history, formation at Gowen Field, Idaho to preparations to close the base. Full crew rosters, original and replacement, and more, are included. For purchase info, patricia.everson@lineone.net.

A Luftwaffe Control Center offered a less friendly target for the group the following day, 18 June. A one-hour delay before takeoff provided the bombers the luxury of a daylight assembly. The briefed route over the Danish peninsula skirted the known flak areas but unfavorable weather over the target forced the bombers to switch targets. Turning away from Fassberg the PFF aircraft led the formation directly over the heavily defended city of Hamburg. Flak thick enough to walk on surrounded the bombers as they passed over the city. At 0954, just six minutes from the coast, flak crippled the aircraft flown by Lt. Leland Beckman. The first burst ruptured the number four oil tank resulting in the engine becoming uncontrollable. More bursts did additional damage and tail number 42-52119 succumbed to the dreaded flak. All ten members, on their fifth mission, bailed out. Sgt. George Copeland exited the plane through the camera hatch. After hitting his back on the plane as he jumped, he pulled the ripcord almost immediately fearing he might pass out from pain. Sgt. Dewy Conn suffered a flak wound in the leg before jumping, and Sgt. Michael J. Eannone jumped with his silk parachute in his hand. Somehow it had deployed in the plane prior to jumping.

Despite those near disasters everyone survived the exit. As Sgt. Copeland floated earthward, he heard gunshots. Assuming they were aimed at him, he plotted his escape. Spotting a forest near his landing area, he planned to hide in the woods. However, after narrowly missing power lines, he landed only to find 'a pistol in my face in very nervous hands.' He spent the remainder of the war as a POW. Less fortunate was Sgt. Dan Waais. Angry civilians killed him after he landed.

While the downed crew tried to evade in Germany, the remainder of the group bombed an airfield near Hamburg as a target of opportunity. After a seven-hour flight, planes landed at Seething where awaiting medics in meat wagons tended to the wounded aboard 42-51079.

June 20, #14: 40 100 lb GPs. Oil refinery, Pölitz, Germany (was in Poland before 1939!) Went up over the North Sea and into Germany east of Stettin. Before we got to the target we could see a lot of flak smoke, and there was plenty of close flak. Twenty-one ships went to Sweden, and our group lost three, one from our squadron. Smoke billowed up to 20,000′. We could see smoke screens at some towns, and Hamburg was still smoking from our raid two days before. I'm writing this a day late so I don't remember too much about it—except that it was a tough, high loss ratio, mission—because today's (6/21) raid overshadows it, especially for our crew. Read on for Big B.

June 21, #15: 10 500 lb GPs. BERLIN. This was really hell. Went up the North Sea and into Germany and until we reached the target. The trip was rather uneventful but then we saw a lot of flak smoke from shooting at earlier groups, and they had our altitude down to the inch. They opened up on us with big guns—bigger bursts than we had ever seen before—probably 105s and 155s, and maybe 240s. Anyway, we could really hear those bursts explode. Practically deafening and we almost had to fly on instruments through the smoke. Then we got a hit in our best engine, #1, and the oil leaked and down went the pressure. Before I feathered it we got a close burst on my side and a piece of flak tore through both panes of the thick bullet proof glass at an angle that also took it through the steel separation between the two windows, and hit me in the back. Broken glass was all over the cockpit, and Al, my copilot, was very busy flying off a left wing and thought I was a goner. I could feel my shoulder hurting so asked the radio operator to see if my clothing and backpack parachute was torn, and he said no, so I felt relieved. All I had was a big black and blue mark... Just as we dropped our bombs I feathered #1 and we dropped below our squadron and sweat out flak for a few more minutes—twelve minutes of it over Berlin. Saw a ship get hit and flip over on its back with the bomb bay doors open and the bombs still in the racks. Saw a couple more get hits in the engines and go peeling off.

We couldn't catch our group again and our engines had a lot of time on them so we didn't dare pull too much power. I called for fighter assistance and we fired some green-green flares. Then, #3 looked very, very bad. Cylinder head temperature high, oil temp high, oil pressure low, and fuel pressure low with oil all over the cowling. About that time, I wasn't so sure. A few minutes before we had discussed Switzerland, Sweden, liberated France (not much of it yet), or home to England. Unanimous—England. So we struggled along, alone, praying for no enemy fighters, and when the 14th wing was passing us we increased a bit more power so we could fly with them to the coast. In the meantime, we were tossing out everything we could. The ball gunner was excited enough to toss out three maybe needed, light first aid packets. But the heavy ball turret was unleashed, so were heavy flak suits and most of our ammunition. Called air sea rescue for a heading to the nearest English shore. Got back after much sweating and our good luck held out because we found a big enough hole in the 900 foot overcast, needed because our flight indicator was out. All in all, we're damn lucky to be back, and I especially so for the thick glass. Thank God we didn't have the normal plate glass or I don't think I'd be sitting here. The path of the flak would have taken it through me at the location of my heart. (I still have the piece of flak with glass embedded, and a photo of me, from the next day, holding the two sections of shattered glass.) We were scheduled to fly again tomorrow, but I saw the doc and got grounded for a rest after the last three missions, and it grounded the whole crew. Had a few drinks and cleaned up and went to church—that one made a Christian out of me. Guess I'll go down and have a bite to eat with Little Olo.

June 22: Grounded today. Censored mail this morning, show this afternoon on the Nazis treatment of the Poles. Tally is 43 bombers lost over and around Berlin yesterday. Darn nice record from nothing much but flak. Heinies are getting pretty darn good shots.

June 24, #16: 10 250 lb GPs. Hote Cote, France. Didn't drop our bombs. Not much flak but got a burst that blew out a hydraulic line. The radio operator called and I finally squeezed it out of him that it was "red stuff," so there was no danger. We got instructions to drop our bombs in the channel, circled our field to let down the nose gear and crank down the flaps. They sure had a lot of meat wagons waiting for us. Landed without incident... George Van Hersett was waiting for me in our hardstand so we went to the party and got damn tight and related 'pushed down the nose wheel and cranked down the flaps.' He stayed overnight and left Sunday noon, and is sweating going home now after finishing his missions.

June 25, #17: 20 250 lb GPs. Airfield twelve miles south of Paris (Orly now?) quite a bit of flak, four holes in ship. Sweated it out, and have since Berlin. Had trouble getting the nose wheel up. Went through a front—more damn clouds. Hit the wrong target, ten miles north of where we were supposed to go, and so ran into more flak to sweat out. Am trying to get a pass now, and then a six-day leave. Payday is needed first, though.

June 26: Stand Down. We almost went to Munich today but it was scrubbed just before takeoff. The clouds run up to 22,000' so we'll surely not fly this afternoon. Will clean up my corner and piddle around.

June 28, #18: 12 500 lb GPs. Rail marshalling yards, Saarbrucken, Germany. Partly cloudy, PFF bombing. Quite a bit of flak, but inaccurate. Was coming home over Belgium and I thought of Amsterdam and The Hague that weren't far off course. Went close to Brussels. Lost two crews in our squadron on yesterday's mission. We didn't go. Three lost from the group. Was an airfield north of Paris. As we were in the pilot's briefing this morning at 0130 a Jerry, probably a JU 88, dropped a couple of bombs on our base. Made quite an explosion, and I certainly wondered what it was at the time.

June 29, #19: Airfield SE of Magdeburg, Germany. 52 100 lb M47 fire bombs. What a horrible day. The leader of the first section aborted, so we went into the third section. Didn't drop our bombs on the primary for some unknown reason, though we made a run on it. Dropped them on some inconsequential field. Came back all alone, ten little ships, and flew darn near over Magdeburg and got flak we shouldn't and wouldn't if we stayed on course. I called the lead and told him but got no answer. After sweating out his leading us crazily all over Germany we came over the coast at 15,000', off course, and got the hell shot out of us. The formation split up all over. The copilot slammed my helmet on my head and I gave it the gun, doing 30-degree banks at short timed intervals. Could see the fire in the exploding flak and hear and feel it. Luckily we got untouched. Issy in the top turret said shortly after we made a turn, there was the flak where we would have been. The guns were the 30-mm. Bofors guns that shoot very fast but can't reach the higher altitudes. Lost Warke and another crew today. Go on pass tomorrow and am sure glad as I know I'll live two more days anyway.

Author's note: On a couple of occasions the lead navigator would come to Frank Erbacher, our excellent navigator, and say, "Frank, where the hell were we today?" The above is an example of terrible navigation.

July 6, #20: 3 2000 lb 489-H (These are BIG babies. We have the room to carry four of them.) Didn't hit briefed bridge. Big front in the way, so hit an airfield somewhere in France. Good mission, little flak. That stuff's got the hell scared out of me now. Guess the

Jerries came up on the boys who went to Leipzig. Glad we weren't there.

July 7: What a delay! Had a two-day pass spent in Norwich. Shot the old .45 the night of the 4th and they shot flares and running lights, a nice try, but a poor substitute for being back home.

July 9, #21: Weather brought us back as we were over Belgium. Were supposed to go somewhere in France. The weather was so bad we lost the formation as we were returning.

July 11, #22: 5 1000 lb GPs. Munich (home and birth of the Nazi party). Were supposed to bomb an airfield east of town if visual, but it wasn't, so we hit the industrial area of Munich. Glad it was PFF or the flak would have been terrific. Were in flak for eight minutes but it wasn't too accurate. A piece of flak got the bombardier in the chest area but the flak suit stopped it. Never saw so many planes on one mission before. The sky was full of Libs and Forts. German radio said bombs fell in town for over a half-hour steady, and I believe it. They reported extensive damage. I feel like we shortened the war a bit today.

Am very tired, was on oxygen seven hours today. We were the first ship to land. Left the formation over the channel and came back under the clouds. Tried to pass four P-38s and was going 270 once but couldn't do it, darnit, but it would have been fun. Navigation was excellent—all pathfinder. Only saw the ground a very few times. Were only ten minutes from Switzerland. First time I brought a pipe along, but I couldn't see spending a year or so without one, though I wasn't pessimistic. However, I was more afraid this morning at briefing than I've been before a mission, but it wasn't bad in the air, thankfully. That's a nuff.

July 12, #23: 6 500 lb GPs and 4 500 lb fire bombs. Where—MUNICH AGAIN! This time rougher, as expected. Flak was much more accurate and I flew in low-left section and we caught hell. Flew right wing in bucket and saw Kuchwara's #4 engine get shot completely off. I moved up and took his place in deputy lead then. Blanton went to Switzerland. Another of our ships crashed at Hardwick. Anyway, he made it back to England. Just heard Kuchwara got back to England. Sounds unbelievable because after he got out of formation they really started working on him, just like they did to us at Berlin.

We go on a six-day pass tomorrow. Am going to Scotland, out of Edinburgh, to a small town, Dollar. (When I purchased the train ticket at Edinburgh to go to Dollar, the male ticket seller said "to Dollar for a dollar." At that time I think there were five shillings for an American dollar.) We were originally going to Berlin today. Glad we didn't, because we are back. Sure getting rough now, though. Sure hope we can make it. I pray enough for it; I just pray a lot in the air. I don't see how we've gotten by this far without getting it. I'm sure God had more to do with it than anyone else. (I no longer believe the almighty interferes with our lives. But under the same stress, if it helps, great.)

Hope we don't have to do over thirty missions too, but they could make us do thirty-five. Well, gotta take a bath and get ready for the big pass. (Kuchwara did not make it back.)

July 23, #24: 40 100 lb GPs. Airfield, Leon, France. GH (radar) mission. Good navigation, good escort, P51s all the way. Little flak at target. After an eleven-day layoff we flew again. Loved the Highlands, and Edinburgh. I'll remember it so won't write it down here. Joe Shogan, my buddy, is up there now.

We've had a lot of wrecks at the field lately. About a half dozen planes smashed up in a week right on the field. Gears have been giving away.

July 25, #25: 40 100 lb GPs. Support of ground troops at St. Lo. We were to saturate the German area in preparation for an American ground offensive. We were to bomb at 16000', but due to weather we went in at 11200. That's too darn low for a Lib. Our troops moved back 1500 yards and their offensive was to start at H plus 55, or 1055. We dropped at 1010. The whole 8th and 9th Air Forces were there. Must have raised hell with the Jerries on the ground. The flak wasn't too thick, but accurate. We had the closest burst ever, right in front of our nose. I ducked as I saw it burst—no safety glass today. It was very audible, the whole crew heard it, and loud. The copilot thought it knocked the nose turret and the bombardier off. I thought it burst between the nose and the flight deck, but it couldn't have unless it went through the ship, but it was too close! We certainly have a lot of airstrips on the beachhead. Our artillery shot a red smoke screen to mark the bomb line and also to cover the withdrawal of our troops 1500 yards. However, as each succeeding group dropped he bombs, the line kept moving back toward the troops. The result was the death of 102 and 380 wounded, including the death of General Leslie J. McNair. Apparently there was no communication between ground and air. (It was a pretty unsophisticated war in comparison to the 21st century) Quite a day, the only time I brought my 45 along as going down amid enemy troops being bombed wouldn't end as a POW.

July 27: No flying last couple of days, only by stand-downs or scrubs did we miss Kiel, and today, close to Friedrichshafen. Got up for briefing at 1230 a.m. Mission was scrubbed just 15 minutes before takeoff. Shogan should be back tonight from his leave.

July 29, #26: Oil refinery at Bremen. PFF—thanks! (Flak less accurate if the gunners can't visually see where their shells are exploding) Hell of a lot of flak, barrage and predicted concentration, eight minutes of it. (Three types, barrage they shoot a lot into a box they think you will have to go through. Looks terrible, but the least dangerous. Predicted concentration, a sort of barrage but more specific in area. And tracking, the most dangerous because they are shooting directly at you and gun crews can get pretty good at this. When you get out of formation, you get tracking.)

Was glad to fly after two scrubs last two mornings. Most flak I've seen so far was, I believe, today, and I can't even imagine what would have happened had it been visual, because it was bad enough the way it was. Lost no planes. One ship had the ailerons shot out but it used A-5 (autopilot) and landed, after taking the precaution of having the crew bail out over Buncher #7. Good for the pilots and probably they also kept the engineer. Had a hard time getting started today. First, a stuck prop governor and then a stuck throttle linkage. Glad we went though—now. Stand down until morning at least.

Author's note:—You can see that the break in mission flying really helped the nerves.

August 1: Started out on #27, but had to abort for the first time. #s 2 and 3 were pretty rough and we lost a lot of oil out of #4, and by the time we got to the final approach we only had ten lb left, but didn't feather it or they might have made us go out over the ocean and drop them. Three engines and two rough ones is not the time for that. It was a heavy load to land with, but we've had some experience doing it a couple of times before. Everybody came back, but didn't hit some oil dump as intended, but an airfield. Gotta go meet Joe and go to the show, He just got back.

August 2, #27: 24 250 lb.??. St. Dizier, France, target of opportunity. Lead navigator got lost so we took a Cook's tour of France. Our section, led by the Skipper (pilot in our barracks), bombed an airfield with JU88s on it. Sweat out fighters all day, no 38s or 51s showed up as scheduled, and we were in a good enemy fighter airfields area, one little group, and for quite a while, just one section, as we lost the other two when we bombed. The Skipper did a good job of leading, and we flew deputy lead. As we left France by La Havre we saw the RAF Lancasters bombing the port. They would come in at different altitudes and headings. Looked like a big mess to us. They got a lot of flak, but did good accurate bombing, it looked. Madden's crew bailed out on returning. Shot up too bad to land it, I guess. Think he got hit where we saw the red flak. We came down close to Paris on the way out. The other two sections finally attempted to bomb an airfield, but for some reason, just one dropped.

August 3, #28: 12 500 lb GPs. Oil refinery, Leon, France. Had 365 hours on the engines. #2s left magneto dropped too much on four separate checks, but we took it as it was a short mission. #2 ran rougher and rougher, and at the IP we had to turn around and feather it, as #4 was getting bad too. We were at 25000' and had to pull too much to try to keep up. Hope we got credit. We dropped our bombs in the ocean, and landed only minutes before the returning formation, who blew hell out of the oil refinery and all got back. Good! Blanck got his thirty-third today. Sure hope he doesn't have to do any more. We go on pass tomorrow.

August 7, #29: 10 250 lb GPs. Brussels oil refinery and storage tanks. Weather was pretty bad and as it was not to be a PFF or GH as it is in occupied territory, we couldn't drop unless it was visual. We hunted for a last resort and sort of went over Rotterdam twice but there were not enough holes in the clouds, so we brought the bombs back.

August 9: Were briefed for Stuttgart but because of dense fog it was scrubbed a half hour after proposed take off time—thanks.

August 10, #30: Oil refinery thirty miles east of Auxerre, France. Had quite a time getting started. It was scrubbed once. We left after the 446th and 95th groups, so I sweat being left wing on the lead, but I got some little friends so we were escorted. This is the same target we tried for a week or so ago and didn't find. Today we found it, but all three sections missed it! Good formation, good navigation, a bit of flak coming out. Capt. Haggin lead the group and for him, his 30th and last.

Author's note: Lead crews should get a break. They are a main target of the opposition.

August 12, #31: 52 100 lb GPs. Airfield NW of Laon, France. Flew over our own battle lines but went too far left of course and got some flak near Avranches where the Germans made a counter-offensive to split our troops, a week or so ago. Our leader's #1 caught fire over England and aborted, so Gibson lead. We really hit the target, and no flak. Had eighteen bombs hang up and one of them was armed—the vane had spun off. So we closed the bomb bay doors and worried for about twenty minutes while the bombardier went back from his forward position and took out the fuses, and then he kicked 'em out. Bombardiers have nasty, dangerous jobs at times like this. Think and hope we only have to do one more, though they are still up in the air about giving us credit for our one and only abortion on the 28th mission.

August 13, #32: 52 100 lb GPs. Road junction south of Rouen. We were to bomb roads to keep the Jerries from escaping a trap. Our group had six targets and each section of six ships was to fine two more. All our bombs were dropped on the first target after which we got the hell out of there, not wanting to through all the flak at Rouen. We hit out for the coast and had an unpleasant ten minutes doing evasive action against ack-ack, but got some bursts right under us, with two pieces of shrapnel as souvenirs. Saw the colonels today and found out we get credit for the 28th mission. Our unliked squadron commander seems to foul up every time he leads a mission. He is trying to make us fly a mission tomorrow. I'm fighting it. (Years later our group had a get-together in Harlingen, Texas, and our former squadron commander was there, and several crews from the other three squadrons voiced their dislike for this fellow.) Carrington (our radio operator) will get grounded. He's not in very good shape. I'm not either but I could take another or more if I had to, but surely hate to.

August 18, # 33: Well, I fought it for four days, but rank prevailed. 10 500 lb GPs. Oil dump two miles north of Nancy, France. Flew over our liberated territory as much as possible. Had good support from 38s, and had 51s at the target. Bombed from 14000′ (too low!), and went right over Nancy for the bomb run, but even though they had 28 guns reported, not one burst of flak did we see. Thanks. Flew over the Falaise Gap on the return and sweat that out. Flew with eleven men—only six ours—four are through—the twins, Hank and Vince. Guess we're through, and it feels damn good, but I'm too tired to get tight. We shot flares, red and green, and that's all we did to celebrate. Go on pass tomorrow. Finis.

Well, I trust that you got through the 33 missions along with me. I was fortunate to catch a tour that occurred during the spring and summer months, and involved undefended targets like bridges. While I have complained about the weather, it was more treacherous during winter months. While there was still plenty of German fighter opposition, nothing like the crews in late 1942 and much of 1943 with little or no fighter escort, and a stronger Luftwaffe. And as the 8th AF grew, more locations could be bombed any one day, requiring more locations to defend. This was somewhat offset by more flak guns as the allies advanced, and more experienced and accurate gun crews. But on any day, I'd rather face a battery of 88s than a determined FW 190 or Me 109, or later on, the German jets. And by this time, you know how I hated and feared flak.

A highly recommended daily operational record of the Eighth Air Force is Roger A. Freeman's *Mighty Eighth War Diary* Jane's Publishing Company, 730 Fifth Ave., New York NY 10019. It includes mission information such as aircraft losses, missing, wounded and killed, the targets, and fighter activity. It is a very complete, valuable historic record.

The Red Cross was wonderful. They had food and lodging

centers in Norwich and at least one in London. They served sandwiches after missions, really appreciated, because churning stomachs couldn't handle lightly fried eggs before a mission.

With my missions finished, what to do. I could go back to the U.S. However, I might be assigned to B29s for a Japanese combat tour. One tour was enough for me. I managed to get assigned as Group air-sea rescue officer. I appointed Joe Shogan as my assistant. I took this assignment very seriously because proper procedures in ditching would save lives. Records showed a ditched B-17 crew would lose one man, as opposed to four in an B-24. The 17 had the advantage of lower landing speeds with a lighter wing loading, stronger fuselage, tail rather than nose wheel, and simply a better configuration for a water landing. I wrote two pages of instructions entitled "Dingy, dingy, let's ditch" (in *Bombs Away! Volume II*) that gave crews pointers for safer water landings.

It was great to be relieved of the pressure of combat missions, to test fly planes after repairs, calibrate air speed, and just have fun flying. Sometimes we would go up and before long a P-38 would join us in formation, and then maybe a British Lancaster, a B-25 or 26, a Mosquito, and we had a great time. We particularly liked the Australian pilots. They attacked life sort of the way we did. We respected the English pilots. They were, it seems, fearless. They would land their big bombers with the gigantic landing gear, just letting them drop in from wherever. I guess their attitude was, airplanes are for activity in the air, and if you are close to the ground, forget it. And the battle of Britain would not be a happy story without the Hurricane and Spitfire guys. Sometimes we would fly over to the coast and dive down on sailboats, pulling up so the prop wash would hit their sails, hoping to give them a bit of a scare. Buzzing—flying low—was exhilarating, but restricted because of accidents. It was kind of accepted to buzz your own base at your completed tour.

As time moved toward the holiday season the urge to be home for Christmas prevailed, and I left our base in November for the relocation base in Stone, England. From there, embarkation on the Queen Mary in Glasgow, Scotland, for the voyage to New York. It was a wonderful trip. No more than three to a cabin, whereas the other way, probably eighteen. No escort—our ship was faster than German subs. We did zigzag a bit. I had never had an ocean voyage. After a few days we got into the much warmer gulf stream, and it was pleasant on deck, watching the restless ocean. The Statue of Liberty was a most welcome sight. I do not remember the train trip to Ft. Lewis, Washington. I arrived home several days before Christmas, and did not have to report back to Santa Ana, California until January 17, 1945, for redistribution. I tried to get assigned to the pink palace, name close to "Don Ce Sar", near St. Petersburg, Florida. It was known as a really nice place for airmen who needed some rest from the emotional rigors of combat. However, I didn't qualify which, of course, was a positive. While most of us were a bit jumpy and a bit resentful of those with no combat, it all wore off before long.

I was unneeded surplus. I was sent to my old B-24 training base in Albuquerque. In 26 days I managed to finagle an assignment to Marana Army Air Base, some thirty miles north of Tucson. They had AT-6 planes, known in the navy as, I think, SNJs, or "The Texan." It had a 650 hp radial engine, a low wing monoplane, retractable gear, very maneuverable, a joy to fly. (Still flown today at air shows). It was the hottest thing I had flown, but pretty tame compared to P51s and the like. Next, it's off to another B-24 base in Walla Walla, Washington, working my way closer to my home in Spokane. I don't recall doing anything at this base except flying a bit of Link and pushing for a better assignment. And it came on July 8, 1945, being transferred to Geiger Field, Spokane. Home at last! Geiger was a base for some 25,000 engineers. It required just three pilots to serve its purpose. A Capt. Matthews, Lt. Brock, and me. The diversity of planes to fly was great. An AT-6, BT-13, L-5, AT-11, C-45, PT-17, and two Ford Tri motor aircraft, used by the forest service for fighting fires. To this day I regret not flying this relic.

I can't understand why I didn't realize the significance of doing so. I flew the PT-17 only once, probably because of a subconscious recollection I had ground looped it in primary training. However, I was much more experienced but still, I passed up more time in this great aerobatic machine. I flew the BT-13 ten times, the AT-11 eleven times, the C-45 eighteen times—mostly on business for the engineers, often to Hamilton Field outside of San Francisco—and my favorite, the L-5VW, twenty times. Rather than the 95 horsepower engine it had 195, and I could hold it on the runway to build up speed and then pull the stick all the way back to my belly and push the flaps full on so that I could go practically straight up for maybe 150'. It had side panels that could be opened and locked in place, leaving an unobstructed view of the countryside below, even allowing to place the elbow out the window, as in driving an auto. I note from my log I didn't waste any time trying it out, July 9 was either my first or second day at Geiger.

My log says that the next day, July 10, I flew to Boeing Field in Seattle. I had no plan to, but a navy WAVE had been hitching rides across the U.S. upon graduating as an ensign at Hunter College in New York. She was stranded in Spokane, and the captain suggested I fly her home to Seattle. I did. Through her I met a Nancy Noble, sister graduate, a great gal that was engaged to one of their favorite instructors. It was easy to see why he picked this one. I took her flying a few times, and also took up my mother and sister Florence. Dr. Fitzgerald, my doctor when I was with Hecla in Wallace, Idaho, phoned and suggested I buzz Wallace. I did, but it was dangerous in the narrow canyon to get over town and on my second pass I narrowly missed the flagpole on the county courthouse. What a scare! How loose things were. Taking friends or family flying would not be allowed now, and buzzing would incur serious consequences.

A sad and unnecessary accident occurred some few months after I was discharged. The captain had ferried the base general, colonel, Red Cross man, and my flying companion on many trips and crew chief, Sgt. Sheets, of York, PA. He named this C-45 "The Pride of York." On returning from San Francisco, in weather, they crashed into a hill, killing all.

I do not believe the captain ever flew a much safer entry to the field that Lt. Brock and I had practiced several times. Years later in going through York I looked up the name "Sheets." There were about ten of them. First one, no knowledge. Well, I'll try the last one. "He was my brother!" I sent him a number of photos of this great, happy Sgt., who had flown with me many times as engineer.

The army doesn't need me anymore. Frankly, they didn't need me after I finished my missions. But the army, at least in those days, was not efficient, working on the level of lowest common denominator. Slowly, within the ability of the lesser, the job gets done. I appreciate and laud the military. If every 18-year-old male had to serve at least a year I believe the discipline and camaraderie that builds self-respect would drastically reduce crime. And then help them with higher education. It will never happen, too bad. I would not include mandatory service for females. They don't need it.

I was discharged in September and my employment at the Hecla Mining Company showed me that more life fulfillment would be achieved from higher education. Stanford had already begun their fall quarter, and the VA (Veterans' Administration) suggested I enroll at the locally located Gonzaga, as their fall semester had not begun. So I, along with a goodly number of other discharges, began our higher education, at ages of 25, more or less. Rah rah was a bit immature for us, but not totally. College spirit is great, and it contends for the happiest, most fun, fulfilling period of my life.

Our Wedding Day

General Jimmy Doolittle Dies

Retired Gen. James H. Doolittle, who became a national hero when he led the first World War II bombing raid on Japan in 1942, died September 27, 1993 at the age of 96. He died at his son's home after suffering a stroke. Doolittle, known as "Jimmy" to virtually everyone, established an unparalleled string of aviation records in the 1920s and 1930s, first as an Army pilot and then as an employee of Shell Oil Co. In 1935 he became one of the first people to earn a doctorate in aeronautics.

But he was remembered above all for leading the April 18, 1942 raid on Japan. The raid on Tokyo inflicted no major damage, and a later Naval War College study could find "no serious strategic reason" for it.

But it stirred American morale just four months after the shock of Pearl Harbor, and it put the Japanese on notice that their cities were within reach of U. S. air power.

When President George Bush gave Doolittle the Presidential Medal of Freedom in July, 1989, he described him as "the master of the calculated risk." General Doolittle also won the Medal of Honor and many other awards.

Shortly after the mid-day raid which stunned the Japanese, Doolittle was promoted from Lt. Colonel to Brigadier General, and by the end of the war he was the youngest Lt. Gen. in the army. He went on to serve in a variety of posts during the war, including commander of the Algeria-based 12th Air Force and later the 8th Air Force, based in Britain, which blasted away Germany's air power.

A Textbook on

Escaping

Lt./Col. Edward W. Appel, 389th

I was first pilot of a B-24 which we flew from the States around the southern route up to England in Feb. of 1944.

After flying 29 missions, I had one to go before my tour was completed. My original crew had already completed their 30 missions by volunteering to fly with other crews when we were not scheduled to fly, so this time I would be flying as command pilot with Lt. Frazee's crew, a crew I had never met.

It was September 5, 1944 and the target was Karlsruhe Marshalling yards. We were to fly deputy lead and I remember we were flying on formation instruments nearly all the way.

Just before reaching the IP we broke into the clear. We had just started our bomb run when the 88s hit. We took a monstrous hit in the right wing which knocked out the right two engines. The last two engines were still going strong but we had no turbos, and the fuel cells were ruptured. The rudder cables were also cut, so we had no rudders. The windshield had come in with the first blast and with gas flowing around I thought we were going to burn.

We managed to get turned around using the ailerons and

headed back, holding direction with ailerons but losing altitude fast. Two engines out on one side, and without turbos and rudders a B-24 is like a falling rock. At this point I was feeling sorry for Capt. Paul Anderson who was a good friend of mine from my hometown of Redfield, S.D., who had elected to fly my last mission with me. He took up a position between us pilots. Being an ordnance officer he wasn't supposed to be on this mission with us and now we were in a position where he, and we, might not make it.

First we salvoed the bombs (must have scared the hell out of some cattle on the ground) and then had the crew throw out anything loose in order to lighten ship. We were at 24,000 feet, but within 25 miles we were down to 10,000. At that point I knew we couldn't make it as our front lines were 100 miles away. Time to bail out, which we all did. When my chute opened it was only seconds until I hit the ground in a plowed field. I found out much later that we had lost four men. The Navigator had jumped before we did and never got his chute open. Also, two of the crew hid out at a French farmhouse (this was in Alsace Lorraine) for about a month but then decided to get out. I understood they got in with the French Underground, put on civilian clothes and tried to make it through the lines. They were caught and shot by the Germans as spies. My friend, Capt. Paul Anderson took up residence in a Stalag Luft.

After landing in the plowed field, I shucked my chute and looking back about a half mile, I could see the last two men running towards each other, but there were farmers running toward them, so I didn't go back there. I hid in a vineyard for a while, but then decided it wasn't a very good hiding place, so I started to get up. I should have looked first.

As I started to get up there was a lot of yelling "HALT!" I looked back and there in line abreast across the fields were German soldiers with rifles. They could have shot me easy, but they kept yelling "HALT!" so I pretended I didn't hear them and kept walking away. I didn't run because then they certainly would have shot. I walked into a clump of trees and then ran like a scared rabbit out the other side and down into a slew where I jumped into the water and hid among the slew rushes. They knew I was in there somewhere because they kept walking around the edge of the water. They would all get together on one side and fire their burp guns through the weeds. Scared the hell out of me!

Finally, they all left except for one man. I could see him standing and watching the place. After a while they all came back and went through the same procedure—shooting and all. Finally, they left and I stayed right there until dark when I sneaked out.

I traveled at night toward the west and the front lines and hid in the daytime using any cover I could find. When I got hungry I would feast from a farmer's field. I also had my escape kit with concentrated rations which helped. Drinking water was another matter, but I found if I walked into a village after dark and stomped around as if I belonged there, I could go up to a pump and pump water into a bucket and carry it out of town and nobody paid attention to me.

Finally, after about ten days, I started walking across a field in daylight. There was a farmer and his wife picking rutabagas and putting them in a wagon. They asked if I was an American and I said yes, after which they motioned me to get into the wagon. I was so darned cold and hungry but at that time that I didn't figure I had much to lose. I still had to get over the mountains to the west where both sides were dug in and shooting anything in sight. After getting in the wagon they covered me with gunny sacks and took me to their home in a little village. They hid me with their son in a hayloft (they were French) as the son was also hiding out from the Germans. We stayed right there until the end of November when the Germans were pushed out and our tanks and trucks came down the road. I was out!

Part 2: Col. Appel's Experience as a Fighter Pilot

I went back to England and while orders were being cut to send me back to the ZI, I decided that instead of going home I would stay and try to hook on with a Fighter Group. I guess I was a little flak happy! I took off for the 56th FG and told Col. Dave Schilling I wanted to fly fighters. He said, "Sure. Come on down."

That was quite a kick getting out of bombers and into fighters. Like getting out of a truck on to a motorcycle. After checking out in the P-47 I flew sixteen dive bombing, strafing and escort missions. My last, the 16th of April 1945, saw me busily strafing Muhldorf Airdrome fifty miles east of Munich.

I came in on the deck and was shooting into ME 109s sitting on the field when I picked up a lot of ground flak and remember seeing holes appear in the wings. Then the engine started running rough and losing power. I started to pull up, which I shouldn't have done over an enemy airfield, and then they really started to get in the hits.

I was soon out of range, but at full throttle I still wasn't getting any power and the airspeed continued to fall off. I tried to get over one last hill before bellying in but as I started to clear the hill the right wing stalled and went under. The plane cartwheeled across the countryside and I thought school was out again. The wings broke off along with the tail, but by some miracle it came down right side up. I cut my knee and elbow a little bouncing around in the cockpit. At first I thought I was all bloody, but it was just hot engine oil from the ruptured oil tank.

I left the Mae West and parachute in the seat and crawled out. Some farmers were watching but they didn't do anything so I took off running. I ran into some trees and beyond there was a little village strung along a road. I had to get past this village as German soldiers were coming from the airfield I had just strafed and were behind me shooting.

As I came to the village two German soldiers came out and drew their guns hollering "HALT!" With all the shooting going on behind me, I thought I'd pretend I was a German running away from the Americans. I yelled back "NICHT HALT, AMERICAN COMEN." They turned and looked back where I came from with wide, startled eyes and I kept on going. Then they swung back towards me again pointing their guns and yelling "HALT!"

I stopped and waved an arm back toward the woods and yelled "NAY, NAY NICHT HALT, AMERICAN COMEN!" They again turned around and watched the other woods for the Americans they thought were coming, and I made tracks. I ran into the woods and actually sat down and laughed, thinking how they would catch hell when the German soldiers came and found out that they had let me get away.

I couldn't find a good place to hide in the woods as the underbrush was all cleaned out, so I climbed to the top of a big tree and just sat there. The Germans soon came a line abreast again, hunting around under the trees with rifles, but they kept right on going. I stayed in the tree until dark, then climbed down and took off northwest toward the front lines.

I walked at night and hid in the daytime, as I had done before. I had a couple of escape kits along with compasses, maps, hacksaw blades and concentrated rations in them. I also had my .45, which was a big consolation even if I didn't fire it.

I would go up to a house right after dark and knock on the door. Usually the man would come to the door and I would tell him straight out that I was an American flyer and that I needed food. Many times they would have me come in and sit at the table and give me bread, meat and coffee. I wouldn't let anybody leave the house while I was there. I would lay my gun on the table and keep everybody at a distance. Then I would leave and make many miles that night so they wouldn't catch me. Actually, some families would give me some food to take along.

I finally got up near the front lines where there was a lot of shooting. I hid under some small, thick evergreens in a hollowed out spot. Looked like an old WWI foxhole, and probably was.

One night, the German Army moved over me and then for two days I was between the two lines that were shooting at each other using mostly artillery. The shells that hit the trees would really blast things around there.

One night the shooting went to the east so the next morning I crept out to the edge of the woods and watched the roads. Finally, I spotted weapon carriers and tanks that were definitely ours. I came out of the woods with my hands held high as I didn't want to get shot at by our own army.

I went back through an Artillery outfit that was the same outfit I came through the first time. The same officers, the same Colonel. The Colonel was a little suspicious of me by this time and thought maybe I was spying for the other side. HOME FREE AGAIN!

By the time I got back to Paris the war was over so I rode an LST across the ocean along with a whole load of ex-POWs.

I was home on R&R helping my dad harvest in the summer of '45 when over the hill comes Capt. Paul Anderson. They had just freed him from a POW camp. His first words were "You son of a gun. You take me on a trip over Germany and you dump me out."

That Specially-Remembered Mission for the 445th

David G. Patterson

From: The History of the 445th Bombardment Group (H), *by Rudolph J. Birsic*

Thursday, February 24, 1944

To the 445th Bomb Group veteran that date stands out above other dates. The mission was Gotha; the results were a Presidential Citation for the Group, but the cost was a black day in the Group's history in terms of casualties. Total casualties amounted to 123; of these, later reports officially listed 54 men as prisoners of war. The 702nd Squadron lost its Commander, Major Evans, and practically its entire operations staff. The 700th operation officer, Captain Waldher, was also lost... Here follows the official descriptive narration as recorded in the Presidential Citation.

'The 445th Bombardment Group (H) 2nd Air Division, is cited

for outstanding performance of duty in action against the enemy. On 24 February 1944 this group participated, with other heavy bombardment groups of the 2nd Bombardment Division, in an attack on the Gothaer Waggonfabrik, A.G. located at Gotha, Germany. On this occasion the attacking bombers met and overcame the fiercest and most determined resistance the enemy was able to muster in defense of this target, so vital to his ability to wage war. Unprotected by friendly fighter cover, the 445th was under almost continuous attack from enemy aircraft for a period of two hours and 20 minutes. Although antiaircraft fire was hurled at the formation along the route to and from the target as well as at the target itself, the deadliest opposition was given by enemy aircraft. For one hour and 20 minutes before "bombs away" savage attacks were made by single and twin engine enemy fighters in a vain attempt to keep the bombers from reaching their target.

On the actual bombing run, that critical period of each bombardment mission, fierce and relentless attacks were unable to keep the bombers from accomplishing their task. Of this group's 25 aircraft which penetrated enemy territory, thirteen were lost to these fierce fighter attacks, which number is approximately twice the loss suffered by any of the other groups participating in this mission. In addition, nine of the twelve surviving aircraft returned from the mission with battle damage. With heroic determination the 445th flew its assigned course, destroying 21 enemy attackers, probably destroying two more, and damaging seven during the long running battle. The target was located and bombed with extreme accuracy and devastating results. This target, the most important source of ME 110s, was so well hit that the enemy air force suffered a most telling blow. The courage, zeal, and perseverance shown by the crew members of the 445th Bombardment Group (H), 2nd Air Division, on this occasion were in accordance with the highest traditions of the military service.

The Hamm Raid,

April 22, 1944

Joseph Broder, 446th

We had a late briefing, a late takeoff, and a return to base after dark at 2130 hours (9:30 PM) and Jerry came back with us. Over a dozen B-24 bombers were shot down, destroyed, and strewn about airfields all over East Anglia, not counting standard aerial casualties. Many ships crash-landed. Our 446th Bomb Group dispatched twenty-four Liberators. Two failed to return, but this does not include miscellaneous casualties.

The objective was Hamm, one of the greatest traffic centers in Western Europe, and the target itself was a complex of railway marshalling yards. While most combat flights are scheduled for the early morning, an exceptional proceeding occurred this day. Within two hours of noon, crews were rounded up from all over the airdrome—mess halls, barracks, flight lines, orderly rooms, officers' and airmen's clubs, and wherever else aviators congregate. At exactly 1200 the 446th (including me) was to be briefed for a major mission. When the target, flight altitude, and ordnance were announced, there were many gasps and groans. It was a surprise, not unlike the late briefing.

Flixton Airfield became a beehive of activity. Vehicles brought personnel from briefings to the aircraft, planes were hurriedly bomb-loaded, ground crews hastened to their specialized assignments, and tarmacs became busy with equipment handling and testing. Cars and jeeps raced back and forth. "Old Hickory" stood at ready, fully war painted and thoroughly inspected by crewmates Elizer and Whaley. Just a few minutes later the pilot's position cackled "thirty minutes' delay." It lasted fifty minutes and the mission was not cancelled.

At 1440, mid-afternoon, we accepted the green-green Very pistol signal from the tower, rumbled awkwardly ahead, raced down the runway at full throttle, finally picked up enough air speed, and barely rose at runway's end. Clearing into a shining sky, we were followed by the rest of the 446th, and our adventure began. Only one aircraft in our 707th Squadron, which led on this day, had to feather a prop and it turned home. He was lucky. We cleared to altitude and droned on.

When met by Focke-Wulf fighters stationed fifty miles south of Hamm, we were clearly able to see the swastika-painted planes become engaged by our P-47 Thunderbolts, dogfight our escorts almost to a standstill and yet still manage to attack our columns. These Germans were very determined. Bitter battles filled the skies as our turrets turned and fired, friends and foes clashed, and two bombers exploded—smoke and debris fluttering earthward. The FW-190s caught it, too, cannon fire exterminating some of them as our friendlies exacted a degree of revenge. Of the three dozen to forty Luftwaffe interceptors, not less than one-third of them were downed by our snub-nosed, fat-bellied friends.

For the first time, I caught a glimpse of an enemy face as he broke off an engagement with one of our nearby bombers. Turning hard and swiftly to his left from what was a ten o'clock high attacking position and then standing on his wing before deliberately hurling himself nose first towards the below, I spotted a dark-haired, squinty-eyed, pale looking youth who hardly looked Teutonic. He looked like me.

As our B-24 formation lumbered on to its target, an avalanche of ground fire exploded in our midst, the black puffs of smoke downing still another Liberator in the wing directly behind us. It was identified by tail gunner Baker as being from the 458th Bomb Group. There was little let-up. Massive bursts of enemy fire continued, chaff drops proved ineffective, and the Ruhr Valley's smoke screen all but obliterated the aiming point and the target. We bombed to unknown results.

Dusk was barely beginning to settle as we land and were hit by Messerschmitt 109s, perhaps seventy predators in all. Luckily, our revolving escort was there. A brilliant defensive effort by an outnumbered group of P-51 Mustangs saved our skins, enabling us to escape with losses of only two bombers in our entire wing... but three more of the giant war birds suffered damage. One aircraft had a section of its right tailfin blown out by a twenty millimeter shell, one had Davis wing damage and was fast losing fuel and altitude, and a third ship had two feathered props. These Libs would barely make it back to base or else ditch in the Channel. They might be rescued by the Royal Navy—they might be rescued by German boats—or they might drown and die. Not an inconsiderable number of our bombers had wounded aboard.

More bad news: I was right... Our ETA to Flixton was almost exact and would take place with darkness falling. But even worse news was yet to come.

Boche ME-410 fighter-bombers, having followed the division's Liberators, beat us back to bases all over East Anglia and wrought enormous damage, confusion, and casualties. The return from Hamm turned into hell. Intruders struck at almost blacked-out airfields, shot down some B-24s in their landing patterns, and caused blazes and bonfires as ships broke up or belly-landed on nearby farms. Pandemonium ruled. Shots were exchanged. One of the 446th's runways was usable; one wasn't. We landed at Seething, a base about a dozen miles away.

When the 446th awoke to Hamm's morning-after, they hadn't the benefit of the reveling, just the hangover. Runways were pot-holed from foreign bombs and had to be smooth-surfaced quickly or the field temporarily closed. Wreckage was removed from what twisted metal remained of what was once a Liberator that had just given up ten charred bodies to an already overworked mortu-ary station. Then another three char burned remains were yielded from an enemy ME-410 aircraft that was still embedded in the B-24. It will never be affixed who destroyed whom on those final fatal yards flown by the young aviators.

The Infamous Kassel Raid, September 27, 1944

George M. Collar, 445th

The 445th Bomb Group was almost wiped out, and I went down on my twenty-ninth mission, during the infamous Kassel raid of September 27, 1944.

It started out uneventfully enough, with 39 planes scheduled to take off from our group. By the time we got into Germany there had been four aborts, so eventually 35 planes dropped their bombs.

The weather over the continent was not very good, with a thick undercast, cloud base about 3,000 feet and tops 6-7000 feet. It was planned to drop the bombs through the clouds using the PFF in the lead ship.

The 445th was leading the 2nd Combat Wing, the other groups in the wing being the 389th and the 453rd. The lead ship was that of Capt. John Chilton, with Maj. Donald McCoy as command pilot. Deputy lead was Capt. Web Uebelhoer, with Capt. Jim Graham as deputy command pilot. I happened to be flying with

Lt. James Schaen in the 702nd BS; we were in the high right squadron.

We were approaching the IP in a southeasterly direction, where we were supposed to make a slight left turn in an east-southeasterly direction toward Kassel, but for some reason the lead ship turned almost directly east, a mistake which would take us past the target city of Kassel, too far to the north. The only explanation was that the radar man had made a grievous error.

Practically every navigator in our group picked up on this mistake almost instantly, but it was too late for the lead ship to correct to the right, as he would have run into the stream of bombers coming out from the rear.

In hindsight we can say that the correct thing to do would have been to make a 360° turn to the left and come in on the rear of the second division, but Major McCoy decided to continue on east and bomb the city of Gottingen, about 50 miles away. As a result, we lost our fighter escort, and flew alone to our destruction.

Some of the pilots contacted the lead ship to report the error, but the only signal they received was "Keep in tight—Keep it together."

We carried on east, and finally dropped our bombs at Gottingen. We then made a turn to the south, and in the vicinity of Eisenach, we made a right turn to proceed west. By this time, we were probably a hundred miles behind the rest of the division.

Just as we made the turn, we were attacked from the rear by between 100 and 150 German fighters. They attacked us line abreast in three waves. Most of these fighters were specially adapted FW-190s equipped with extra armor, and both 20 and 30mm cannons. They were accompanied by a smaller number of ME-109s.

The battle probably lasted only a few minutes, but it was a horrendous attack, as the FW-190 assault fighters passed through the bomber formations with 20 and 30mm cannons blazing, and the 50 cal. machine guns of the B-24s responding. The skies were full of bright flashes from the exploding shells. Burning and exploding airplanes were plummeting earthward; debris from the planes was spinning through the air. Bomb bay doors floated down like leaves.

In between, many parachutes were blossoming out and carrying flyers toward the under cast and an unknown fate below.

Now I wasn't supposed to be on this raid, and I was due for a three-day pass and was scheduled to leave for London that morning, so I was surprised when they arrested me out of bed at 3:00 AM and told me that I was to take the place of Lt. Jim Schaen's bombardier, who had failed to return from London on the evening of the 26th.

We were the lead plane in the low left element of the high right squadron. I was in the nose turret. The first inkling that we were being attacked was the sudden appearance of many small flak bursts just ahead of the plane, and at the same time a sound like sledge hammer blows hitting the plane. The left wing was hit and on fire, and at the same time there was an explosion under the turret. About this time, the FW-190 that was attacking us streaked overhead not more than a few feet above us. I tried to shoot at him, but the turret controls were inoperative. The explosion under the turret had probably severed the hydraulics to the turret.

After the fighter had passed, I glanced down at the lead squadron and watched with horror as the fighters attacked them. At least two of the bombers were on fire, including the lead plane. At about this time the bail-out bell rang and I descended from the turret. As I glanced around, the nose section looked like Swiss cheese. It was a miracle that neither the navigator nor myself had been hit. Lt. Bean, the navigator, opened the nose wheel door and we both bailed out.

When the smoke of this great battle had cleared, 25 of our bombers had crashed into German soil. Two of our planes crash-landed in occupied France. One had crashed near Brussels, Belgium. Two made it across the Channel to make forced landings at the emergency strip at Manston. One crashed near the base in Norfolk. Only four were able to land at Tibenham.

Of the 238 men aboard the 25 bombers which went down in Germany, 115 were KIA or subsequently died of injuries. One was killed in the plane which crashed in Norfolk and one was killed in the crash in Belgium, for a total of 117.

Another American killed that day was Lt. Leo Lamb of the 361st FG, who belatedly came to our rescue. He collided with an FW-190 in midair.

During the battle, the German air force lost 29 planes, with 18 German pilots KIA. And it is true that five American airmen were murdered that day near the village of Nentershausen. The murdered airmen were second Lt. Newell W. Brainard (Lt. Carrow's crew), T/Sgt. John J. Donohue (Lt. Elder's crew), 2nd Lt. John W. Cowgill, 2nd Lt. Hector V. Scala, and T/Sgt. James T. Fields, all from Lt. Baynham's crew. The perpetrators were civilians, the main culprits being camp bosses at some hard labor camps near a copper mine in the vicinity. The killers were apprehended after the war and brought to justice at a war crimes trial. They were found guilty, and subsequently executed.

One would have thought that with a battle of this magnitude, more would have been written about it. Aside from a paragraph in Roger Freeman's book *The Mighty Eighth* that stated this was the greatest single loss of any group in the Eighth Air Force, it received no other publicity. This is understandable, since this had been a failed raid, and a big defeat for our side. It is possible that everyone was trying to forget it. But it was certainly not forgotten by those who survived it, nor by anyone who happened to be at Tibenham that day, nor by the next of kin of those who perished.

Being Jewish Was an Extra Risk for This Kassel Survivor!

Larry Hobbs, Staff Writer, Palm Beach Daily News

Editor's Note: This story, slightly modified, first appeared in the Friday, January 19, 1996 issue of the Palm Beach Daily News.

"I stand here and I still get a feeling about seeing that airplane," said Weinstein, who was a bombardier/navigator in a B-24 with the 445th Bomb Group during World War II.

The restored B-24 "All American" serves as a flying museum for the Collings Foundation of Stow, Mass. They fly it to about 150 cities a year. The plane is kept in the air largely through sponsorship contributions that range from $24 to $5,000.

He was not always this nostalgic about his war years. When World War II was won, Weinstein returned to Chicago and did his best to leave the experience in his past, he said. He never talked much about the day his ten-member crew was shot down over

Germany, or his harrowing ordeal as a Jewish American in a Nazi prisoner of war camp.

It has only been within the last ten years that Weinstein began searching out fellow Air Force veterans to swap war stories.

"Most of us did try to forget it for about 50 years," said Weinstein, who was awarded the Distinguished Flying Cross, the Purple Heart, and the Air Medal. "It's only about the last seven or eight years that I got back to it. It's fun to talk to these guys. We have so much in common, all the guys who flew in these things during the war."

When Weinstein entered the war in 1941, the magic number was 25—that's how many bombing missions you had to survive to complete a tour of duty. (It was increased to 35 missions later in the war.) The odds of not landing safely back in England were 1-in-3 to 1-in-20 every time you took off on a mission—you never knew the odds when you went out.

Weinstein's crew beat the odds until his 25th and final mission on September 27, 1944. Only five of 35 bombers returned from that mission, three of which crashed on the way back. Weinstein's B-24 was flying at 20,000 feet when they were shot down over Kassel, Germany.

As the plane nose-dived, Weinstein climbed from his tiny cubbyhole in the front and jumped. But his parachute got snagged by equipment inside, leaving him dangling outside the plane.

"I bailed out, but the straps got caught," Weinstein said. "I had to chin myself back into the airplane and jump again. By that time, we were only about 2,500 feet above the ground."

He spent two weeks trying to reach Switzerland before being captured and sent to POW Stalag Luft 1 in Kassel.

"After I bailed out, two weeks later I was captured and taken to a small compound where there were about a dozen other crew members who had also been captured, and we were all being held in a small cell or room. In that group there were two badly wounded airmen who had received no medical attention. One had a badly shot up leg and the other was completely burned down one side of his body. I was the ranking officer in the group, and I asked the guard to take me to see the commandant. Don't ask me where I got the nerve or guts to do that, but I did!

"I was taken to the commandant's office and gave him my name, rank and serial number and told him that there were two badly wounded men who needed medical attention. I said that according to the Geneva Convention, they were entitled to some help.

"The commandant (a major) was a very militant looking and well-dressed officer. He got up and came around from his desk and hit me several times on the cheek with a riding crop. It split my cheek open, and why I don't have a 'dueling scar' there today is a miracle. He proceeded to tell me that we, the Jews and the American airmen, were bombing churches, schools and hospitals, and that is how much he cared about the Geneva Convention.

After I picked myself up from the floor, he had the guard take me back to the cell. In a few hours they came and took the two wounded men out, hopefully to a hospital.

"When I bailed out, my flying boots came off. I was only wearing a pair of wool socks under them. When I landed I hid for a few days trying to make my way to Switzerland. I cut a piece of my leather jacket apart and made myself a pair of moccasins. That's the way I was dressed when I was taken into the commandant's office. Several hours after I was back in the cell, the guard came and took me back to the commandant's office. I stood there at attention while I heard him say to the guard in German, "Take him out and *schiessen* (shoot) him." Since German and Yiddish are very much alike and I had a very, very fleeting knowledge of either, I assumed he meant for the guard to take me out and shoot me.

"The guard marched me out of the building. We were in a walled compound, and I thought he was going to line me up against the wall and shoot me. I saw a gate about 100 yards ahead and thought when I got there, I would make a run for it. If he were going to shoot me, he was going to have to shoot me in the back, not up against the wall.

"About 25 yards from the gate, there was a small building. The guard shoved me in there and proceeded to give me a pair of shoes! Another few yards and I wouldn't be here to tell this story.

"Obviously what the commandant had said was something about *schuhe* (shoes), but in my fear it sounded like *schiessen* (shoot).

"The first thing people always ask me is what is was like to be a POW, and the second thing they ask is what it was like to be a Jewish POW in Germany," Weinstein said.

Nazi Gestapo leader Heinrich Himmler visited the camp of 27,000 POWs and issued a death sentence for its 1,100 Jewish prisoners, Weinstein recalls.

"Himmler came to the camp and left word that all Jewish officers were to be separated and shot," Weinstein said. "Our commander said, 'You march one Jewish guy off this camp and we'll riot.'"

The Nazis backed down, Weinstein said. However, Jewish prisoners were segregated from their fellow American soldiers. They were interrogated often, but the Germans never carried out their threats and intimidation. The camp was liberated on May 11, 1945.

Operation Market

Garden

Lt. Col. Robert E. Oberschmid, 93rd

We were flying twenty feet above the ground, engines howling in protest of a power setting far above normal and the engine instruments in the "red" or close to it. We had an indicated air speed of 205/210 with the wind whistling through more holes than anyone would ever count, still taking hits from small arms fire and no effective means of fighting back. I didn't even have my trusty 45. Where and when, you say? OK, follow me where angels fear to tread but where "all those fine young men" would go so many, many times.

We had been briefed for a practice mission with a real twist—a number (18?) of 93rd BG aircraft together with approximately 102 B-24s from other 2nd D Groups would assemble and fly a loose bomber stream to an area north of London, descend to treetop level and return to our home base on the deck, individually hedge hopping all the way. What a fascinating opportunity that turned out to be. About as much fun as I ever had flying a B-24, and I'm sure there are bovine descendants that still cringe when a plane passes overhead.

Several days later (18 Sept. 44) we were called for another such flight, but this time we were going to Holland. Arnhem to be exact, and we would be dropping parachute supplies to our airborne troops who had gone in the day before. It was to be a "no mission credit" kind of trip. No flak vests or steel helmets but they added a load master for some obscure reason. It wasn't going to be as much fun as the practice mission either, because the trip would be at 500 feet instead of on the deck and we would have fifteen P-51s to intercede for us. They wouldn't be necessary of course, but just in case. I was decked out in a pair of oxfords, pink pants, green shirt, A2 jacket and thirty mission crush hat. Piece of cake. An early day version of kick the tire, light the fire, every man's a tiger.

We were doing our pre-flight when jeeps began running all over the place, picking up our navigators to re-brief. Somebody somewhere had decided we were going to the wrong place. Seems we were not going to Arnhem after all—now it was Oosterbeek. Talk about confusion—if ever the alarm bells in my head had gone off this would have been the time, but no matter, away we went, we were invulnerable, we were good and this was gonna be fun, at least someone said that.

At its best, the North Sea is an ugly, incredibly cold, foreboding body of water. This day it was fairly calm, but the debris of war was scattered from England to Holland. At the top of the list were several Horsa gliders awash in the sea and one of them had at least three British troops sitting on the wing. We reported their plight to "Colgate" (air sea rescue) but the troops were a long way from shore and had already been in the sea at least 24 hours. Poor odds, I'd say.

Landfall was on time, uneventful, on course and at 500 feet, very beautiful. Holland in the fall is truly a poet's inspiration. It was a clear day with the Dutch countryside before us when all hell broke loose. It started with a loud bang from the front of the plane and our nose gunner, Nick Flueras, said he had been hit and the turret was knocked out. Now anyone who flew 25 or 30 missions with the Mighty 8th knows how such an event can focus one's attention. Our bombardier, Al Faulhaber, gave him first aid and said the injury wasn't very bad, but we had lost the turret we would so desperately need. On to Oosterbeek —but now we were really on the deck in a very loose gaggle rather than a formation. A number of the planes had been hit and the radio was alive with the concerns of the various crews, to wit; what the hell's going on and didn't they say this was going to be a fun "no mission credit" trip and where and where are our little friends and hey, a guy could get hurt doing stuff like this. I was flying ten to fifteen feet above the ground and was pulling up to cross dikes and roads. I could see some large electrical transmission towers ahead and I made the decision to fly *under* the wires rather than pull up again. Now just sit back and reflect on that maneuver for a few minutes, and you can't help but wonder where you and I and all the rest of us got the courage to make a decision like that. And the courage of my crew was equal to or greater than mine—they knew what I was going to do and no one uttered a peep. Our top turret gunner Glenn Thompson says he still has a tendency to duck his head driving under a high line.

From here on things just got worse. We came to a guard tower at the corner of a large fenced area which turned out to be a Prisoner of War camp. I lifted the left wing over the first guard tower and flew the length of the fence, waving at the prisoners who were really animated at the thought that deliverance was at hand—little did they know. At the end of the fence, I lifted the wing again to clear a second guard tower and there, not more than thirty feet from my face and eyeball to eyeball were two German soldiers with a machine gun in full automatic. They stitched our plane from end to end but didn't hit anything vital; however, my navigator Jerry Baughman developed a blister on the back of his neck from a round that passed a bit too close.

From then on things just got worse than worse. We were flying about thirty feet above a canal that ran along one side of a small town. My left wing was over the street and the right wing over green fields. Soldiers of all nations gravitate toward towns, and this idyllic village was no exception; it had German soldiers every place I looked. One guy on a bike going our direction looked over his shoulder when he heard us coming and somersaulted but came up on his feet with a pistol in his hand and put a few more holes in us.

There were soldiers walking, riding in trucks, half-tracks and tanks and they were all shooting at us. We passed a church and a priest was in the belfry waving down at us—at least he wasn't shooting.

Approaching Oosterbeek, we pulled up to 500 feet, formed up, opened the bomb bays and made the drop on target. Two of our bundles did not release and our engineer, Fred Johnson, did his usual circus trick of going into the bomb bay without a parachute to release them. As we made a left turn away from the drop zone I could see that the trees across the river from our drop point were sprinkled with the parachutes of our paratroopers and many of those men were still hanging there.

As we headed home, it was obvious that a disaster of major proportions had been brought down on our heads. We never did see our little friends but were told later that they had been devastated on the way in and the trip out was just an extension of that mess. We were on the deck indicating about 210 when a terrific explosion occurred in the cockpit. A fire broke out in the fuse panel on my left and the cockpit area was full of smoke and debris. It took me a few seconds to realize I was still alive, if somewhat rattled. When I turned to our engineer Fred, who always flew standing between our copilot Art Antonio and myself, I saw a picture of total amazement. Fred had been wearing a baseball cap and the visor was gone. The only remnants were a few threads hanging down his forehead. Anyone who believes "close only counts in horseshoes" has never been shot at and missed.

Over the North Sea headed home we watched one of our Group go in the water. Technically it was a perfect ditching, but there were no survivors. Not even a cushion floated after the second impact which also broke the plane in two. We also saw another B-24 and a C-47 go down in the water. Approaching Milfoil (Hardwick) I requested an ambulance for my nose gunner but it proved unnecessary as his injuries were quite minor. So minor that my recommendation for his Purple Heart wasn't even acknowledged. Because of my request for the ambulance we were greeted by a number of staff and medical personnel whose curiosity immediately shifted to questions such as "Where is everybody?" When we informed them that "everybody" was scattered and splattered from Hardwick to Arnhem, Nijmegen, Oosterbeek and back, the mood became somber indeed. In the final analysis Montgomery's end run across the Ruhr was an utter disaster. Inadequate planning, ineffective staffing, confusion and timid leadership led to one of our greatest defeats of the war.

After the war I visited the battle area on the ground and flew over the drop zone several times retracing that portion of the mission. It became obvious we and our paratroopers were victims of incredible error. Simply put, our resupply drop zone was not in an area controlled by our forces.

Operation Market Garden eventually proved to be a military operation based on political considerations and thus doomed from the start.

For an exceptional account of Market Garden, read Cornelius Ryan's *A Bridge Too Far* and Geoffrey Powell's *The Devil's Birthday.*

Our crew consisted of myself and copilot Art Antonio, navigator Jerry Baughman, radar navigator Elmer Pearson, bombardier Elwood Faulhaber, engineer Fred Johnson, radio operator Eugene Clement, gunners Nick Flueras, Glenn Thompson, James Duprey and Allen Sorenson.

With the exception of our radar navigator who joined our crew on mission #14, we did our phase training, flight over, 30 missions and return to the ZI together. Jerry Baughman and Nick Flueras are now deceased but the rest of us, and Jerry's widow Mary Baughman, have a reunion every year.

"Ordeal" in Paris

Donald F. Baumler, 445th BG

Reprinted from the *Kassel Mission Chronicles*

On September 5, 1944, we flew a mission to Karlsruhe, Germany. It was a nine-hour mission. The weather was bad and the results were very bad because of the flak, fighters, the fact that the leader got shot up, and we missed the target and dropped our bombs on an alternate target. So three days later, on September 8, 1944, we had to go back to Karlsruhe.

On September 8, the weather was again bad. We ran into a front that was 27,000 feet high. Our leader decided to climb over it. After passing it, 100 miles from Karlsruhe, we dropped down to 20,000 feet to bomb. Then we turned around and were faced with the same front.

We couldn't possibly climb over it again and have gas to get home, so our brilliant leader decided to go under it. He put the whole group of some forty planes into a very steep dive. I was indicating over 300 mph when my windshield iced up and I couldn't see the plane I was flying on, so I pulled off to the side and leveled off and gradually let down to 500 feet to get under the clouds. I was scraping ice off the windshield. One of my crew in the back reported a line of concrete emplacements (The Siegfried Line).

Right at that very moment a shell (probably 40 mm) hit us mid-ship, just back of the wing and ahead of the side waist window. The force of the blast apparently went to the front and destroyed all our radio equipment and oxygen bottles, and cut the rudder cables completely. It also put the plane into a severe nose down position. I thought the tail was blown off and yelled for Johnny to put on the automatic pilot. He was in such shock that he handed me my steel flak helmet. I knocked it away, pulled the nose up, and tried to make a sharp turn, only to have the rudder pedal clank on the floor with no resistance. I thought we were goners.

So I called on the intercom to "bail out," but realized everything was dead. However, we were in a flat aileron turn and still flying, so I headed for the cloud base. Many more caliber shells hit us, but I finally made it into the clouds and proceeded to fly blind in a southerly direction toward Switzerland. Then the wings iced up and I had to lower our altitude. Eventually, after several hours, we broke out and recognized what could only be the Alps. We were way too far south.

Harold Parson, our regular navigator, was not with us, and Leon White, the bombardier, offered to try to get a fix on the "G" box. He said he knew where we were and gave me a heading toward Paris. I knew Paris was captured about four days previously, so I took the heading. About an hour later, lo and behold, there was Paris. We circled the Eiffel Tower and then tried to find an airfield. About ten miles south, at Bretigny, we saw an old German airfield with one runway, now a 9th AF fighter base. Unfortunately, the wind was blowing crossways and strong. We shot off red flares (emergency) and made my approach. But without rudders to crab into the wind, I could only hold direction by lowering the wing (up to a point). When we got near the ground, I had to level out and the plane started going sideways. When we hit, the left landing gear partially collapsed. We did a pretty hard ground loop.

Afraid of fire, I went out the top hatch and ran up the wing. When I jumped, it must have been 20 feet off the ground. Fortunately, I suffered only a slightly sprained ankle. They pulled the airplane off the runway, and only then did I see the rudder cables cut in half and hanging down. There was a three-foot diameter hole in the side of the plane, and it was a miracle that the waist gunners were not hit.

I reported to the base commander, and he was supposed to radio my base. The message never got there. He reported my name as "Roger Barton," and sent it to the 8th AF Headquarters.

The next day, the base engineering officer said he could fix the landing gear, and Johnny, my copilot, said he could splice the cables together, since he had worked for the telephone company. The base radio people had the know-how to fix the radio equipment. So, we went into Paris.

When we hit downtown, many people recognized our flying clothes and began to cheer us and follow us down the street. They gave us wine to drink while we saw all the sights, and eventually it turned dark. We were walking down the street when suddenly bullets started ricocheting off a building. We holed up in a doorway and found out there were still die-hard German snipers around.

A civilian in the next doorway (probably an American deserter), offered to take us to a place for drinks. All we had was invasion money. It turned out to be a "House of Pleasure" and the madam was an American from New York City. We filled her in on how the war was going, and she supplied drinks, no charge. Later, we went to General Ike's Hotel HQ, and they let us sleep in the lobby and gave us coffee and toast for breakfast.

Back at the airfield two days later, our plane was ready to fly.

I gave the fighter pilots a buzz job and headed for England. I didn't have the "Code of the Day," and English gunners started shooting ahead of us.

When I got over the base and called "Arton Tower," they said that the plane was not listed. Then I identified myself, and when we landed, all the jeeps from Headquarters came out to meet us. We were debriefed and the Engineering Officer told me that a 4" Channel main bulkhead was cut in half, and said if I had put any stress on it, the plane could have broken in half. I didn't tell him about the buzz job when I left France.

When I got to my hut, they had divided up all my clothes and taken my personal possessions to Father Quinlan, who was going to send them to Peggy. They didn't officially notify next-of-kin for about two weeks, so Peggy never knew.

Because of our "ordeal," we were given a week's leave. We went to Edinburgh, Scotland, played golf at some course that was like a cow pasture, and kissed all the Scottish lassies at the USO. It was a tough life!

Prisoner of War: Henry Morris' Last Flight

The following condensed account, written by a friend of Henry Morris over a period of several years, was recently forwarded to us by his son. Sergeant Morris was on his 33rd mission, 12 September 1944, to Misburg. His aircraft "LAMBSY DIVEY" (44-40170) exploded just after bombs away. He was the sole survivor and finished the war as a German POW. This is his story as related by a friend.

"Gaining speed rapidly, the LAMBSY DIVEY rolled down the runway and lifted off, flying low over the end of the runway with a load of incendiary bombs destined for an oil refinery at Misburg, Germany. Gradually gaining speed, Lt. Sparrow banked to the left and headed for forming altitude.

"With a sigh of relief, S/Sgt. Henry Morris, waist gunner, felt the tension ease as he listened to the steady drone of the engines. There was always a tight feeling in his stomach on takeoff.

"At 0700, the 852nd Squadron formed with the other

Squadrons of the 491st Bomb Group and headed east to join the other Groups of the 14th Combat Wing. A bright sun was glinting off the plexiglass nose of LAMBSY DIVEY as they bored through the cold morning air.

"The 491st headed east toward CP-1 on the coast of France where they would pick up their fighter escort. Lt. Sparrow's voice came over the intercom, 'Clear your guns and keep your eyes peeled for enemy fighters.' The 50 caliber machine guns clattered as they were fired to ascertain if they were working properly.

"The fighter escort picked them up just before the formation entered enemy territory. P-51 Mustangs were flying area cover, the heavy bodied Thunderbolts, flying 3,000 feet above, were giving close support to the 491st. They were a welcome sight.

"Puffs of black clouds suddenly erupted up ahead, marking the spot where the German AA batteries were firing. The propellers clawed through the cold air as the bombers went up to 26,000 feet to get away from the flak. It was cold, but Henry could feel the cold sweat run down his back.

"They had been in the air over four hours now, and Henry was tense as he watched the little black clouds of death move up towards them. 'Just like the others,' he thought. This was his thirty-third mission and he had never liked to see those flak bursts reaching for his plane. 'Well, they are putting out the welcome mat again,' said the pilot. Henry thought about an earlier mission he was on with LUCKY BUCK and how they had caught a flak burst in the tail section. So here he was, in another B-24, being bounced around by the concussion of flak bursts.

"As they moved deeper into Germany he searched the sky above, seeking to locate the enemy fighters which he knew were there. Without his Polaroid sunglasses he would never be able to look directly into the sun, but they were up there. He saw the

P-47s drop their auxiliary gas tanks and go looking for the German fighters.

"He saw an ME-109, but the German pilot made no move toward his plane. Suddenly a hole appeared in the wing of LAMBSY DIVEY. A B-24 went out of control and headed earthward spinning. He saw no parachutes.

"This was the hottest reception they had ever received. AA fire seemed to intensify as they made their run over the target. 'Let's get the hell out of here,' said the bombardier. Lt. Sparrow banked right, put the nose down and headed for the rally point. Just off the target, LAMBSY DIVEY took a hit in the #2 engine from a flak burst. The plane began to burn, leaving a trail of black smoke. Flak was tearing holes in the fuselage. Henry had shrapnel wounds in both legs. Then it happened. With a deafening roar, LAMBSY DIVEY exploded.

"When he came to, he was falling through space. His was the only chute in the sky. 'I've had it,' he thought. Then he pulled his ripcord. With a jolt, he found himself drifting slowly toward the ground. As he dropped, he could see an AA battery close to where he was going to land. He could see the men scurrying around with their weapons. He had heard stories of parachutists being machine-gunned as they came down. But, if anyone was shooting at him, they had missed—so far.

"Remembering his air crew training, he hit the ground and rolled. With pain stabbing through his legs, he started to run for cover but he was caught by an angry mob of German civilians. They kicked and beat him to the ground and hit him in the back of the head. When he revived there was a rope around his neck. He was being dragged towards some trees. They were shouting at him, but he did not know what they were saying. He thought of the irony of it all, being shot down and escaping from the burning plane, to end his life at the end of a rope at the hands of a lynch mob.

"At that time a squad of soldiers ran up and rescued him, removing the rope. Cursing both Henry and the soldiers, the civilians followed them until one of the soldiers aimed his rifle at the mob leader.

"The soldiers shoved him into the back of a truck and took him to a bomb-damaged building to be interrogated. Although he could hardly walk, he was interrogated relentlessly. Consistently he gave only his name, rank and serial number; then the two guards would punch, slap and beat him. The interrogators then changed tactics. They offered him better treatment if he would talk. When that failed, the Major jumped up and shouted, 'Dumpkopf, don't you know we will exterminate your Air Force if you continue to bomb us?' The Major nodded to the troops and said, 'Take him away.'

"They half dragged, half carried him to the truck outside. In a few minutes the truck stopped in front of a barbed-wire enclosed stockade. He was put into a half-lighted room where he could see the forms of men sprawled against the walls. The men were also survivors of the air battles of that day.

"Henry didn't sleep much that night. Hunger pains reminded him that he had not eaten for hours, and his wounded legs throbbed painfully.

"In the early morning they were separated into two groups. Men not wounded were marched away. The wounded men were taken to a bomb-scarred building for medical treatment. Some of the German medical personnel evidently disliked the idea of giving medical treatment to enemy airmen. One, who could speak English, told Henry he thought it was a waste of medicine to give it to them when so many civilians were dying as a result of their bombing. They were given food and loaded into trucks, taken to a railroad station and put into a boxcar. After many hours of traveling they came to a stop.

"The sight that met their eyes was none too inviting. The unpainted buildings of the POW compound stood out starkly against the bare earth. This was to be Henry's home from September 1944 until March 1945.

"They had roll call every morning and every night. They didn't stay outside long, as dogs patrolled the compound until morning. They slept on the floor, huddled together to keep warm all through the cold winter. They were guarded by German soldiers, SS troops, and Hitler's Youth Organizations. The Hitler Youth were detested by the prisoners, mostly because of their habit of jabbing the prisoner with bayonets as they guarded them.

"Food was rationed and there was no medical attention. They all suffered from malnutrition with barely enough food to sustain life.

"Early one morning the men were ordered out of their camp and forced to march westward. Rumors were that the Russian armies were near. On the third day they were the target of strafing planes and Russian artillery. A little later they were attacked by Russian tanks. As the guards fell under the Russian fire, the prisoners grabbed their guns and joined the battle to take their revenge on the German guards.

"Now the former prisoners were faced with another problem. They didn't know what the Russians would do with them, so they formed their own unit, equipped with weapons taken from the Germans. They demanded to fight their way to meet up with the American forces advancing in Germany. This was a new way of life as Henry fought along with the ground forces. They learned how to live off the land as the Russians did.

"After the battle of Berlin, Henry made contact with the soldiers of the 101st Airborne Division. After delousing and a bath, Henry was given some clean clothes.

"Once again Henry was on his way, but this time it was en route to home in the USA. Henry was the only member of LAMBSY DIVEY to survive the war."

Regensburg

Sammy Schneider, 485th BG

This Mission Write-Up Is from the Publication "Bomber Legends"
After the raid on Regensburg, February 16, 1945, another drama
took place through the Brenner Pass. The following is an account as
told to Jo Haden Galbraith, daughter of Lt. Robert (Bob) O. Haden,
Navigator from the 831st squadron who passed away in 1995. He was
on Glenn Hess's crew and they were on the raid to Regensburg. The
target was the Obertraubling Messerschmitt assembly plant. It was
the largest plant of its kind in Europe and turned out 200-300 ME-1
09 fighter aircraft each month.

The crew was on a mission to bomb the Messerschmitt Plant
at Regensburg, Germany. As they began the bomb run through
heavy flak the number one engine took a direct hit, blowing the
prop into the sky and causing the plane to buck like a wild bronco.
It was immediately thrown into a severe left bank as the pilot,
Lt. Hess, struggled to regain control. Unnerved, and now flying
with only three engines, they courageously pressed on toward the
target. The bomb bay doors were opened, and within seconds the
number two engine was hit, blowing off the turbo charger. Fortunately, it did not explode, but the impact caused the plane to bank
hard to the right out of control. To make matters worse, it threw

them into the prop-wash of another bomber, causing the plane to flip upside down. The order was given to bail out, but the centrifugal force caused by the fierce spinning kept the men pinned to the airplane floor and walls frantically trying to pull themselves out of the hatches and waist windows. Caught in a death trap and unable to budge, the crew began their final prayers when the plane (aided no doubt by a little Divine intervention) miraculously righted itself in enabling the pilot to pull out of the spin and regain control. Now at 10,000 feet and with a limited amount of fuel the crew was forced to make some quick decisions. They had two choices: fly to Switzerland, which was doable, or take their chances and try to make it to the allied border in northern Italy. If they landed in Switzerland, a neutral country, they knew they would be interned there for the rest of the war. This did not sit well with the men, as there was no telling how long that might be, possibly years. They were also concerned that they might be classified as M.I.A. (missing in action), causing undue stress on their families. Unable to maintain an altitude higher than 10,000 feet with only two engines, the navigator, Lt. Haden, searched for a route to Italy that would cut through the 15,000 ft. Alpine mountains. He found it in Brenner Pass, a valley which connects Innsbruck, Austria with Bolzano, Italy.

Brenner Pass is technically at the border between Italy and Austria. The crews always considered it to include the entire valley that snakes through the Alps Mountains with Verona at the South end and Innsbruck at the North end. In places the valley is just wide enough for a river, a road and a railroad. It was a main connection between the Axis. The valley is well over 100 miles long and every foot was heavily defended by 558 large antiaircraft gun installations. Under the best conditions in peacetime a journey through the Alps at that altitude would be considered treacherous. For a crippled bomber low on fuel and being shot at from all sides, it was darn near suicide. To further complicate matters much of northern Italy was still occupied by the Germans. Which meant even if they made it through the Alpine pass in one piece, they would still have a considerable flight over enemy territory.

Fuel was a major concern. Before takeoff the tanks were topped off at 2750 gallons and the planes were loaded to the hilt with bombs. On the way to the target, the group tried to gain as much altitude as possible, consequently burning about 3/4 of the fuel by the time they reached their mark. This meant there might be as little as 600 gallons of fuel left after the run. However, if they made it over the Alps it would be downhill the rest of the way.

Haden calculated that if the Gods were with them (and if they didn't hit a mountain or get blown out of the sky) they would have just enough fuel to eke across the Allied border into Rimini, a coastal town on the Adriatic with an army base and runway. With no time to ponder the idea a vote was taken, and trusting their navigator, the captain and crew opted to take their chances and go for it.

Needless to say it was a harrowing flight through the snow-covered Alps, (pilot Glenn Hess likened it to guiding an elephant through the eye of the needle under fire). But somehow, against all odds, their badly crippled plane managed to make it through the Pass, cross the allied border on fumes, and hobble to a stop at the tail end of the Rimini runway. Hess checked the fuel gauge—it was empty.

Stunned and badly shaken by their ordeal, the men crawled out to inspect the plane. Hess recalled: "The plane was so badly shot-up that you couldn't lay your hand anywhere on it without touching a flak hole. We hadn't been out of the plane more than two minutes when this General came flying down the runway raising all kinds of Hell about us landing on his airstrip. It was a fighter strip and the General was screaming at me to get my f—— plane off his runway! I stood there and took his insults for a while until finally exasperated I stopped him by saying 'Sir, would you like to inspect my plane?' We looked at each other for a moment and then I just walked away. Once he got a good look at it we heard him yell, 'Hell this thing ain't worth movin'!' He then ordered a bulldozer to shove it over the nearest embankment, and that's where it stayed."

"I Remember Billy"

Jack McKenzie

My name is Jack McKenzie and I was a First Pilot in the 735th Squadron of the 453rd Bomb Group. I flew eleven missions from February 25, 1945 to April 10, 1945. I am a ham radio operator, NSMFG, Extra Class, and have a more-than-passing interest in Morse Code. The attached is about my boyhood friend, Morse Code and the fact that it resulted in his death over Japan—the day after the war was over!

His name was Billy Smith and we grew up in the little sleepy town of Mesquite, Texas.

After high school, we both went to Texas A&M. This was during World War II and we both hitchhiked to Dallas and volunteered for Aviation Cadet training in the Army Air Forces. We entered service the same day at Shepherd Field, Texas, where we were assigned to different barracks according to our last names. When we left basic training, Billy went to Aviation Cadet Pre Flight at San Antonio, Texas, whereas I was sent to Maxwell Field, Alabama. In preflight we both had to learn to copy five words per minute Morse Code.

I did... he didn't.

After preflight, I went to Primary Flight School, followed by

Basic Flight School and Advanced Flight School where I received my commission and pilot wings. I then went to the Four Engine School back at Maxwell Field, where I learned to fly B-24 bombers. This was followed by crew training and eventually to the 735th Squadron of the 453rd Bomb Group (Heavy) of the 8th Air Force in England from where I flew missions over Germany.

In the meantime, Billy repeated another two months of pre-flight whereby this time he had learned to copy Morse code at twenty words per minute or so. And then, for reasons that would only be understood by someone who has served in the military, he did not ship out again and was held back for another onerous two months of preflight! By this time the need for pilots had declined, and as soon as he got to Primary Flight School he washed out. He was sent, where else, to Radio School.

Radio School took a long time and then he was assigned to a B-29 crew. Crew training took a long time, to the end that his crew did not make it to the Pacific Theater of Operations until the war was nearly over.

On V-J Day all combat crews were stood down and further missions were flown by crews like Billy's who had not been in combat. His crew was assigned to a low level mission to drop food parcels to American prisoner-of-war camps in Japan, a mission for which they were not trained. They flew into a mountain, and Billy was killed along with his entire crew.

Thus Billy died the day after the war was over, and all because of Morse Code.

Life sometimes doesn't seem fair.

Our Unforgettable Mission 23 Was Worth Every "Penny" Of It

Lt. Col. James R. Maris, 392nd, with Vickie J. Maris

After assembly, we headed our B-24s to the coastal departure point, making scheduled turns where other squadrons joined the long line of departing bombers. The B-24s tracked out over the North Sea passing Heligoland. Near Kiel we turned to the southeast assuming a heading toward Berlin. This turn was to throw the fighters off course and make them think the target for the day was Berlin. As we were making this turn, the wings changed the formation and split into squadrons in trail—sixteen B-24s per squadron. Soon after this maneuver, we made a turn to the northwest that put our airplanes on course to bomb the oil refineries at Hamburg.

The antiaircraft guns at Hamburg were not firing at individual aircraft, but instead were set up to fire in predetermined grid blocks over the target we were to bomb. They would wait until a complete squadron was overhead and fire into their assigned grid. This type of firing made a large block of smoke and fire over the target. For a moment, an entire squadron would vanish in the thick, black blanket of smoke.

But the moment didn't last long. Planes would disrupt the layer of smoke as they spun out of formation or blew up before us. With each squadron, we anxiously counted the B-24s that would fly free of the smoke on the other side of the target. Ten, eleven, maybe twelve planes from each squadron survived the flak barrage. The sky was filled with parachutes descending airmen into uncertainty. As many as 40 to 60 men per squadron made the jump.

We now approached with a vivid picture of our near-certain destiny. I was so overcome by this skyline display of death and destruction that I vomited into my oxygen mask in the cockpit. My copilot had to take over for a few moments as I cleaned up the mess, repositioned my mask and steadied my nerves for the task ahead.

We entered the flak storm over our target and were immediately tossed by the severe turbulence created by the exploding 88mm flak. The "Bad Penny" was bathed in brilliant flashes of light and peppered with exploding shells. She rocked and shuttered with the jarring impact of every burst.

The biggest jolt came when the number one engine was blown off. We rolled hard to the right and it was all that my copilot and I could do to right our B-24. Not long after, a second blast stripped the cowling and supercharger off engine number three on our right wing. An engine oil fire created an expanding plume of white smoke that trailed our aircraft.

But even at half-mast, our "Bad Penny" was determined to get us home. As the airmen had been dislodging the bomb and closing our bomb bay doors, Herbie and I had been carefully watching our descent. We had dropped from 22,000 feet to 18,000 in our recovery process. After calculating our ground speed and rate of sink, we estimated that we would probably cross the English coast at about 1,900 feet. This would allow us to go the remaining distance inland to RAF Station Wendling—home.

There were a lot of "ifs" involved, though. Because of this, we decided to lighten the load and improve our chances. Anything loose was thrown out of the aircraft. Flak vests. Flak helmets. Machine guns. Ammunition. Cameras. Aircraft manuals. The bombardier had a few choice words to say about his binoculars going overboard.

The "Bad Penny" strained to hold altitude while her engines—the two that had survived the attack—were running extremely hot. I continued to be amazed that our number three was hanging in there. She was running, but without cowling and supercharger. Then, out of the blue, she kicked in with enough additional power for us to cross the English coast at 1,400 feet. I had never dreamed of flying a B-24 on two-and-a-half engines and with a full crew across the North Sea.

When we identified our landfall, Herbie gave us a heading for Wendling. We broke out the red flares and were standing by to shoot them off as we neared the base.

Our problems were not over yet, though. Our electrical system and hydraulics were inoperative. This meant we had to manually lower the landing gear. If we lowered it too early, the gear would create too much drag and cause us to fall short of the landing field. So we worked out the timing as best we could and started to crank when the base came into view. Herbie and our bombardier unlatched the nose gear and with the help of Fitz, pushed the nose gear out. It fell in the locked position.

In the bomb bay, the flight engineer organized the gunners into a team to crank down the mains (landing gear). I put the gear handle in the down position and gunners took turns on the crank. Since the bomb bay doors weren't fully closed, they again used the parachute harness lifeline when lowering an airman into the bomb bay to turn the crank. When an airman would slip or be thrown off balance by the force of the wind blowing in through the doors, the others would pull him to safety with the makeshift line. After many more turns than the 71 defined in the manual, the gear locked into place. We were at 500 feet on the downwind side of the runway. The airmen fired our red flares to announce our arrival.

Just when we thought we were home free, Mother Nature dished up one more challenge. Since the "Bad Penny" had been at high altitude for hours, her surfaces were extremely cold. This caused our forward glass on the nose and windshield to ice over during our descent through the moist air near the ground. I had to peer out the open side windows to judge height and direction. With some divine assistance, I was able to hold our aircraft steady as she settled onto the runway. With no hydraulics and consequently, no brakes, we rolled the entire length of the runway before the "Bad Penny" came to a stop.

I had ordered the crew into crash positions before landing. Everyone was somewhat dazed with the realization that we were safely on the ground. I had to shout to them to get them to quickly exit the aircraft and run to a safe distance. The "Bad Penny" was primed to blow at any minute. According to procedure and to prevent imminent fire, the copilot and I shut down the cockpit and then scrambled down, through the front of the bomb bay and out onto the open tarmac under the right wing. There we found our entire crew, ignoring instructions to flee, waiting for us to make sure we could get out. Once again, I had to motivate them to hurry away from the aircraft!

They were off like a shot. The copilot and I were close behind. At a safe distance, we turned and looked at our "Bad Penny." Her tires were flat. Gasoline was dripping from her battered fuselage and wings. Her pain fell to the tarmac with each drop of ice melting from her aluminum skin. Tubes, pipes, broken metal fairings hung down in tangled disarray. Her once overheated engines now crackled and popped as parts began to cool and shrink. This valiant bomber safely brought us home. But she would fly no more.

My crew was checked over at the infirmary and all were unharmed. I, on the other hand, had been wondering what I would find under my flight vest. I had tried to ignore the pain that was wildly spreading across my side during our return trip, but suddenly it seemed to grow more quickly now that we were on the ground.

After removing my flight suit and flight jacket, we found a piece of flak embedded in a steel plate in my flak jacket. It had bent the plate and severely bruised my side, but beyond that, I was uninjured. Today, touching that steel plate with its embedded flak is an instant reminder of all the events that attempted to end Mission 23 that day in August.

The following day, we returned to the "Bad Penny" to tell her goodbye. We counted 85 holes in her fuselage from nose to tail. Her number one engine was somewhere in Germany along with pieces of the number three. The hole in her left wing was large enough to lower a man through.

My crew and I always felt that the "Bad Penny" shed her own blood to save ours. We are certain that she was running with a power far greater than the lift in her wings to carry us safely home.

Let's Not Forget What Happened to Lt. Edwin M. Helton's Crew

Walter J. Mundy, 467th

As Group Vice President of the 467th BG, I was asked by the Roll of Honor review committee to verify that a short list of 467th combat crew members were Killed in Action or Killed in the Line of Duty. The names on the list were those crew members who were not verified as deceased in either classification and official verification is necessary to have them named on the Roll of Honor at the Second Air Division Memorial Library.

Through correspondence with the Army Total Personnel Command, I was able to verify that S/Sgt. Rufus C. Davis on Lt. Charles D. Harrison's crew was Killed in Action on May 8, 1944. I have requested verification of eight other 467th crew members and of this date have received verification of one other that I want to pass on to the Roll of Honor committee and to the members of the 467th and the Second Air Division Association.

The story that follows is one that will stir many emotions of those of us who flew in combat and those Americans and English people who will never forget the sacrifices of the men of the Second Air Division. This is a story of a crew that should be here alive with us but instead must remain always in spirit in our hearts.

This story not only answers the requirements of verifying that Lt. Helton and his crew were Killed in Action, it also provides the vital information concerning the mission, the aircraft, the crew, and the history for inclusion in the electronic database of the 467th BG.

These brave men are no longer Missing in Action. They will always be on the Roll of Honor.

THE DATE: 21 June 1944

THE TARGET: Genshagen Industrial Works near Berlin (Mission #60)

THE AIRCRAFT: B-24H # 4252497

THE CREW MEMBERS:

1st Lt. Edwin Helton, pilot, 0687592; 2nd Lt. Maurice R. Nelson, copilot, 0699712; 2nd Lt. Richard J. Ludka, bombardier, 0694919; T/Sgt. Warren G. Rankin, engineer, 35575827; T/Sgt. Frank Borchick, radio operator, 13171042; S/Sgt. Thomas A. Gensert, ball turret gunner, 35766187; S/Sgt. Charles L. Knowles, Jr., gunner, 18189980; S/Sgt. Carmine Margiosso, gunner, 12037871; S/Sgt. Stanley Brzezowski, tail gunner, 32862091.

THE DOCUMENT:

Lt. Helton's B-24 was damaged by flak over the target and was last seen going down under control with one engine on fire and one engine's prop feathered. Reports indicate that the aircraft crashed on the west bank of the Muritz near the village of Klink, Germany. All nine members of the crew were rescued and captured. Seven crew members, except Lt. Helton and Lt. Hudka, were taken into the town of Waren where they were turned over to the Security Police, who executed (MURDERED) them and had them buried in a common grave in Poppentin, Germany. The remains of these seven were subsequently disinterred and sent to the U.S. Cemetery at Saint-Avold, France where they were identified. German reports indicate that all seven had been shot in the head.

Lt. Helton and Lt. Ludka were turned over to SS Police Commissioner Stempel in Fürstenberg-Mecklenburg where they were similarly executed (MURDERED) and allegedly buried in Drogen/Stargard. The remains of Lts. Helton and Ludka have been determined to be unrecoverable.

This wartime atrocity was investigated and The Gauleiter of Mecklenburg, one Friedrich Hildebrandt, the Nazi criminal who ordered the murders of these airmen, was tried as a war criminal and hanged. Other German SS police and officials who participated in the atrocity are dead by suicide or were detained by the German police and prosecuted as war criminals.

YES, THIS IS A STORY THAT HAD TO BE TOLD!

A Viking in the 8th Air Force

Major Kenneth L. Driscoll, 801st "Carpetbaggers"

He was a Norwegian national hero, but most Americans, including Army Air Force veterans, do not even recognize his name. Yet he was both an American and an 8th Air Force B-24 pilot!

Yes, Col. Bernt Balchen was one of the most talented and knowledgeable aviators of the 20th century. He was a superb aircraft mechanic, a precise navigator, and probably the most talented Arctic pilot of his time – and it is time you know the "whole" story!

He was born in 1900 in a small southern Norwegian town named Kristiansand. When he was about 21 years old, he got his wings in the Royal Norwegian Air Force. He spent several years gaining a vast amount of Arctic type flying throughout snowy, rugged, mountainous Norway.

In 1926 he was at Spitzbergen, an island about 500 miles north of the tip of northern Norway. He was there as a member of the expedition of the famous Norwegian polar explorer Capt. Roald Amundsen. They were preparing to be the first to fly across the North Pole (by dirigible, not aircraft).

While they were at Spitzbergen, U.S. Navy Commander Richard Byrd's ship arrived carrying a trimotor aircraft which was to be used by Byrd's expedition to fly across the North Pole. Byrd's pilot was Floyd Bennet.

Members of both expeditions, although rivals, became friendly. Bernt Balchen, since he was an expert in snowy, cold weather flying conditions, improvised and modified the skis on Byrd's aircraft so that it could safely take off under overloaded conditions.

Byrd's aircraft got to the North Pole first and then returned to Spitzbergen. When he returned to the United States by ship, he took Bernt Balchen with him. Balchen then became Byrd's pilot.

In the spring of 1927 there was a race on to see who would be the first to fly across the Atlantic Ocean. While Lindbergh was planning his flight from Roosevelt Field, Byrd was also planning his at the same time from the same airfield. Balchen was one of the two pilots of Byrd's aircraft. Lindbergh made the first successful Atlantic crossing. Byrd's aircraft flew across a month later. Balchen's extensive experience in instrument flying made it possible to safely cross the ocean under very adverse weather conditions.

Although he still loved his native Norway, he took out his first papers to become a citizen of the United States after he returned from France.

From 1920-30 he spent much of his time with Commander Byrd preparing for and successfully completing the first flight of an aircraft across the South Pole.

The crew of the expedition had a tremendous welcome when they returned to New York City in June, 1931. They then went to Washington D.C. where they were honored by President Hoover at a reception at the White House.

Soon thereafter, Balchen was served a subpoena by the U.S.

immigration authorities. He had broken his residence requirements, after getting his first papers, by being with the Byrd expedition for two years outside of the United States, and was to be
deported!

The story made the headlines that evening in all of the Washington D.C. newspapers. New York State Representative to Congress, Fiorello LaGuardia (later to become mayor of New York
City), after discussing the matter with President Hoover, introduced a special bill to Congress the following day to grant Bernt
Balchen full citizenship. That bill was passed and signed by President Hoover.

Balchen stayed very active in aviation activities during the
rest of the 1930s. Some of his close friends and associates during
that time were Charles Lindbergh, Amelia Earhart, Wiley Post,
Floyd Bennet, Hap Arnold, Tooey Spaatz, Ira Eaker and Eddie
Rickenbacker.

On June 30, 1941, six months before the U.S. entered into
World War II, Balchen was in the Philippines delivering a PBY to
the RAF when an urgent telegram came from General Hap Arnold,
Commanding General of the U.S. Army Air Forces, requesting his
immediate return to Washington.

On July 3, 1941, in a meeting with General Arnold, he was
asked to join the Army Air Forces for a very special assignment.
Balchen agreed, and was granted the rank of Captain.

His first assignment was to plan and supervise the construc-
tion of an airfield in southwestern Greenland. This airfield was
named Bluie West Eight. It was later used by hundreds of aircraft
going to and returning from Europe during WWII.

While there, he led rescue missions to save the crews of two
B-17 type aircraft that had crashed hundreds of miles away on the
icecap of Greenland after becoming lost.

He was directed by a top secret message from General Marshall, Washington D.C., to seek out and destroy a German weather station that had been secretly set up on the barren northeast coast of Greenland. He successfully accomplished that mission by using four bombers flying from Iceland.

In September 1943, Balchen was still in Iceland when General Arnold stopped over. Arnold asked what type of assignment he would like next. Balchen told him that he would like to assist the Norwegian resistance movement against the Germans occupying Norway.

Back in Washington, he had a meeting with General William (Wild Bill) Donovan, the head of the O.S.S. One of the missions of the O.S.S. in Europe was to train spies, saboteurs and organize resistance forces in German occupied countries. Balchen was briefed by O.S.S. in Europe personnel on some projects and sent to England.

With the backing of Generals Tooey Spaatz and Jimmy Doolittle of the 8th Air Force, and the O.S.S., Balchen was given the top secret project to organize and implement an airlift between Stockholm, Sweden and Scotland using modified, stripped-down B-24s.

There were thousands of military-aged men, Norwegian and others, stranded in Sweden, who could be used in the Allied war effort.

Armament was removed, and the B-24s had seats installed also. The exterior was painted dark green, without any identification. Crews in civilian clothing were issued passports and visas to enter Sweden, Finland and Russia.

The 801st Prov. Bomb Group (code name Carpetbaggers) supplied the B-24s, crews, and support to complete his missions. This group had been flying top secret night missions working with the O.S.S. dropping agents and supplies to resistance groups in German occupied countries, mostly France, at that time.

(Note: Just by chance, I was a pilot in the 801st BG (Carpet-baggers) from May 25, 1944 to August 27, 1944. I had 30 night missions during that three-month period flying from Harrington Air Base.)

Five modified B-24s were prepared at Bovingdon Air Base, north of London.

Due to its unique nature, this unit was assigned to headquarters, European Air Transport Command.

Although his mission was approved in late January, 1944, Balchen ran into much red tape (primarily from the English) in getting a suitable airfield to set up his operations. Finally, about the end of March, 1944, the King of Norway asked Winston Churchill to intervene, cut the red tape, and provide Balchen with facilities at a Royal Air Force Base for his operations. Within two days, Balchen got permission to operate out of Leuchars RAF base on the east coast of Scotland, north of Edinburgh. The code name for his project was "Sonnie."

About 5,000 people were evacuated from Sweden to Scotland. Balchen's aircraft also flew hundreds of people and many tons of war material into Sweden, finding its way across the border to be used by the Norwegians resistance forces.

When the war started in Europe, Sweden stayed neutral. It had close ties with Germany and with its neighbor, Norway. But by early 1944, the Swedish people, and government, became pro-Allies and anti-Nazi.

Early in the summer of 1944, while Col. Balchen was in Stockholm on one of his many flights, he was contacted by an old friend who was pro-Norwegian and held a position very high up in the Swedish government. The Swedes had recovered, almost intact, a top secret experimental German V-2 rocket. Two were launched from the German coast into Sweden. Rather than make a diplomatic protest to the German government and let the Germans know where they landed, the Swedish government decided to turn one of the rockets over to the Allies. Balchen borrowed a C-47 cargo aircraft from his headquarters and his executive officer Lt. Col. Keith Allen picked up the three-piece V-2 rocket in Sweden and flew it back to Leuchars. It was then delivered to the English government at Farnsborough Air base near London.

This same Col. Allen was shot down and killed while on a secret mission (code name "Project Ball") to northern Norway a short while later. His mission was to drop an agent near the great German battleship Tirpitz, which was hiding in a deep narrow fjord. The agent was to spy on the Tirpitz and report back to England via radio any movement of the battleship.

After the agent was dropped, the aircraft developed engine problems over northern Norway. Rather than flying the long overwater flight back to Scotland, he elected to fly on to Murmansk, Russia for an emergency landing. As his aircraft was flying over the heavily defended seaport of Murmansk, it was shot down by Russian naval ships. Ten of the crew bailed out and were returned to Scotland by the British battleship HMS Rodney, which was at Murmansk. Col. Allen went down with the aircraft.

Around May, 1944, it was brought to Col. Balchen's attention that additional war supplies were urgently needed by the resistance forces in Norway. He got direct approval from HQ 8th Air Force to set up a miniature "Carpetbagger" operation to drop military supplies and agents into Norway. The code name for this secret operation was "Project Ball." It was also directly supported by the 801st B.G. (Carpetbaggers) from its base at Harrington, England. Around August 13, 1944 this group became the 492nd B.G. (Carpetbaggers).

Because of its very secret and sensitive nature, little has been published about Project "Where and When." This operation took place in Sweden in early 1945. Its mission was to transport over

1400 Norwegian police troops (trained in Sweden), a field hospital, and supplies from Kallax, Sweden to Kirkenes, Norway and other Norwegian towns when the Germans withdrew from northern Norway. Col. Balchen had ten C-47 cargo planes operating in Sweden before the end of the war in Europe. Prior to the day that the war ended there, he was in the Norwegian town of Kirkenes, which at the time was occupied by the Russians.

After World War II ended, Balchen returned to Norway and was president of Norwegian Airlines (DNL). He was also one of the original directors of Scandinavian Airline System (SAS).

In 1947 I met Col. Balchen a number of times; in fact, he was a guest at my wedding in Oslo, April 21, 1948. Here is the background:

In February 1948 I was a captain, USAF, stationed at a training unit at Westover AFB, Massachusetts. I was then assigned to the U.S. Air Attaché Office, American Embassy, Oslo, Norway as Assistant Air Attaché.

About a week after I got to Oslo, about the end of February, on a Saturday morning as I was walking into the embassy office building in downtown Oslo, I met the U.S. Ambassador to Norway, Charles Ulrick Bay, who was also entering the building at the same time. I recognized him, and since I was in uniform, he recognized me as the new Air Force captain assigned to the embassy. He asked me if I had my family with me, and I told him that I was single but was thinking about getting married to my girlfriend who was back in the States. He said, "If you bring her over, I will give you a wedding." I decided to take him up on his offer. Since I was newly assigned to the embassy, I knew very few people in Oslo. The ambassador and my boss, the Air Attaché, Major Dale Jensen, decided who should be invited to my wedding at the ambassador's residence at Five (5) Nobles gate, Oslo (this was a mansion given to the U.S. government by the famed Nobel family). The guests they invited were VIP from the Norwegian Air Force, U.S. Embassy, prominent Norwegians and Col. and Mrs. Balchen. We had a captive audience. I do not know of anybody in Oslo at the time who would not have accepted an invitation from the U.S. Ambassador to attend a function at the ambassador's residence.

Over an eight-month period in 1948, I met Col. Balchen at numerous social events. I really did not get to know him well, however. Our paths never crossed other than at social events. He was about 21 years older than I. He was a bird (full) colonel and I was a captain. He was deeply involved in rebuilding the Norwegian Airline (DNL), and being a director in starting a new international airline, Scandinavian Airline System (SAS). I remember him as being quite stout and speaking with a very distinct Norwegian accent.

Around November 1948, he was recalled by the U.S. Air Force and was assigned as commanding officer of the Tenth Rescue Squadron, Fairbanks, Alaska. He had been recommended to the Army Air Forces many years earlier, and was instrumental in establishing a base at Thule, Greenland. This did become a reality, and that base is part of the DEW LINE now protecting the northern approaches to the United States.

He was an advisor to King Haakon of Norway on aviation matters prior to, during, and after World War II.

He was honored for various achievements by Presidents Coolidge, Hoover, Roosevelt and Eisenhower.

He was the American Viking!

Hap Arnold: America's First Airman! Army Air Force, WWII

Jack Stankrauff, Historian of the Yankee Air Force

Reprinted with Permission from Yankee Wings, July-September 1995

On June 20, 1941, the U.S. Army Air Forces officially came into being, replacing the Army Air Corps. Hap Arnold began organizing and staffing an organization which now was much closer to his vision and to those of air power advocates. Arnold's title was changed to Commanding General six months later, with an added star.

DECEMBER 7, 1941—WAR!

Arnold inspected two B-17 squadrons at Hamilton Field, California prior to their departure for the Philippines on Saturday, December 6, 1941. These same aircraft arrived over Pearl Harbor in the midst of the Japanese Navy's surprise attack. When Arnold

Hap Arnold

learned of the attack, he exclaimed, "How could the Japs be so stupid?"

As America entered the war, one of Arnold's first major objectives was to bring the AAF up to strength in aircraft, facilities, and doctrine. This job was made easier by the reorganization of the War Department, which he and Spaatz had proposed long ago. Pearl Harbor was the catalyst for this reform. Under the reform completed in March of 1942, the War Department was split into the air forces, ground forces, and supply. Now the AAF was not only equal with the Army ground forces, but was also one step closer to independence.

In the days following Pearl Harbor, Arnold spent many hours poring over maps. He painstakingly noted small details of islands, mountains and peninsulas which would be vital and strategic in the coming war years.

Arnold tried to follow an established office routine during the war. A typical Arnold duty day was described by Geoffrey Perret: "He would arrive for work around 7:30 each morning and tackle the stack of cables that had come in overnight. There would be as many as 1,000 messages from around the world. All would have been reviewed; the most important 40 or 50 were on his deck. There would be a pile of plans, studies, and reports to read, but Arnold insisted that the contents of each be reduced to a half-page summary. He'd read the summary. Occasionally, he'd ask for the original document. The hundreds of letters that arrived each day were reduced to a list of one-sentence summaries. He'd scan the list and decide which letters he wanted to read in full. Reading alone would keep Arnold occupied for much of the day. When he had finished with the cables and correspondence, the briefers would come in and offer a 30 to 45-minute rundown on operations in theaters of war throughout the world during the past 24 hours. They'd offer a statistical breakdown on what the AAF had done and its state of readiness. They'd also provide him with the latest top-secret information from spies or code-breaking that affected the air war. The rest of the day was spent mainly talking to people, in person or on the phone. Arnold was blessed, moreover, with an ability to read an official document while holding a conversation. That enabled him to continue reading as documents flowed non-stop across his desk."

Arnold hated staff meetings, committees, and other military routine. He issued informal directives—typically a quick note scrawled on a single sheet of paper and passed to an officer with orders to expedite it. He possessed a brilliant mind, which enabled him to go straight to the heart of a complex matter. He abhorred the red tape of military bureaucracy, with its myriad of time-consuming paperwork. "Hitler won't wait that long," he said, "and neither will I!"

Arnold impulsively drove himself, and as a result, suffered five heart attacks during the war. One historian wrote, "To many, at the time and later, Arnold *was* the Army Air Force. He threw himself into his work in a way that was both impressive and deplorable. He didn't delegate anything, unlike Marshall, who had freely delegated to mere majors and lieutenant colonels powers that few generals would ever possess. Every day Arnold got involved in decisions large and small, like a man suffering from deprivation. Instead of having deputies with real authority, he had five aides with fancy titles, but they were little more than messenger boys. Marshall, by way of contrast, chose strong, able and decisive staff officers, such as General Joseph McNarney, whom he made deputy chief of staff. Like Marshall, they believed in the power of well-run organizations to get results and he trusted them to make decisions in his name, often without telling him what they'd done. Arnold couldn't bring himself to do that. The pivot of Arnold's management style was his legendary impulsiveness. He would stop people walking past his door and tell them to drop everything they were doing and go across the country or overseas, and tackle some problem that had just landed on his desk. On one famous occasion he ordered the chief air surgeon to head for Wright Field and work the bugs out of a troublesome engine. He'd noticed the brigadier general's stars, but not the medical Corps insignia. The impulsiveness was a form of stress management. A problem was stress, and by dumping it into someone's lap he'd gotten rid of it for now."

THE "CHART TRICK"

As the war went into 1942, the AAF was threatened by superior fighters—the Zero (code-named *Hap* early in the war until Arnold ordered it changed to *Hamp*) and the Messerschmitt

ME 109. The press picked up on this, belittling our airplanes as inferior and causing the deaths of young, brave American pilots.

Determined to set the record straight, Arnold had a chart posted in his office showing the performance of the world's fighter planes, although the planes were not identified. "Then he asked one of the country's most outspoken aviation writers to examine the chart and tell him which aircraft the AAF ought to buy. The writer's first choice turned out to be the P-47; second was the P-38; third was the P-51. His newspaper, *The New York Herald-Tribune*, went overnight from being one of the AAF's fiercest critics to being one of its most reliable friends. When Arnold pulled the chart trick on another hostile aviation writer, the man was so thoroughly converted that he gave up his job and joined the AAF."

"SPECIAL AVIATION PROJECT"

In the first six months after Pearl Harbor the Allies sustained a string of defeats which had a significant adverse effect upon the public's will to win. A bold stroke was needed to jolt public opinion and that stroke began as the "Special Aviation Project." Navy Captain Francis Low conceived a plan to attack the Japanese capital with twin-engined bombers launched from an aircraft carrier. Arnold assigned to the project one of his most experienced and innovative staff officers, Lt. Col. Jimmy Doolittle. Although Arnold did not want him to lead the mission, Doolittle took charge of all USAAF support, from the selection of the North American B-25 as the bomber, to the recruiting and training of the crews.

Upon giving the Chief a progress report, Doolittle asked to lead the mission himself. Arnold told him to check with his Chief of Staff, General Millard Harmon. "I smelled a rat," Doolittle recalled later. Expecting that Arnold would phone Harmon and forbid him to lead the mission, Doolittle hurried to the Chief of Staff's office before the call was made. Using all of his persuasive abilities, Doolittle told Harmon that he wanted to lead the Tokyo mission, implying that if it was all right with him, it was all right with Arnold. "Sure, Jimmy, it's all yours," Harmon replied.

While not a great success in terms of a blow to the enemy's war-making potential, the Doolittle Raid was a tremendous boost for Allied morale, as well as exposing the vulnerability of the Japanese homeland to aerial attack. It also forced Japanese Admiral Isoroku Yamamoto to develop a plane to draw out and destroy the American carriers missed by the Pearl Harbor attack. The resulting Battle of Midway in June 1942 severely crippled the Japanese carrier forces, which led in turn to a shift in the balance of power in the Pacific Area. After the raid Doolittle was promoted to brigadier general and awarded the Medal of Honor.

ARNOLD AND "THE MURDERER"

Arnold used Doolittle's piloting skills for another task, too. The Martin B-26 Marauder (variously nicknamed "The Murderer" and "Widow Maker") was causing the AAF problems. Propellers over speeded on takeoff, causing spins into the ground. "One a Day in Tampa Bay" became the ominous slogan at a Marauder training field in Florida. Arnold sent Doolittle to demonstrate the Marauder to trainee pilots, as well as the famous aviatrix, Jacqueline Cochran. After finishing a flight, she said anyone afraid to fly one was a "sissy." (Arnold and Doolittle ensured Marauder crew safety by getting the Martin Company to make wing and engine changes. As a result of these changes, the Marauder became one of the finest aerial weapons of the war.)

MacARTHUR AGAIN

If Arnold thought that after the Mitchell court martial and the Alaskan flight he could avoid further encounters with Douglas MacArthur, he was mistaken. ISAAF General Harold George, who headed air operations in the Southwest pacific, continually fought with MacArthur over tactics, supplies, and practically everything else. The air war suffered because of their bickering, so Arnold proposed that General Frank Andrews replace George. MacArthur wouldn't hear of it—he had given Andrews a written reprimand in 1935 for extolling the B-17. Arnold then nominated Doolittle, which also angered MacArthur because the Navy used an entire carrier task force to position Doolittle's bombers to raid Tokyo, yet couldn't send reinforcements to his beleaguered forces in the Philippines. Arnold then sent General George Kenney, who the imperious MacArthur finally accepted.

"ARNOLD LINE"

Arnold was a genius with logistics. With AAF bases scattered over the world needing supplies, he initiated the Air Transport Command to not only carry vital material, but also to ferry planes. (Today's Air Force reflects Arnold's concept of a worldwide logistics system.) To ferry planes to England, routes were carefully surveyed and landing fields built, complete with refueling and weather facilities.

WASPs

Arnold concurred in the formation and support of the Women Air Force Service Pilots (WASP) organization. WASPs performed admirably during the war, ferrying all types of planes—from fighters to bombers and other training missions, including searchlight and radar tracking, gunnery and mock attack missions on ground troops. Arnold lauded their accomplishments: "It is on record that women can fly as well as men. We will not again look upon a women's flying organization as experimental."

Arnold chose his old flying comrades, Carl Spaatz and Ira Eaker, to respectively command the Eighth Air Force and its bomber force. They saw their vision of a strategic bombing force attacking the enemy's industrial heartland in accordance with the Mitchell gospel. Arnold organized the Committee of Operations

Analysts to study German and Japanese industry and transport and to recommend targets for attack missions.

MISADVENTURE?

During 1940 and 1941, German operations in Holland, Belgium, and Crete interested Arnold. In February 1941 he ordered Wright Field to develop "a glider that could be towed by an aircraft (capable of) transporting personnel and material and seizing objectives that cannot normally be reached by conventional ground units." Then he sent Col. Michael Murphy to formulate tactics. The USAAF and Army had few gliders available and practically no training programs underway. Furthermore, few military leaders believed in the canvas and wood gliders, which were slow, easy antiaircraft and ground fire targets. One Arnold staffer worried: "The man who sold General Arnold on gliders is Hitler's best friend!" Wright Field designers came up with the CG (Cargo Glider)-4As.

Arnold witnessed an impressive display of the glider's combat capabilities in North Carolina on August 4, 1943—the famous "Pea Patch Show"—orchestrated by Murphy. After briefings and dinner, the VIPs were bussed to the demonstration as twilight turned to darkness. They thought they were going to another briefing, but Murphy had planned a demonstration of night glider operations. This was a very touchy subject in view of the debacle at Sicily a few weeks prior, when a breakdown of inter-service coordination had resulted in the destruction of numerous gliders and their tow planes by U.S. Navy anti-aircraft fire.

As Murphy extolled the virtues of gliders, ten CG-4As cut loose from their tow planes in the dark sky several miles away, and headed for a dim light which was concealed from the VIPs. Murphy's booming voice prevented the audience hearing the muffled thumps as the gliders landed and disgorged their loads. On command the field was brightly illuminated, to reveal the gliders and combat-ready troops arrayed practically in the VIPs' laps. Ever the showman, Murphy had saved the best for last. As the audience stared at the scene, a nine-piece band exited, playing the Air Corps' song. Arnold returned to Washington convinced that fully loaded gliders could be effectively employed in darkness.

THE COMBINED BOMBER OFFENSIVE

Early in the war Arnold urged the British to cooperate with the Combined Bomber strategy. Relations were strained with the Royal Air Force, but Arnold mollified them. England's Prime Minister Winston Churchill believed in air power too, but wanted the USAAF to join the RAF in night missions. Due to the urgings of Spaatz and Eaker (as instructed by Arnold) the Prime Minister changed his mind and agreed to the USAAF bombing by day and the RAF by night.

Arnold vehemently disagreed with the British on the grounds of inhumanity when they suggested carpet-bombing German cities. He believed in crippling air strikes on German military and industrial targets. The "Round the Clock" plan was finally agreed to by the British and Americans at the Casablanca Conference in 1943. Now respected on both sides of the Atlantic, and supported by President Roosevelt and the Joint Chiefs of Staff, Arnold received his fourth star in 1943.

Arnold and the entire Eighth Air Force command hierarchy originally believed that heavily armed bombers in massed formations could easily defend themselves without fighter escort, a doctrine from the 1930s, until the Luftwaffe destroyed this fallacy with their cannon. In a letter dated August 24, 1942, Arnold wrote Spaatz that Eighth Air Force bomber operations "...can be extended, as soon as the necessary size force can be built up, into the heart of Germany *without fighter protection* over the whole range of operations." Actually, as late as 1943 USAAF production priorities were bombers first, medium and light bombers second, then reconnaissance planes, transports, and finally, fighters. The USAAF desperately needed a long-range fighter that could accompany the bombers all the way to and from the targets.

To solve the problem, Arnold sent General Barney Giles to North American to find ways to extend the range of the P-51 Mustang. Giles' suggestion to increase the fighter's fuel capacity by 300 gallons was met with healthy skepticism by the Chief Engineer, Dutch Kindelberger, and the company's president, but an attempt was begun. In conjunction with design changes to install the Rolls Royce Merlin engine, additional fuel capacity was added in the wings. The increase in performance was phenomenal, and the Mustang was changed from a cart-horse into a thoroughbred.

"DECLARATION OF INDEPENDENCE"

The use of Eighth AF units to support the North African invasion in November 1942 greatly incensed Arnold, Eaker, and Spaatz. They were further upset by continual command difficulties between the Army ground forces and AAF personnel. With the insistence and support of Arnold, Marshall issued Field Manual FM 100-20 *Command and Employment of Air Powers* on July 21, 1943 which stated that air and land forces were: "...co-equal and interdependent forces, neither is an auxiliary of the other. The gaining of air superiority is the first requirement for the success of any major land operation...Land forces operating without must take such security measures against hostile air attack that their mobility and ability to defeat the enemy land forces are greatly reduced. Therefore, air forces must be employed primarily against the enemy's air forces until air superiority is obtained. The inherent flexibility of air power is its greatest asset. Control of available air power must be centralized and command must be exercised through the air forces commander if this inherent flexibility and ability to deliver a decisive blow are to be fully exploited. Therefore, the command of air and ground forces in a theater of operations will be vested in the superior commander charged with the actual conduct of operations in the theater, who will exercise command of air forces through the air force commander and command of ground forces through the ground force commander." This doctrine worked well for the rest of World War II. Just as important, FM 100-20 signaled a separateness of the USAAF from Army ground forces.

While Arnold gave of himself during his career and especially during the war, he expected the same from both the forces he commanded. He increased bomber crew missions in the European Theater from 25 to 30 and later to 35. Statistics proved that the more experienced crew was more effective and would survive. This was especially true when the Allies gained air superiority in Europe.

General Carl Spaatz always carried bomb strike photos with him to show world leaders and VIP visitors. Arnold picked up this habit. An idea struck Arnold: A magazine for AAF personnel all over the world. In 1943, *Impact* was born, a monthly magazine classified confidential which carried stories and pictures of military aviation, intelligence information, operational data, new aircraft developments, and tactics written by ex-newspapermen and magazine writers with deadline immediacy. *Impact* was a popular morale-builder at AAF facilities all over the globe.

CHENNAULT

While morale was important to Arnold, some personnel were not, including Claire Chennault. The two locked horns in (1933?), when Arnold commanded March Field. Back then Arnold subscribed to the theory that heavily armed bombers "...would always get through." Arnold never forgot Chennault's abrasive challenges of this dogma. "Who is this damned fellow Chennault?" he sarcastically asked.

Frustrated with the generals' hide-bound attitudes toward fighters, Chennault resigned from the service in 1937, after which

Madam Chiang Kai-shek hired him to organize and train the Republic of China's air force. Concerned over Japanese advances in China, President Franklin D. Roosevelt intervened on several occasions, and at least twice in matters involving the U.S. Army Air Force. An April 15, 1941 executive order allowed US. military pilots to resign their commissions to fly to China for a year, and then return to their respective rank and service. These pilots manned Chennault's American Volunteer Group (better known to the public as the Flying Tigers); however, the U.S. military brass regarded them as paid mercenaries. Just as badly needed in China were modern fighter aircraft. After Chennault's appeals for aircraft were turned down by both the Army and Navy, FDR and Navy Secretary Frank Knox intervened to arrange for the transfer to China of 100 Curtiss P-40s. For this Arnold would pay Chennault back later.

Arnold promoted Clayton Bissell, a World War One fighter ace and one of the pilots who bombed the German battleships in 1921 with Mitchell, to major general with a date of rank *one day* prior to Chennault's. Bissell was ordered to command the 10th AF in the China-Burma-India Theater, where he outranked 14th AF Commander Chennault.

Colonel Robert L. Scott was another who felt Arnold's wrath. A combat veteran who stayed on after the Flying Tigers were disbanded in July 1942, Scott performed brilliantly as Commanding Officer of the 23rd Fighter Group. When his tour was over, however, Arnold ordered him back home for a nationwide publicity tour in connection with his book, *God Is My Copilot*. When Scott continued to request a return to China, and aware of his close relations with Chennault, Arnold sternly lectured him: "We are in the military profession. We do not dabble in politics. Go down there and tell those ladies [of the American Legion Women's Auxiliary in Orlando, Florida] about the Air Force. If you talk about political matters, I will send you to South America where there is no war!"

When Scott gave his talk, the nation was immersed in controversy over labor leader John L. Lewis and his United Mine Workers, whose strike was threatening to slow down the war effort. In response to one persistent woman's questions about the strike, Scott finally relented and said it was only his personal opinion, but he'd shoot down the labor union leader for slowing war production. This comment made nationwide headlines the following day. Months later Arnold cornered Scott in a bar, and snapped, "Scott, I damn well thought I'd find you here. I've watched you all evening, but with all the amenities here, there hasn't been time to ask you a question which has been troubling me for almost a year. It's about that talk you gave to those ladies in Orlando. Before I leave I want the ungarbled truth from you. You weren't really stupid enough to shoot down that labor leader with six .50-cal machine guns, were you?"

"Sir, I said it," he replied, "but I explained both before and afterward that it was just my personal opinion and not that of the War Department."

Arnold, now livid, retorted, "Personal opinion hell! Son, as long as you wear that uniform, *you don't have a personal opinion!*"

On the other hand, Arnold could treat his top flyers with paternal humor. When he wanted Major Richard Bong, the highest-scoring AAF fighter ace (40 kills), out of combat, Arnold wired Fifth Air Force Commander General George Kenney: "Major Bong's excuses in matter of shooting down three more Nips noted with happy skepticism at this headquarters. Subject officer incorrigible. In Judge Advocate's opinion, he is liable under Article of War 122." (Article 122 referred to a willful or negligent damage to enemy equipment on aircraft.) Bong had been ordered to fight only when attacked, and not to seek out enemy planes to shoot them down. Bong was later awarded the Medal of Honor. Arnold saw to it that Bong was brought home.

Arnold was just as quick with action as with his tongue. When German V-1 and V-2 rocket attacks were terrorizing England in 1944, he came under pressure from British and American military and civilian officials to destroy the launch sites using air power. Arnold first wanted low level attack tests made. Weary of Material Command at Wright Field dictating to him what he could or couldn't do, Arnold had set up his own research and development center at Eglin Field in Florida. Here were created remote-controlled gun turrets, Azon Guided Bombs, napalm, and other innovative aerial weaponry. He phoned the commander of Eglin Field and ordered him to build test sites: "I want the job done in days—not weeks. It will take a hell of a lot of concrete...give it first priority and complete it in days. Weeks are too long!" The sites were completed and the tests were flown, and they aided in the destruction of the German rocket installations.

BETTER HIS CAREER

As early as November 1939, Arnold wanted a bomber with a 5,000 mile range to replace and be superior to the B-17 and B-24. The first candidate was the Douglas XB-19, but it was underpowered. Boeing's XB-29 Superfortress design was accepted in 1941. Just in case the Boeing bomber didn't work, Consolidated built roles of carrier-based and land-based aircraft. No land or sea campaign could have been won without the command of the air. While air power alone did not defeat the enemy, it was critical to the outcome of the sea and air battles. Thus, Arnold shrewdly wrote the evaluation to disarm the critics of his dream of an independent air force.

The Chief of Staff was ready for retirement, but who would succeed him? The top candidates with four-star rank were George Kenney, Joseph McNarney, and Carl Spaatz. Kenney was experienced in tactical, not strategic, air power. McNarney had served throughout the war as a staff officer. Spaatz was chosen based largely on his wartime strategic experience in the European and Mediterranean Theaters. Arnold retired on February 28, 1946 and moved to Sonoma, California in June. He and his wife Bee raised four children, one girl and three boys (one son died in 1927). Arnold relaxed at his 50-acre ranch, raised prize cattle, and enjoyed his hobbies of furniture making and quail and pheasant hunting. (During a wartime leave, he was accidentally shot in the head and shoulders. He wasn't seriously injured, however, since the shot came from a long distance away and he was protected by his glasses and a heavy hunting coat.)

A DREAM COMES TRUE

Thanks to his pre-war efforts, astute maneuvering during World War II and the USAAF's wartime performance, Arnold's dream of an independent air force came true on July 26, 1947 with president Truman's signature on the National Security Act of 1947.

While Henry Arnold spent billions during his military career, by 1949 his personal financial resources were very low. He appeared in beer advertisements and even tried to get back on active duty. His royalties from *Global Mission* weren't enough. Arnold died of a heart attack on January 15, 1950. His estate was a $20,000 insurance policy. His wife struggled along on a $75 per month widow's pension and supplemented her meager income by selling real estate.

Arnold was unique in aviation history annals. One historian summarized Arnold's significance in aviation history: "Arnold provided firm but often erratic leadership. He was such a strong and singular figure that it is impossible to imagine anyone like him ever leading the Air Force again. Modern military bureaucracies, dominated as they are by committees and staff studies, don't allow men who are so idiosyncratic to rise to the top. For every fault, though, Arnold offered a compensating strong point, such as his belief in and his love of innovation and improvisation."

Over his career, Arnold received many decorations, including two Mackay Trophies (1912 and 1934), the Distinguished Flying Cross (1936), the Collier Trophy (1942), the Distinguished Service Medal (1943) with two Oak Leaf Clusters (awarded later), the Victory Medal, three theater ribbons, plus numerous foreign decorations, awards and medals. He was inducted into the National Aviation Hall of Fame at Dayton, Ohio in 1967.

Author's note: Ann and I and our 7-year-old son Clark met Mrs. Arnold by chance, and Clark knew of her husband, and she was impressed. Here are the contents of a letter she wrote him July 23, 1965. "Mrs. Henry H. Arnold, El Rancho Feliz, Sonoma, California—Dear Clark:- Thank you for your card from the Air Academy. I wish you could see a parade when the whole regiment is there. It's an inspiring sight. The enclosed is a replica of the tracking ship the USAFS 'General H. H. Arnold' and has taken part in the latest space flights. My boys use these pins as tie pins but you could put it on that wonderful blouse of yours. Please give my regards to the family and thanks again. Sincerely, Sharon P. Arnold. Mrs. "Hap" Arnold."... Another time she sent Clark a couple of the general's personal insignia—which we still have—with the comment she would have sent more but some Sgt. took most of the items.

Patricia's Enduring

Mission

Angi Kennedy

From EDP Sunday, November 10, 2007 448th BG

For Patricia Everson, remembrance isn't only something that only happens every November; it is part of every single day. She tells how a whispered promise on a deserted 448th BG Norfolk airbase helped shape her life.

The wind rattled the doors of the empty buildings, as Patricia Everson stood silently staring down the distance of the airstrip. Where the B-24 Liberators of the USAAF had once thundered to their takeoffs, now tufts of grass and weeds were insolently breaking a way through. Natural decay was slowly but surely reclaiming this deserted airbase at Seething, southeast of Norwich.

The village teenager had gone there in search of wild cowslips, but instead found herself pledging a promise that, many years later, would set her on a remarkable, life-changing mission. Patricia remembers that April day clearly. "Everything was so charged up with what had happened there. There and then, I swore I would never forget the men who had been based there."

Life and the years rolled on. Soon there would be little clue to the airbase's story left to catch the eye of anyone passing through Seething. Only the other people of the communities around the base would share the frisson of excitement whenever a trans-Atlantic accent was heard from a rare American visitor to the villages.

It was the early 1980s, and moves were afoot to create a memorial in the village and at the airfield to the 400-plus men, based at Seething, who had lost their lives in the Second World War. Patricia Everson, by then in her mid-40s, offered her help, raising funds for the event at which some of the former airmen and their families would be present.

For her, this would be a chance to fulfill a secret longing that had been burning away at her since childhood.

Patricia was a five- year- old schoolgirl when war was declared. She was one of the generation who can even now summon up the smell of the claustrophobic gas mask and the dank, stale air of the shelter in the garden. She grew up in the days of rationing, of course, of cod liver oil and malt supplements for undernourished youngsters, of sanctioned days off when she and her fellow schoolchildren would pick soft fruit, rose hips to be made into syrup, acorns to feed the pigs, and to collect aluminum foil and metal scrap to help the war effort.

Her father, Fred Knights, had joined up as a driver with the RAF. Patricia and her young brother, Reggie, did their best to help their mother, Jean, grow vegetables for their meals and collect water from the well.

Although she has no memory of hunger in those days of hardship, Patricia certainly recalls a sense of drabness. But that was to change in 1943. America had entered the war, and East Anglia was ideally placed to become its "airbase." Airstrips were being carved into the landscape, accompanied by mess halls, billets, and control towers. A mile outside the little village of

Seething, the 58th Station Complement Squadron turned acre after acre of open field into a new airbase, ready for the arrival of the aircraft and flight crews of the 448th Bomb Group of the USAAF.

"I was nine years old when they came," Patricia said. Suddenly we went from the 300 to 400 people in the village to having 3,000 young Americans down the road with these huge B-24 Liberator bombers.

"We had been at war for quite a few years by then and, to some extent, we were still living under that sort of Victorian thing of us children being seen and not heard.

"But now the Americans treated us like equals, and they really endeared themselves to us children, happy to spend a lot of time talking to children like us. They were so friendly to everyone. They made quite an impression on the older girls too!

"They would cycle through the villages, and because all the road signs had been removed to confuse the enemy, they were forever asking where the nearest pub was and if we had got a big sister at home.

"You must remember, many of them were only young boys themselves. Their average age was 19—anyone in their mid-20s was called the old man of the crew!"

Many were astonished by the tough conditions that the English had been living in. "They wrote begging letters home, asking for things to give to the children," said Patricia. "They were extremely generous. When they heard that the Jenny Lind Children's Hospital was running short of supplies, they took things there, and they had a choir that would go singing round the wards.

"One of the Americans said he never realized how bad things had been here. He had an orange in his pocket and decided he would give it to the first child he came across. He gave it to this little boy who'd never seen one before, and he bit into it—he didn't know you had to peel it first.

"Most of the children wanted chewing gum, they called them 'the gum chumers', but I loved the comic strips out of their newspapers the most."

"The highpoint was the Thanksgiving and Christmas parties though, when the children of the surrounding villages, homes and evacuees were invited to the base. For the Thanksgiving party in 1943, they came down to the school in their trucks and I can remember even now the excitement of being lifted over that tailboard.

"When we got there it was the first time I had heard live music outside church, and the food was so different to ours—even the gravy was a different colour.

"I wanted to ask a lot of questions because I didn't know much about America. But I was seated at a long table with all the young Americans and they were firing questions at me. Suddenly I was too shy to ask anything and I just said yes and no and thank you."

The regret at this missed chance stayed with Patricia, and resurfaced all those years later in 1984 as the preparations took shape for the memorial service. This time, she told herself, she would have the courage to talk to the Americans about their lives.

"I was so looking forward to it," she said. "But two and a half weeks before the service my brother and mother were killed outright in a car crash at Kirstead."

For the tight-knit family, who had lived just doors apart at Seething, it was a terrible blow, and a shock for the community too which had been so focused on the memorial that it was about to see put in place for the U.S. airmen of four decades earlier.

"I went to the service, but I wasn't emotionally able to do what I wanted to," said Patricia. "After the Americans had gone home, I really felt I had failed myself for a second time.

"So I managed to get the names of the people in America who

had sent contributions for the memorial. I wanted to write to them to ask them about their experiences.

"There was no one more badly equipped than myself. I couldn't type or write letters, but there was a drive inside me pushing me to carry on.

"First in my letters I had to clear the air so that they knew I wasn't an illegitimate child or an ex-girlfriend trying to track them down. Sometimes I would send out fifty letters and not get back a reply.

"Some of the men just weren't ready to look back. But the first time I got a letter with some black and white photos of when the man was at the base, I thought 'Yes, I can do this.'"

And gradually the letters began to arrive through the post, some just a few notes or names, others pouring out wartime memories. Today she has some fifty albums of their writings and hundreds of photographs, from official poses to relaxed off-duty shots of Americans on and around the base. Over the last twenty years, Patricia has gradually pieced together the jigsaw of names, numbers, memories and missions to build a comprehensive picture of life at Seething airbase from November 1943 to June 1945, when the Americans left. And in the process she has brought about reunions of old crewmates, friends, colleagues and, of course, people from the villages around the base.

"I was able to reunite a whole crew of ten and to put them in touch with the young boy from the village whom they sort of adopted while they were here."

For her too there have been many revelations. Although she lived through the war, she saw it with a child's eyes; it was not until many years later that she was able to comprehend the true toll on the men who were at Seething.

"As a child it was exciting. It is only when you are older that you realize how many people had died. There was one particular night when we lost two whole crews, twenty men, including one man who had been shot down just two days earlier and saved by the air-sea rescue.

"How brave they had to be. They were so young and I am sure a lot of them never thought it would happen to them."

Since hearing from Patricia, many of the old airmen have visited Seething to see the base once more and to pay their respects at the memorials to their fallen colleagues. And she has also gone over to America to take part in the large reunions there as the historian of the 448th Bomb Group collection. Her husband, Ron, has also played an important part in the Seething airbase story. He was part of a small group that restored the base's near-derelict control tower which is now a "living memorial," home to a collection of memorabilia, donated uniforms and equipment from its wartime days, as well as being a focus for those making pilgrimage to the airfield.

Opening the latest letter to arrive at Stanmare, her home on The Street at Seething, Patricia never knows what to expect, although more often these days they are the requests of grandchildren and great-grandchildren eager to discover information about their elderly or late relatives' wartime experiences.

"Some of the families say they didn't even know he was in the forces in the war," she said. "I think that quite a lot of the men buried it inside themselves when they returned home. Because so many of them were quite young, a lot had to go back to education and then get themselves a job so that they could start paying for their house and to get their children through their education.

"When they stand on the runway and think of their friends who didn't make it, yes, it is very emotional," she said.

"I have worked hard to get as many records as I can, but I can't get the personal details unless the men tell me them. But they do talk to me because although I was a child then, I knew what it was like for them in some ways.

"Sometimes their families will stand there with their mouths open because they have never heard him tell these stories before. They say 'Why didn't you ever say anything?' and the men say 'You never asked.'"

"It's hard now because so many of them have become personal friends and we are losing them fast," she added, "but I feel I was able to share their golden years with them and put them in touch with each other when they hadn't been in contact since they finished their missions."

Author's note—it was some twenty plus years ago that I received a letter from Pat saying she was a nine and ten-year-old school girl when we were there, and would like anything we had to offer about our Seething days. We have corresponded for years, and met Pat and Ron several times, both in England and the U.S. She has been and is the catalyst for the archives of the 448th Bomb Group.

A Post-War Talk

with Top Nazi Albert

Speer

Lt. Gen. Ira C. Eaker, USAF (Ret.) and Arthur G.B.
Metcalf

Reprinted from AIR FORCE Magazine, April 1977

On October 21, 1976, retired Air Force Lt. Gen. Ira C. Eaker, who commanded both VIII Bomber Command and then Eighth Air Force in 1942-43, and Dr. Arthur G.B. Metcalf, Chairman of the Board of the United States Strategic Institute, met with Albert Speer, Hitler's minister of armaments production, at Mr. Speer's home in Heidelberg. These highlights of their discussion concerning the effects of Allied airpower on German production were made available to AIR FORCE Magazine by General Eaker and Dr. Metcalf. The insights that were revealed in the conversations are a significant contribution to understanding the development of strategic airpower and its contribution to victory in World War Two.

EAKER: Mr. Speer, it seems we worked at cross-purposes in the last war. It was your mission to supply the weapons for the

Nazi land, sea and air forces. It was my job to prevent your accomplishing that by bombing your munitions factories and their supporting systems—oil, ball bearings, power, and transportation.

If I had had a more accurate estimate of your problems, it would have improved our chances of accomplishing our mission.

Now, more than thirty years after Allied bomber operations began in World War II, there is a renewal of interest in airpower operations in that war. One of the major current interests concerns this question: Which hurt you more, the RAF night bombing or the American daylight bombing? Or was it the combination, called "round-the-clock bombing," the most effective Allied strategy?

SPEER: At first, of course, it was the British night bombing. We had that to deal with a year before the American daylight raids began, and a year-and-a-half before you made significant attacks with a hundred or more of your daylight bombers.

After the British night bombing raids on our industry in the Ruhr, and especially their heavy raids on coastal cities like Bremen and Hamburg, I was directed to concentrate on night fighter production. Eventually, we began to take heavy toll of the British night bomber force as a result of devising tactics and techniques and developing equipment to deal with the night bombing effort.

I often wondered why the RAF Bomber Command did not continue their thousand-plane raids on our cities. Had they been able to do so, the morale of the German population and the German labor force might have been significantly weakened.

Of course, one reason why the burning of Bremen did not hurt the morale of our people more was because they did not know at the time the full measure of that catastrophe. Hitler's Propaganda Ministry had full control over all communications. Naturally they did not play up bad news. I, myself, did not know the full extent of the firebombing of Bremen, the horrible loss of civilian life, until much later.

Later on, when American bombers came in daylight in ever-increasing numbers, attacking our munitions factories very effectively, our military leaders repeatedly told Hitler that unless the daylight bombers could be stopped, the end of war was clearly in sight. So I was ordered to concentrate on day-fighter production. For a time, we held our own, often causing your raids heavy losses, as at Schweinfurt and Regensburg on August 17, 1943, but eventually you overwhelmed us. So I should suppose that it was the combined air effort that destroyed our means to wage war, and eventually the will and resources to continue.

You will note that in my book Spandau I pointed out that you in fact had started a second front long before you crossed the Channel with ground forces in June 1944. Air Marshal Milch told me that your combined air effort forced us to keep 900,000 men tied down on the so-called "West Wall" to defend against your bombers. This, of course, included the fighter defenses, the antiaircraft artillery people, and the firefighters, as well as a large number of workmen needed for repairing damaged factories. There was also the large number of artillery pieces required all over Germany because we never knew which of our industrial cities you would attack next. It was your freedom of target choice and our uncertainty that enabled a limited number of bombers to tie down such tremendous numbers of people and equipment in our defense effort.

I suspect that well over a million Germans were ultimately engaged in antiaircraft defenses, as well as 10,000 or more antiaircraft guns. Without this great drain on our manpower, logistics, and weapons, we might well have knocked Russia out of the war before your invasion of France.

EAKER: Your view of the bomber offensive as constituting a second front is one I have never seen advanced elsewhere. Which of the target systems—shipbuilding, fighter plane and engine factories, oil, ball bearings, or transportation—was most decisive?

SPEER: It was the combination. At first I was most worried about ball bearings. If you had repeated your bombing attacks and destroyed our ball bearing industry, the war would have been over a year earlier. Your failure to do so enabled us to get bearings from Sweden and other sources and to move our damaged ball bearing machines to dispersed localities.

EAKER: There were several reasons why we did not repeat our attacks on Schweinfurt immediately. In the first place, the strike photos showed great damage. Secondly, we sent out 376 bombers that day against Schweinfurt and Regensburg and lost sixty. No air force can sustain that loss rate. We always tried to hold our operational losses below the programmed number of replacement bombers and crews. I was determined that our bomber force should always be a growing force.

In addition, we had other target systems of high priority, such as aircraft production, oil, transportation, etc. If we had continued all our effort against one of these systems, you would have concentrated your defenses around that system, and our resulting losses would have been unacceptable. Further, we always endeavored to send our daylight bombers against a high-priority target, which was for that particular day free of cloud cover. All these conditions naturally diversified our bombing attacks.

SPEER: You are quite right. Ball bearings were not our only critical weapons production system. Your attacks on our petroleum supply, for example, were also decisive in our pilot training program. After your successive raids had severely damaged Romanian oil sources, you followed up by mining the Danube and by constant attacks on locks and barges so that eventually our supply of gasoline and oil from natural sources was greatly diminished. Then you turned, quite logically, to our synthetic oil production. By that time, you had such overwhelming air superiority that your long-range fighters were not all required to protect your bombers, but began very disastrous attacks on fighter planes on our airdromes.

Your air attacks on our transportation system were also very effective. They not only interfered with transport of troops and their equipment, but also disrupted my weapons production system. We often were producing engines and planes in required numbers, but we could not get them together from our dispersed factory sites. This was particularly true with respect to rail and barge transportation throughout Germany, especially in critical locations like the steel making Ruhr, which also supplied coal and coke to other critical industries.

The Allied attacks on our shipping did much more damage than you apparently realized at the time—not only the destruction of the shipbuilding facilities in our coastal cities, but the attacks on our submarine pens in the occupied Channel ports as well. And, of course, it was your long-range air reconnaissance over the Atlantic sea lanes that eventually reduced our submarine effectiveness and enabled the Americans adequately to supply those vast invasion forces. Sir Arthur Harris undoubtedly was correct in his contention that the so-called Combined Bomber Offensive was critical, perhaps decisive, in the three campaigns he described: land, sea and air.

EAKER: Aside from the bombing of German industry, a very high priority with the Allies was the destruction of the Luftwaffe. Since the Luftwaffe did not show on June 6, 1944, when that great naval armada appeared off the three French invasion beaches, we thought we had positive evidence that our Allied air offensive had largely destroyed the Luftwaffe.

SPEER: I think your surmise was essentially correct. I was still turning out the required number of fighter planes, but by that time we were out of experienced pilots. We were so short of fuel that we could give the incoming pilots in our flying schools only 3 ½ hours flying training per week. These poorly trained and inexperienced Luftwaffe pilots, by that time, were suffering heavy losses. A pilot only survived for a maximum of seven missions against your bombers and their accompanying long-range fighters in 1944 and '45. This was very discouraging to German pilots. It represented an attrition of fourteen percent for each mission. I do remember Hitler had ordered that 1,000 fighters take to the air on the day of the invasion. I do not know the reason for their not showing up. Perhaps General Galland [chief of German fighters] could tell you.

METCALF: Do you believe, as some do, that the Luftwaffe was misused?

SPEER: Yes, I do. First of all, the performance of our fighters and bombers, which had been developed well before the war, was inferior to your military aircraft. Hitler insisted that the Me-262, the twin-jet fighter we developed, be converted to a bomber, since Hitler was interested only in offensive weapons. It was a great mistake. I believe that as a fighter, it would have offered much more serious opposition to your bombers than the fighters we did use. When we removed the guns, ammunition, and other fighter armament from the Me-262, it was capable of carrying only a single 500-pound bomb, which was hardly worthwhile. Also, the shift of our aircraft industry from the production of bombers to the production of fighters and then back to the production of bombers was a nightmare. This disruption was hardly conducive to producing the aircraft we needed with which to fight the war.

METCALF: Was Goering's leadership of the Luftwaffe bad?

SPEER: One would have to say yes. After all, he spent most of his time at Karinhall, his country estate, dressed in long, exotic robes, heavily bejeweled, etc. As you know, he was on drugs for a long time. At the time of the Nuremberg trials Goering was, of course, off the drugs and he had lost a great deal of his excess weight. At that time, he behaved like a new person and exhibited many qualities of leadership and clear-headedness. It was quite a surprising transformation.

METCALF: Was the German failure to execute the cross-channel invasion of England ("Sea Lion") due to your inability to gain command of the air over Britain?

SPEER: Yes. And here again, the need was for a superior fighter capable of knocking down the Royal Air Force, which would have played havoc with our invasion flotilla and our troops on invasion barges during the long passage across the Channel.

METCALF: Was it a mistake to interrupt your campaign against the Royal Air Force, whose fighters were having such telling effects on the Luftwaffe during the Battle of Britain, in order to bomb population centers? That shift in strategy gave the RAF a breather—a chance to recover from the systematic attrition of its fighter forces.

SPEER: Yet, it was. Here again was seen the influence of Adolf Hitler.

EAKER: As I remember, you were charged at the Nuremberg trials with the use and abuse of a so-called slave labor force of some 6,000,000 conquered people.

SPEER: The foreign labor force was guarded, housed, fed, and under the general supervision of Himmler. I only made requisitions and was allotted the labor required in our factories. In hindsight, I should have been more concerned about the treatment of this labor force. My factory managers complained about the training program resulting from the frequent loss of labor, probably due in part to lack of proper housing, feeding, and care.

This labor force had some distinct limitations. As you probably know, the loss of our code machine, which enabled your Ultra process to intercept [and decode] our radio communications, was due to this labor. There were many factory fires that probably were set by the laborers, and continual reports of sabotage.

How much wiser you were to bring your women into the labor force. Had we done that initially, as you did, it could well have affected the whole course of the war. We would have found out, as you did, that women were equally effective and, for some skills better than male labor. We never did, despite our hard-pressed munitions production in the late years of the war, make use of this great potential.

METCALF: Was foreign labor worth the number of occupations troops you had to use to combat local resistance activities that were heightened by taking those workers out of the countries?

SPEER: We had an expression that "Sauckel [Fritz Sauckel, Gauleiter of Thuringia, who was in charge of all foreign labor] was the greatest ally of the French Maquis," whose activities pinned down large numbers of military manpower. On balance, I guess it was not worthwhile. It was also a management problem within our own country to guard these people to prevent sabotage, etc. It was through [Polish workers] that the cryptographic machines for Ultra were handed over to the enemy. No, I don't think the foreign labor program did as much good as it did harm.

EAKER: In your book you refer often to the unity of effort of the whole German people behind Hitler and his war effort.

SPEER: Your premise that the German people were all united behind Hitler I do not believe to be entirely valid. You will recall, there were many attempts to assassinate him. As the dreary war years wound on, there was great disaffection about various phases of his leadership. Undoubtedly Hitler's early successes in the Low Countries and in France gave our people hope that all Germany would again be reunited, that all the territories lost in the First

World War would be recovered. Also, as you may remember, we had been suffering great economic depression and deprivation with many people out of work and the tragic depreciation of the mark. With the Second World War, all that changed, of course. This undoubtedly made a tremendous impression on our people, and I can see where you, on the other side, would get the idea of our united effort.

There was great doubt about the wisdom of attacking Russia. I believe most of our military leaders and knowledgeable citizens doubted the wisdom of fighting on two fronts. After 1944, we frequently heard of Churchill's remark that Hitler was the Allies' secret weapon, and that was probably true.

Now I would like to ask some questions about the Allied air effort in World War Two. I have often wondered why you began your bombing attacks with such limited forces. Would it not have been better to have waited until you had several hundred, perhaps a thousand, bombers available?

EAKER: We did not have that option, for several reasons. After Pearl Harbor, there was great pressure, both at the political level and among the military leaders, to send all our bombers against the Japanese. If we had not begun operations against the Nazis, according to our prewar plan, this Pacific deployment would have taken place. The RAF bomber force would then have been left to deal alone with the Luftwaffe and German weapons production. It was only by demonstrating, as early as possible, that the daylight bombing offensive against Germany was feasible and productive that we were able to sustain our bomber buildup for operations out of Britain, as originally planned.

We learned during those limited early operations how to operate bomber forces under the conditions that then prevailed. If we had waited for the arrival of a thousand bombers before making attacks on German-occupied Europe, it probably would have been a tragic disaster. We learned how to deal with the weather, what kind of training we would have to give our combat crews, what types of formations to fly, and what communications we would require. We also learned that significant changes would be required in our aircraft.

Here is another consideration you may not have taken fully into account. Armies and navies have clashed for centuries, and their battles, strategies, and tactics have been recorded, studied, and analyzed by historians and war colleges of many nations. Prior to World War II, airpower had never had similar experience. Although Lord Trenchard of Britain, General Douhet of Italy, and Gen. William Mitchell of the U.S. had prophesied that strategic airpower could exercise a decisive influence on warfare, those theories had never been tested.

The airplane was less than fifty years old. Flying machines with the power and capacity to test the visions of Trenchard, Douhet, and Mitchell had not been developed. For the first time, the U.S. Eighth Air Force, operating out of Britain, and Britain's own Royal Air Force were to be given the resources to test those theories of the use of strategic airpower.

Gen. H.H. Arnold, head of the U.S. Army Air Forces, was a dedicated Mitchell disciple. His instructions to Gen. Carl Spaatz and to me were clear-cut, specific, unmistakable. We were to take the heavy bombers General Arnold would send us and demonstrate what airpower could do. Could it, as he hoped and believed, exercise a decisive influence on warfare by destroying the weapons-making capacity of an industrial nation like Germany?

General Spaatz was diverted from the test temporarily when he was ordered, in October 1942, to accompany General Eisenhower to Africa to conduct the campaign against Rommel and to seize North Africa. I moved up from leading VIII Bomber Command to be Eighth Air Force Commander for six months. This responsibility for the vital test of airpower fell upon us for the next two critical years.

So, during 1942 and '43, this process continued, cooperatively, out of Britain—the RAF by night, the U.S. Eighth Air Force by day.

SPEER: Why did you not attack our sources of electrical power upon which our weapon production so largely depended? We were always apprehensive about the vulnerability of our dams, our transformers, and our electric grid, so essential to continued war production.

EAKER: Our target planners had suggested electric power as one of the critical Nazi targets. However, the operational people, including myself, pointed out that the bomber was not an effective weapon against electric power production and distribution. We had no bombs available of a size and characteristic needed to destroy your water power. Transformers could not be seen at night, or even in daylight from bomber altitudes, and they were much too small to be attacked successfully. The power lines were discernible, but any bomb damage could be quickly repaired, and we realized you undoubtedly had provided for quick repairs of lines and transformers.

You will recall that the British spent a great deal of effort on the development of a bomb large enough to damage your dams. But the work of the dam-busters, though spectacular, did not accomplish decisive results.

As late as the Vietnam War, with the great technical advances that had been made in the meantime, the North Vietnamese power plants, transformers, and electric grid did not become especially lucrative targets until the smart bombs were available. Of course, with nuclear weapons, power sources of the enemy would be productive, perhaps decisive, targets.

SPEER: Why did you not join the British in attacking civilian industrial centers and our labor force?

EAKER: Airpower pioneers, including Lord Trenchard, General Douhet, and General Mitchell, had long believed that bombardment aviation might be able to reduce the will of civilian populations to resist. Our own doctrine held that the way to reduce civilian morale was not by killing people, but by depriving them of the resources for further resistance.

The U.S. airpower doctrine, which covered the employment of the Eighth Air Force out of Britain, never contemplated attack on civilian populations, other than that incidental to attacking munitions factories. A letter I wrote to General Spaatz in 1943 contained this often-quoted observation: "We must never allow the record of this war to convict us of throwing the strategic bomber at the man in the street."

I do not imply any criticism of the Royal Air Force bomber effort. Their position was entirely different. German planes had brutally attacked London, Coventry, and other cities, inflicting heavy loss of life. When the RAF began to retaliate with the limited resources available, all they could do with their night operations was to hit German industrial areas. As the bomber force grew, they were able, as you have said, to effect considerable destruction of your war effort by bombing German industrialized areas.

METCALF: At what time in the war did you feel that the Allied bombing was becoming unbearable to the German people?

SPEER: The best answer I can give is that the gradual buildup of your bombing attacks permitted the German people to become accustomed to and fortified against the great increase in destruction. So it is difficult to say at what point the tolerance of the population may have shown signs of being exceeded. Of course, the fire bombings of Hamburg, Dresden, and the like were great disasters locally. It would have been better if you had been able early in the war to have abruptly increased the size and weight of these bombing raids.

EAKER: I believe you expressed some surprise that there was not closer cooperation between the British night bomber and American daylight operations. It was realized early that the British and American bombers had differing characteristics and limitations and crews with different training and experience. This made it advisable for each to be assigned the distinctive air task that each was best qualified to perform. Occasionally there was close collaboration. The RAF attacked targets we had hit and set afire in daylight, bombing on our fires. We in turn made daylight attacks on installations they had hit at night and which were discernible, even in bad weather, by the fire and smoke.

There was close cooperation in the exchange of target data, operational data, and in logistics and communications. This was necessary with so many planes operational in such a limited airspace as the British Isles. I would not want to leave the impression that there was any lack of mutual support and cooperation. Seldom, if ever, have two national military forces cooperated as effectively as did the RAF and the U.S. Eighth Air Force in the war years.

Albert Speer was convicted of war crimes in 1946 at Nuremberg and spent twenty years in prison for his role in Hitler's Third Reich. Within two years after becoming munitions minister in 1942, he almost tripled production of armed vehicles, quadrupled that of large guns, and more than doubled aircraft production.

Speer won a measure of respect at Nuremberg when he alone among those on trial confessed general responsibility for wartime crimes.

Caught in the gravitational pull of the megalomaniac's magnetism, Speer spun in Hitler's orbit until the end. His diaries are a valuable contribution to the knowledge of Nazi Germany and the personalities of the imprisoned top Nazis when stripped of power.

The late Lt. General Ira C. Eaker completed pilot training in 1918. Prior to World War II, he served as Executive Assistant to the Chief of the old Air Corps and participated as a pilot in many pioneering flights, including the "Question Mark" endurance flight and the Pan-American flight of 1926. During the war, he commanded successively VIII Bomber Command, 8th Air Force, and Mediterranean Allied Air Forces. General Eaker flew on the first heavy bombing raid against occupied Europe and the first shuttle bombing mission to bases in Russia.

Dr. Arthur G.B. Metcalf is the Chairman of the Board and President of Electronics Corp. of America, the founder and Chairman of the U.S. Strategic Institute, and Strategic Studies Editor of "Strategic Review." A former faculty member of MIT and Harvard, Dr. Metcalf has been a test pilot and was a pioneer in the field of aircraft control and stability. During World War II, he served as a lieutenant colonel. He is the author of many articles in the fields of mathematics, aerodynamics, and strategy and doctrine.

Despite the Air Force Magazine's claim, General Eaker did not fly on the first heavy bomber raid against Europe. His was the first 8AF raid from England by B-17s on August 17, 1942. The first raid by heavy bombers, B-24s in fact, occurred on June 11, 1942 by 12 "HALPRO" Liberators from Fayid, Egypt, bombing for the first time, Ploesti, Romania.

Unsung People

This is added to honor the millions of persons who shower kindness, help, and counsel to others in need, with little or no recognition. One example that comes to mind is Virginia Lollar, Chico, California, who has, over the 40 years of our friendship, always had a passion to aid others. Fill one need, she finds another.

The Virginias of his world are mostly unrecognized, and to whom I wish to pay respect – and to regret not being blessed with the intense love and care to act for less fortunate.

The Saga of Seething's Flying Dog - 448th BG

As the B-24 Liberator crews prepared for the group's 100th mission to Siracourt, France on 21 June 1944, an amusing sidelight was experienced during the four hours which followed.

The successful efforts of a local terrier dog to fly an operational mission was completed from Seething Airfield that particular day.

'Bomb Boy' as the black and white was affectionately called by his ten co-masters who formed the crew of the Liberator 'Hit Parade' was often referred to around the base as the 'washed out Air Cadet.' The crews never took him up for fear the of the ill-effects that might have resulted at high altitudes.

He had often, in the past, sneaked into the plane right before the take off in order to fly over Germany, but had always been found in time to be put out before the start of the mission.

Through trial and error, 'Bomb Boy' finally found a perfectly camouflaged spot right near the nose-wheel. Immediately before takeoff he managed to jump into the plane, when everyone was checking last minute preparations, and stowed away in his concealed hiding place.

He didn't move until the Liberator had gained altitude. Then he made his way along the flight deck right between the pilot and copilot as the plane headed out over the channel towards enemy territory.

The Pilot, cursing roundly when he saw the dog, decided to take him along. This being the Pilot's twenty-first mission, he didn't want to turn back to Seething.

In the meantime, he handed 'Bomb Boy' over to the crew and told them that they had better prepare him for the trip.

The first big problem was to give oxygen to the terrier. Fortunately, the crew always carried a spare mask. 'Bomb Boy' wouldn't let the mask be fitted at first. After a time, he became a little dizzy from the rarified atmosphere, and yielded. The radio operator tucked him into his heated flying suit to keep him warm.

'Bomb Boy' acted like a veteran throughout the mission. Occasionally, he cleared his ears by moving his jaws and yawning. He stood before the open bomb bay doors and watched Hit Parade's bombs fall away to blast the target.

And he ate his share of chocolate D-ration, never once suffering any air sickness, or other ill effects from high altitude flight.

'Bomb Boy' was with the crew when they were interrogated by the Intelligence Officer after they had landed, and occasionally put in his comment with a few well pranced barks. He was accepted as an honorary observer of the crew and was voted to receive flying pay with 50% increase in his weekly allowance of chocolate from the crew's ration.

Major General
Andrew S. Low, Jr.,
USAF—Retired

A. Edward (Abe) Wilen, 453rd

Andy Low led the 453rd Bomb Group and in turn led the 8th Air Force on May 8, 1944, on a mission to Brunswick, Germany. The 453rd was badly hit by German fighters. Among the planes that went down was Crew #8, Pilot Richard Witton, copilot Wallace Croxford, Bombardier Walter Conneely and Navigator Abe Wilen. Thirty-nine years later, May 1983, in Indiana, Pennsylvania at Jimmy Stewart's 75th birthday celebration, Andy Low on reuniting with me said, "Wilen, you were badly hit on May 8, 1944, I saw you rammed by a German fighter and then your plane went down."

In mid-May, Witton, Croxford, Conneely and I wound up at the West compound in Stalag Luft III, Sagan, Poland. This is the camp that the movie "The Great Escape" was about. Two months prior, seventy-six men escaped through a tunnel. Only three made it to England. Of those captured, 50 were shot at Hitler's orders.

On July 29, 1944, on a mission to Bremen, Germany, Andy

Low was shot down. He was badly hurt and wound up in a hospital for 16 days. He almost lost an arm but was fortunate to have a South African doctor save it for him.

In mid-August, Andy wound up at Stalag Luft III also, but in the North Compound. From that date until the 27th of January, 1945, POW life went on for Andy, myself and the rest of our crew. On January 27th, with the Russians advancing in our direction, we got orders to march.

About six inches of snow had accumulated and the temperatures went down as low as ten degrees below zero. We were all handed Red Cross parcels and started our march. We in the West Compound left about 11:30 p.m. to midnight. Andy, in the North Compound, left about 3:00 a.m. on the 28th. Snow fell and created blizzard conditions. Men froze, men fell out, some were shot. Andy Low and we marched together, not knowing the other was there.

There are some good books on Stalag Luft III and the march. The important thing was that Low, Witton, Croxford, Conneely and Wilen survived it together.

At this point, Croxford and Conneely went on to Stalag VIIA in Moosburg, Germany. Andy Low, Dick Witton and Abe Wilen wound up at Stalag XIIID in Nurnberg, Germany, a mile away from the marshalling yard.

This target was bombed repeatedly by the 8th A.F. in daylight and the British at night. Late in February our own 453rd bombed us. Many bombs fell near our camp. There was little food, and rats, mice and bugs were everywhere. There were not enough beds, so some slept on the floor. At night during the bombing, we were told that anyone trying to get out of the barracks would be shot. We saw the flashes, counted the seconds and could determine how close the bombs came.

Eventually, on April 4th, as Patton's Third Army was moving toward us, we marched south to wind up at Stalag VIIA in Moosburg. On the way, we were strafed by our own fighters as we marched on the road. We had to tear up anything white and work out the letters POW in the field to warn our fighter planes away.

When we got to Moosburg, Dick Witton and I were in a large tent with many others. Andy Low was in a smaller tent next to ours.

On April 29, we were liberated together and we in the tents were flown out first on May 3. Many years passed until our paths crossed again.

When I think of Andy Low and his relationship to our crew and myself, I feel that the thread that ties us together is best expressed in a quotation from a veteran's magazine:

"I know why men who have been to war yearn to be together. They long to be with men who once acted their best. Men who suffered and sacrificed. Who were stripped raw, right down to their humanity."

The Ballantrae

Disaster

King Schultz, pilot 448th Bomb Group, and representative to the 2nd Air Division

With the war in Europe having ended in the previous month, in June 1945 the personnel at Seething were making preparations to return home and hand the base back to the RAF. All four squadrons drew lots for those who were to go home by air. Twenty airmen were allocated to each B-24: ten air crew and ten ground crew in each bomber. It was cramped but practicable.

On 10 June the first departures started. The route home was via RAF Valley in Anglesey, then on through either the Azores or Iceland depending upon the route weather. During the following twelve days, 64 bombers of the 448th BG, complete with 640 airmen aboard, took off and days later arrived back safely in the U.S.

The sixty-fifth and very last B-24 departed a little after daybreak on the morning of 12 June, pounding down the 2000 yards of runway 24 for the last time as Capt. Jim Blank eased the 27-ton bomber into the air. His orders were to avoid the RAF Valley route because of poor weather brewing up in the west. He was directed instead to fly via Prestwick, Ayr. So he set course from Seething for Splasher Beacon at Louth in Lines, and on to Marske Beacon and then Middlesbrough, achieving excellent reading on each radio compass. However, as he approached Cheviot Hills on the Scottish border, weather and cloud conditions begin to deteriorate rapidly. Inside the aircraft, the occupants could hear the heavy rain battering the fuselage as the doomed B-24 droned on through the eerie mist towards its destination.

The pilots could no longer get a satisfactory reading on the radio compass. They sensed that the wind had probably backed and that their estimated drift had changed. The navigator, Lt. Bernard F. Pargh, advised that they should continue on course and await improved visibility. Prestwick reported low clouds and rain, with more to come.

The bomber collided with a hillside four miles southeast of Ballantrae whilst making a controlled descent on instruments. Disintegrating as it went, the Liberator slid along on its belly for some 125 yards, scattering debris along the way and throwing some of its packed occupants out onto the moor as it came to an abrupt halt. Only the tail and center bomb bay sections were still recognizable as aircraft components; the rest of the aircraft was totally wrecked.

Of those on board, only four survived the initial impact, and all were badly injured. After laying unconscious for a considerable period of time, one of the four passengers (all of the aircrew were dead), S/Sgt. John R. May awoke to find a scene of utter devastation. All he could remember was that just prior to impact, someone had yelled, "Hey! There's the ground!" In great pain he lapsed into unconsciousness and only recovered that evening. Everyone else had been killed. During the night, one of the survivors, Pfc. George Gaffney, died.

As soon as he could muster the strength, Sgt. May, despite the acute pain he was experiencing from a broken back, attempted to hobble down the hill, tripping and lapsing into a state of unconsciousness after he fell and struck some rocks, which created a gaping hole close to his temple. Eventually he was found by a gamekeeper for the Lagafater Estate. The RAF and police were informed, and ambulance teams were soon on their way. Dick Pokorny and Ken Nelson together with Sgt. May were rescued and taken to Prestwick Hospital. While there, T/Sgt. Pokorny had a visit from an English Land Army girl, returning his wallet which had been found at the crash site, still with his money inside. "Our British allies are very honorable," he remarked. Irony often plays a part in tragedies such as this.

The pilot, Capt. James Blank, prior to takeoff had placed his wife's and baby daughter's photograph above the instrument panel. Then, after his usual request over the intercom of "no smoking in flight," he added, "This is one mission that we want to be perfect." Perhaps the aircraft crashed at the height of only 1400 feet on Pildinny Hill because the waters of Loch Ryan were mistaken for Ayr Bay. The accident report states an occasional sight of water prior to the crash. Perhaps a stronger-than-anticipated tail wind caused an underestimated ETA at Prestwick and they thought they were on the final approach for the airfield. Whatever the cause, the consequences were tragic, as another seventeen of America's finest lost their lives.

Crew members: Capt. Jim Blank (pilot), Lt. John K. Huber (copilot), Lt. Bernard F. Pargh (navigator), Lt. Frank Y. Pollio (bombardier), T/Sgt. Morris L. Kanerak (radio), S/Sgt. Louis Menred (gunner), S/Sgt. Cris C. King (gunner), S/Sgt. John Wildman (gunner), S/Sgt. William T. Harriman (gunner).

Passengers: Ten enlisted men and two officers, Capt. Harold L. Earmant (713th Squadron pilot), Lt. Col. Heber T. Thompson (448th BG Ops Officer, a very experienced top veteran who had come over with the original unit in 1943 as a young 2nd Lieutenant pilot).

Author's note: "When weather's ahead and you're in doubt, be sure to make a 180 about."

Crossing the U.S. on our way overseas, I obeyed this advice for a safe trip.

Mission 23:

Baumenheim,

Germany—19 March,

1945

Mission Diary of Lt. Col. Harold H. Dorfman, 448th

This mission was an extremely interesting one from a sightseeing point of view. Again I flew as pilotage navigator. I love that nose turret position, most comfortable seat in the plane. But this time it was really worthwhile. CAVU all the way in, and most of the way out. Flying time eight hours and five minutes.

Takeoff was at 1030 hours. Much too late for a mission of that length. We were to lead the 20th Combat Wing today. Colonel Westover was flying with us as command pilot. Still Lt. Voigt and crew, Lt. Block, the D.R. navigator, was finishing up, so after this I'm to be D.R.

Forming was in Belgium, just south of Brussels. It went over extremely well. We went into Germany somewhere around Strasbourg and headed for the target near Munich, a jet aircraft parts factory.

We bombed visual. Bombs away at 1448 hours, altitude 17,900 feet, temperature -47°F. We really plastered the target.

Coming out we passed north of Frankfurt and then across the Rhine south of Coblenz. Frankfurt was a mess. Coblenz was leveled, just nothing there, no blip on the radar. You could see north to Cologne and Düsseldorf. One of the two was really burning; at that distance, I couldn't tell which it was. I could see the flashes of the artillery on the west bank of the Rhine and the shells bursting on the east bank. Up at Remagen, where our troops had crossed the Rhine, you could see the heavy artillery marking the area. We held on the east bank. It looked like hell down there from here. We passed directly over Aachen. That was another pitiful sight. It was beaten to a pulp.

Hit from behind by a jet, I took in a picture I would rather forget. From then on the trip was uneventful. I almost went to sleep in that nose turret.

Lt. Block put on quite a flare show in the traffic pattern, celebrating the end of his tour.

That was it for #23.

Duneberg

Gordon M. Baker, 566th Sqd., 389 B.G.

I thought the Duneberg B April 7, 1945 raid was a closed issue with the March *Newsletter*. But, with the additional two articles in the September *Newsletter,* I thought I might as well add my bit to the confusion.

When the ME-109 was inserted into our box of four aircraft, I was standing with one foot on the raised deck between the seats of the pilot and the copilot on the plane flying the slot position in the lead flight. So I had an excellent view (and no duties) of the ME-109 and its destination of two of our aircraft.

When I was first aware of the ME-109, I saw him flying at the same elevation and at the same speed as our element of four planes. He had entered the formation from its rear. The fighter was flying to the left of the tail turret of the lead plane and therefore slightly to the left and ahead of our nose turret. The ME first would fire its guns at the lead plane and then would pull its nose up slightly. Then it would fall back into its level firing position and let off more rounds of ammunition. I have always figured the ME had armor plating on its belly and that the pilot was using this jiggling tactic so as to avail himself of the protection afforded by his armor plating. On the other hand, it may have had something to do with its speed since the ME-109 must have been close to its stalling speed.

It was amazing, considering that at least twelve 50-caliber machine guns were firing at his plane, that the Germans pilot was able to hold his position within our formation as long as he did, which seemed to be minutes, but wasn't. At any rate, smoke then started to steam from the engine nacelle of the ME and at this point the (wounded?) German pilot must have realized that he had had it. So he accelerated his ME under his left wing of the lead plane and flipped it into the lap of its pilot.

Two things happened next. First, the 3-bladed prop of the ME-109 was detached from its engine and floated directly towards our plane. Luckily, it dropped out of sight before our plane ran into it. I mention this because it had stopped rotating and seemed to be suspended in the air, right in front of us.

The second action involved the engine of the ME-109. It rolled along the top of the right wing of the lead plane and dropped off its end directly onto the deputy lead plane. The German pilot must have wanted to commit suicide, else why would he have flown formation with us, presenting himself as a sitting duck? One German for 20 Americans; one ME for two B-24s.

The bomb damage was quite impressive as viewed through the left blister on the flight deck and through the open bomb bay doors. And the top turret gunner should remember my presence on this flight since I repaired his intercom (a loose wire in his plug-in junction box) and enabled him to claim an enemy plane.

However, I was impressed even more to see a German plane, without any propeller, coming down almost vertically to the right of our formation. This was the first jet aircraft I had ever seen, and it wasn't one of ours!

I had persuaded the CO to let me fly with the crew as a flight engineer that morning, although my MOS was that of Squadron

Engineering Officer. After landing at Hethel, I figured that I was not getting enough (any) flight pay and therefore I would forego any more combat flying; especially after witnessing two B-24s out of four (50%) going down over enemy territory. However, the flight did give me a better outlook on what it was like to fly a mission over Germany.

Unfortunately, after some 40 years I cannot remember our plane designation nor any of the names of the crew. Perhaps someone whom I flew with that morning can tell us.

Duneberg—April 7, 1945

John B. (Buff) Maguire (389th BG)

My crew also flew that particular mission to Duneberg on April 7, 1945. In fact, that target was an ammunition and dynamite dump, and we carried 12-500 lb. GP bombs, and I flew a D+ plane that day. This particular mission was my eleventh mission, and it was my third mission as a deputy lead pilot. As stated in the Earl Zimmerman article, the 389th BG was leading the entire 2nd Air Division to Duneberg, and the 566th Bomb Squadron was flying the low left position.

This particular mission is still very vivid in my mind—I guess it is because of the importance of our leading the entire 2nd Air Division on the mission that day, and we still were able to completely destroy the target and I had a ringside seat for the action. At the time, and during interrogation, I was never able to figure out how the ME-109 was able to get through the P-51 fighter cover. I remember the ME-109 diving from above at almost a 180-degree angle between our three squadrons in the 389th BG, then pulling up into formation so that it was flying off the right wing of the lead plane and the left wing of the deputy lead plane. The ME-109 just sat there firing its guns until it was put out of commission, at which time it did a roll over and smashed into the cockpit area of the lead plane and then into the deputy lead ship.

The Zimmerman article stated that one of the P-51s was hit by our fire and the pilot bailed out. I remember that. The one thing I was most afraid of during this action was being hit by fire from our own guns, because the ME-109 attacked us at the IP and flew in formation at the beginning of the bomb-run until the ME-109 pilot was apparently killed. We then used the bombardiers of the high right squadron and the low left squadron to still make the bomb run, drop the bombs, and destroy the target.

Even being so close to all of this action, we went over our plane with a fine-toothed comb after landing, and nowhere could we find any holes or hits from any guns. I guess the Old Boy upstairs was looking out for us since we did not even receive a scratch.

Another thing which is very vivid in my memory is the talk or speech that James N. "Jimmy" Stewart gave at our interrogation, telling us what a fine job we did of destroying the target when the lead plane and the deputy lead plane were both lost at the IP commencing the bomb run. At the time, Jimmy Stewart was either a Lieutenant or full Colonel and was the Deputy Wing Commander. I remember his remarks were just as impressive as any movie I have seen him in.

The article in the March newsletter is accurate. My notes further say that we were also attacked by jet fighters coming down the bomber stream, and that the 389th BG lost two crews and three planes. One of the planes had the crew bail out.

The Zimmerman article stated that he was doing nothing with the waist gun because he was so busy watching all of the action. I just want him to know that my ringside seat was so close

to the action, when we returned to base I had to change my underwear.

After The Mission Is Over

Patrick J. McGuckin - B17, 389th BG

Over the last several years there have been written many stories about the April 7, 1945 raid on Duneberg, and probably each one clouds the story as much as clearing it up. We all see things differently; I remember at debriefing, several gunners lined up to claim the "kill."

The story I want to tell is what happened AFTER the attack, but to review briefly:

I was the left waist gunner on the Kiser crew, in the High Right formation. Saw the German fighter coming in a pursuit curve at about 8 o'clock. I, along with about 60 other gunners, started to fire. Then things really happened in a hurry. The fighter shot out an engine in one plane, forcing it to abort and land at a base near Paris. Then he crashed into the lead plane and bounced off into the deputy lead plane. Both planes were lost. The German just seemed to disintegrate. We lost Col. Herboth in the lead plane.

Now for the story I wish to tell. It's about the pilot on the deputy lead, Lt. Kunkle. I wish I could locate him and have him tell his story, but after checking all the rosters over the years I haven't been able to find him, so here goes.

About a week or so after the mission, it was announced on bulletin boards on base that a survivor of that raid would be in the Aero Club to tell his story. He didn't remember leaving his plane; he only knew that he was in a chute with the ripcord in his hand, and was at about 3000 feet. (He was probably blown out by one of the explosions.) One of his boots and the felt slipper was missing from one foot. He could see three or four other chutes and tried to remember how to pull on the chute cords so he could meet up with the others, but at the last minute it looked like the others were heading for a Stalag, so he quit trying and landed in a forest. He said he was so confused that he ran toward the road instead of going deeper into the woods. It was lucky for him that he did, for at that time some trucks arrived bringing a German search party to look for him. They found his chute and naturally assumed he went deeper into the woods, so that's where they looked while he was hiding under a low branched pine tree. He knew if he was caught he was only obliged to give his name, rank and serial number. He could remember his name and rank, but he was so confused he couldn't remember his serial number.

The Germans didn't find him, so he stayed in the forest trying to think what he would do next. He thought he might make it back if he traveled at night and rested during the day.

That night he heard voices from two men that jumped off a train that went through the woods. Not knowing whether they were friend or foe, he still had his Colt 45 so he confronted them. Seems that one of them was a Lt. in the Russian Army, the other was a young Hulk civilian slave laborer. They had been in Germany for so long that they could speak German, and Kunkle was of German descent, so he could also speak the language.

Lt. Kunkle's bare foot was sore, sprained when leaving the

plane, so while traveling that first night they broke into a German farmhouse. The Russians stole food, window drapes (for blankets) and went into the bedroom where the farmer and his wife were sleeping and got boots for Lt. Kunkle. (He said most of the canned food was American.)

On one of the nights they came to a river, with no boats to be had. The Hulk pulled fence posts out of the ground, and with the fence wire they fashioned them into a raft and crossed. When reaching the other side, they had no more use for the raft so they let it go down the river, only to find when they had traveled a short distance that they were on an island. While exploring the island for a way off, they found a bombed out bridge. They could travel from girder to girder, but the Hulk couldn't swim, so they had quite a time getting across.

On one of the days they even went into a train depot and bought tickets to get a little closer to home. Another night they were about to bed down for the night when they discovered that there was a German Tank Corps also bedded down in the woods. Needless to say, they went to the next woods.

When they were getting closer to friendly lines one evening, they ran into a German officer and two enlisted men. They thought they were done for, but the Germans were probably deserters, knowing that the war was over as far as Germany was concerned. The officer asked if they had matches; he had cigarettes, but no matches. Kunkle tore off part of the striker and gave it to him. He in turn asked Kunkle if he could do anything for them. Kunkle said they could use some bread or any kind of food. The German left, and a short while later came back with a loaf of white bread. They all bedded down a short distance from each other, and when they awoke the Germans were gone.

Getting closer to the British lines they were crossing a bridge when Kunkle felt a wire with his foot. They all scrambled for a ditch when a very English voice called out, "Who's there?" When they identified themselves they were allowed to cross. It seems that the bridge was zeroed in with two machine guns. If they had tripped the wire the gunners would have to pull the trigger.

I don't know what ever happened to the Russians. Kunkle was held long enough to be identified by American forces, spend a day or two in Paris, and then return to Hethel to tell us his story.

This story may have a twin, because the left waist gunner on the lead plane, Jim Kratoska, and two others from the same crew survived. I don't know if they were the people Lt. Kunkle saw when he was coming down or if there were other survivors.

It's been 45 years now since all this happened, yet so much of it is still clear. Only wish I could remember this morning and yesterday.

The Final Flight of the Original "Bird Dog" Crew

William H. Counts, Sr., 467th

It would seem our final flight on Thursday, June 29, 1944 was, indeed, jinxed from the beginning. We supposedly were "standing down," but at the last minute were called to fly this mission. At the time we were awakened, around three a.m., none of us were enthusiastic about flying on such short notice. We quickly dressed and rode our bicycles over to the mess hall to eat. After eating, we went to get our flying equipment and dressed for the flight. We were pressed for time, and rather than change into a flying suit, I simply put my electric suit over my dress uniform, and went to mission briefing.

We were one man short because the enlisted men had informed me that Sgt. Thomas Hansbury, our tail gunner, had been on guard duty the night before. The thought of placing a combat crew member on guard duty and then expecting him to fly the next day was irritating to me, and I had the word passed along to Hansbury to remain in the barracks and I would credit him as being on this mission.

Our takeoff was to the southwest and we were on instruments almost as soon as we were airborne.

While over the Channel, and before getting over enemy territory, it was customary for each of us to use the "restroom" since we would not be getting out of our seats until we were again back over neutral territory. This was not as simple as it may sound, because of the procedure involved in disconnecting and reconnecting oxygen, electric suit, flak vest and pants, steel helmet, and radio connections, etc. When I sat back down, I reconnected everything except I FORGOT TO FASTEN MY SAFETY BELT AND SHOULDER STRAPS! I had never done this before, and it was to be the major factor later in my not perishing inside the ship.

As we continued inland toward our target, at an altitude of 21,500 feet, I kept eyeing the deputy lead's position, hoping someone would fill that slot. No one did, however, and I waited until almost the last minute before sliding our ship down into that position. This maneuver was accomplished between Wing IP and Group IP. (Wing IP means Wing Initial Point where the Combat Wing breaks up into individual groups and proceeds to that group's target. Group IP means the Initial Point for the individual groups to proceed to their own target.)

As we approached our target, the JU-88 factory at Aschersleben, visibility was good and we could see no flak or fighters in the area. We were not more than 30 seconds from "bombs away" when the first burst was fired, and they hit us with that burst and every ensuing burst. We could hear the flak tearing through the aircraft each time one of the 88mm shells exploded. As I reflect on this, I am amazed that our bombs were not hit in the bomb bay. Just before "bombs away," Sgt. Francis Van Veen, our radio operator, tapped my right shoulder and said, "There's a fire in the bomb bay." I looked back over my shoulder and saw the fire, which appeared to be hydraulic fluid burning. I told Van Veen to try to put it out, and returned to trying to keep the aircraft in formation and clear of other planes. At almost the same time Van Veen reported "fire," I had felt the controls go slack and my oxygen supply was extremely hot. I jerked the oxygen hose loose to avoid inhaling flames, in case that system was on fire—as it is sure death if this happens. Eyewitnesses later reported seeing the men in the back of the plane slump over and fall to the floor, and flames streaking out of the waist windows. It is my belief that they died from breathing the deadly flames from the oxygen system, but there is no way to know this for certain. They could have been hit by flak fragments.

Because of this fact, Sgt. John Murphy may not have been able to get his customary brick thrown out. On every mission he carried one addressed, "to Adolf with love, from Murph," and threw it out somewhere over Germany.

It was Robby's custom to call out "bombs away," and I didn't hear him as I felt the ship rise as the heavy bomb load was released. Our radio was out but I didn't know it at the time. Immediately after bombs away, I fed the two left engines in and cut back the right engines, in order to avoid midair collision with anyone else and clear the formation. As we cleared the formation, in a diving right turn, I fed all four engines back in and the plane began heeling to the left. I felt that we were going to go down, and told the boys on the intercom to abandon the aircraft. I repeated this twice before I realized the radio was out, as I didn't get any "feedback" through my headset. As I reached for the alarm bell to alert the crew to bail out, Lt. Bill Greble, my copilot, had risen from his seat and was stepping around the control pedestal, when, it felt to me like the right wing came off. I don't know if the wing did come off then, or there was an explosion, or exactly what happened; but for lack of a better expression—"all hell broke loose." I believe the top turret came loose and crushed Greble and nearly got me, as something grabbed my left leg and held it tight enough to pull my flying boot, electric sock and regular sock completely off.

The aircraft gyrated viciously, with a whipping motion, that I find difficult to accurately describe. I was being tumbled about inside the fuselage like a pea in a rain barrel, and could not maintain any sense of direction, up or down, center of gravity or anything else might think they could do under those circumstances. I had previously thought what I might do if something like this were to happen, but I couldn't even put my hand in front of my face, so violent were the forces. After what seemed an eternity, during this period, I realized I was not going to get out and that I would be smashing lifeless upon striking the ground. I was almost unconscious from the beating I was taking inside the plane when the violent oscillation suddenly stopped and the plane continued falling with a rolling motion—similar to the rotation of a mixing machine, such as a concrete mixer. After an indeterminate time in this condition, I suddenly felt fresh air blow across my back, and I knew that the next time the plane rotated I would be thrown out—and sure enough, I was thrown out of some hold, like a shot, into cool, fresh air. I estimate the altitude to have been about 2500 feet, and as I got my feet pointed towards earth, I looked down and saw our aircraft fuselage falling below me, rolling over and over, with no wings on it. It appeared to me that the plane had quit burning.

I remember our briefings on being shot down, to delay opening your chute until you could see trees start to spread rapidly and you would miss some ground fire at you. I did this and when I thought it was time, I grasped my "D" ring with my right hand and pulled, but was unable to pull the rip cord. I had injured my right elbow and hadn't realized it until that moment. I then put my left hand over my right hand and pushed, opening the parachute. I swung forward and then backward and started another swing forward when I hit the ground face down in a plowed field, about 100 feet from where the fuselage of our plane hit. I wanted to run over to it, but couldn't because Germans were already coming toward me from across the field.

Thinking of escape, at some later time, I unbuckled my chute and ran about 100 feet into a clump of trees, about the size of a very small house. I quickly broke open my escape kit and hid a tube of condensed milk and an escape compass in my only boot—the right one. My left foot was completely bare. I buried the rest of the kit, containing Germany escape money and other items that I didn't want the Germans to get. As the Germans approached me, I came out of the woods toward them and fell down on my stomach, pretending to be hurt more than I actually was.

The next thing I knew they were standing all around me, both men and women. They looked to be some sort of civilian watch force whose purpose was this very thing. One woman asked me if I had a "pistola." I pretended not to understand. Another one looked at my clothes and asked a man if I was a civilian. He replied, "Nix, officere." They brought my parachute over and the women were feeling the material and looking as though they were thinking of what they could make out of it. They handed it over to some of the men.

They took me over to a road where I sat down. It wasn't until later, when I saw myself in a mirror, that I realized how terrible I must have looked. My head and face were totally covered with blood from head wounds that went to the skull and my face was totally covered in blood; you could see no skin, except for my eyelids. My left foot was also burned and cut, especially on my heel and my right elbow was injured. I was very fortunate, though!

One old man pointed a rifle at me and indicated that he

wanted me to start walking down the road, away from the others, and I had no choice but to go. I firmly believed at that time, and do now, that he intended to shoot me when we were out of sight of the others. I made up my mind that I was not going to just walk along and be shot, and I was trying to formulate a plan, in my mind, of how to jump him first, when the regular Wehrmacht soldiers came down the road in a pick-up truck and put me in the back with two of them. During this time, they were apparently checking the old man out good, which included threatening hand gestures. It was during this trip, where they took me to an airfield we had just bombed that I saw two B-24s from other groups on the ground burning and two other plumes of black smoke that I am almost certain were either other aircraft burning, or the wings from our aircraft which contained the fuel tanks. On the way to the field, as we were passing along a high bluff, someone apparently threw a brick at me from the top of the cliff and it landed in the bed of the truck. One of the young German soldiers drew his pistol and I believe he would have shot at whoever threw the brick if he had located them.

It was at the airport that I saw myself in a mirror. They took me to a room where there were three other American fliers. One of them was named Fred, and he was seriously injured in the back. Another one was named Feldman, who later turned up at Stalag Luft III with me. He was from Tulsa, Oklahoma. If I was told the name of the other flyer, I do not remember it. We were not allowed to speak to one another. I remember that the clocks in the building were stopped at 10:32 from our bombs. They took everything I had away from me, except for my handkerchief, which they must have missed. That handkerchief was really good to have, especially when I was in solitary confinement later. When I went down the corridor to the bathroom, I would wet it and carry it back to my cell and dab it around my face the best I could.

From the room at the airport I was taken to the local jail where I was put in a dark room (cell) that had a wooden bunk with nothing but boards on it. It was made to slant upwards for a pillow. (The Germans didn't mollycoddle their outcasts.) Believe it or not, I actually went to sleep, I suppose from a combination of shock and loss of blood. Later that same day I was transferred to a regular jail at Bernburg, where a German doctor supposedly tended my wounds. He put something on gauze that burned like fire and just scrubbed my head and face wounds with much unnecessary vigor. I decided he was trying to make me show pain, but I was determined to show none, and didn't. I almost fell out though, as when I was standing there everything went slowly black, but I didn't fall. I probably would have if the doctor hadn't stopped scrubbing on my wounds when he did.

I had been asking about any other fliers, hoping some of the crew might have made it, but a German major who interrogated me drew me a picture of the fuselage of our plane, showing the location of the bodies of the crew members that they had recovered. They also told me where Bill Greble and Don Hudson had been found. Greble hadn't opened his chute, and Hudson was thrown out with no chute on. He was found over half a mile from the fuselage where the others were. They showed me Greble's Zippo cigarette lighter, which was crushed like a wad of tinfoil. They also brought me Don Hudson's left flying boot to wear. I knew Bill and Don didn't make it. But I could not tell, from the information they were giving me, whether it was the truth or not. They were very cunning at obtaining information from downed fliers and we were warned about this. They could not account for the tenth, or missing man from the crew. It puzzled them. They kept asking me if I had a boxer on my crew. I told them no. It seems, as they said, they had shot and killed an airman that day who had tried to fight when they captured him. He took a swing at one of the Germans and was shot to death. I have no way of knowing whether that was the truth or not.

I was kept at Bernburg one night and sent, along with others, to Wetzlar, which seemed to be a distribution center for prisoners. I, along with others, was taken there by train. After a couple of days at Wetzlar, they loaded a whole bunch of us on another train. Those of us in my car were sent to Dulag Luft, the infamous inter-rogation center at Frankfurt on the Maine. The RAF finally fire-bombed this place because the Germans were obtaining so much intelligence from captured fliers. It was reported that only one Allied Prisoner of War lost his life in the bombing.

At Dulag Luft, I was placed in solitary confinement in room 4C. The room was about five or six feet wide, and about 8 feet long with one barred window that had wooden shutters that were kept closed, making the room quite dark. I never got out of the room except for going to the restroom and to daily interrogation in the mornings.

I was kept in this place a long time, perhaps ten or twelve days—maybe even fifteen, as I completely lost track of time. This was in violation of the Geneva Convention, which restricts hold-ing a prisoner in solitary confinement more than three days. As I was taken back and forth down the long hall to interrogation, I noticed there was a white card tacked up on my door, where only one or two others along the corridor had them—and even those would disappear after two or three days. One day I asked the guard why the card was on my door and in broken English he replied, "Why don't you speak?" He conveyed to me that they would keep me there until I was too weak to get up off the straw bunk with-out fainting, if I didn't tell them what they wanted to know. The guard seemed to be trying to warn me and I sensed that he didn't agree with my treatment. They deliberately fed starvation rations to prisoners as that was a part of the breaking-down process.

In the morning I was given a warm cup of ersatz coffee and one piece of black bread, which was thinly spread with some kind of marmalade; at noon they brought me the coffee and a small bowl of warm, watery soup; at night, the coffee with the bread again. Sometimes at night, they would bring two pieces of bread. I saved the hard crusts of the bread to scrub my teeth and washed out my mouth with the so-called coffee.

The very next weekend, after I had the talk with the partially friendly guard, I wasn't called in to be interrogated. When I asked why, I was told that my personal interrogator, a German Hauptmann (Captain) was on leave. I then said to the guard, "Why, he told me I was going to be released this weekend." To my surprise they believed me!!! They opened my shutters on my window, let me shave and clean up and even gave me a book to read. That very afternoon I was released from Dulag Luft and transferred to Stalag Luft III at Sagan, Germany. I should mention that it was obvious to me the reason they kept me for so long was because they were trying to find out where the tenth man on our crew was. They knew very well there should have been ten men on the airplane as they probably had the papers showing Hansbury as being on the flight.

Before I went outside, another POW handed me a draw string tobacco sack with enough tobacco in it, along with the papers, to roll two or three cigarettes. For the first time since I was captured, I was free to walk from a room by myself and go to another location unattended. I sat down by the side of one of the buildings with my cigarette in the warm sun and was enjoying my smoke when I heard a slow, southern drawl beside me, asking, "Can I have a draw off that cigarette?" I handed him the tobacco sack and papers and we struck up a conversation, learning we were both from Arkansas. He was Lt. Roy Dale Thompson, from Clinton, and I was from North Little Rock. We became lifelong friends and were separated only by his death by heart attack in 1984. When Tommy and I returned to the States, his fiancée introduced me to her best friend, and we have now been married for almost 44 years. I feel sure the effects of the war cut his life short some fifteen or twenty years, as he came out of prison camp with heart problems and a nerve condition.

For the longest time, after I was in Stalag Luft III, I lived in fear they would discover my absence when my interrogator returned and come to Sagan and take me back to Dulag Luft. But they never did. It may be, by that time, the war was so advanced they couldn't keep up with everything. I never gave up hope that someone other than me made it out of our plane that dreadful day, but each time a new group of "Kriegies" (prisoners) came in, I would question them, but never received any hope from anyone I talked with.

Incidentally, while I was at Dulag Luft, one of the threats they used was accusing me of being a spy. I didn't wear my dog tags and they used that as an excuse to tell me that since I had no identification, that anyone could get clothes like my uniform, and therefore they had no way of establishing that I was an American serviceman so I could be executed for spying.

Before daylight on January 28, 1945, we were marched out of Stalag Luft III because of the advancing Russians from the east. This was a miserable journey of some two to three weeks in the bitter cold and deep snow. Our German guards (some of them) were in worse shape than we were. There was one old man who got to the point where he couldn't put one foot in front of the other. He would drag his left foot, up to his right, one step at a time. The whites of his eyes were solid red with blood, and I have seen some of our own men carry the old man's rifle for him. We had orders not to escape during the march. These orders were from our own leaders. The reason was that all of Germany had been declared an area that any unauthorized person could be shot as a spy.

We walked from Sagan to Spremberg. During part of this journey two German intelligence men walked with us. They talked to us about the Russians and made the statement that they had killed fifteen million Russians and couldn't whip them—and that we (the Americans) couldn't either. They stated that we would have to team up someday to fight the Russians.

One night on this trip we stayed in a barn, and it was so cold that we stayed up and walked around most of the night to stay warm. We only had one light blanket each that we carried with us. Another night they packed so many of us in a church that the air grew stale, and we all became groggy and some men passed out. We stayed two or three nights in a pottery factory, where we were actually warm inside the building. They had some unique pottery containers there in which a man could crawl inside, and they were said to hold 1,000 liters.

At Halbau, Germany, we were standing in line in the street with snow on the ground, and it was still snowing. An old German woman kept bringing us hot water, in defiance of a Nazi party member. Each time she went back and forth by him, she would toss her head up. The party member was standing over on a corner, by a post, with his hat brim pulled down over his eyes, like a movie gangster. Out in the country, we were stopped for a rest, and there was a house close to the road. I went over to the house and traded some soap for a bag of potatoes—kartoffels in German. I asked the lady in German if she had any food she would trade me. She said she had some kartoffels and asked me what I would give her for them. I told her soap, and we made a trade. I carried the potatoes all the way to Moosburg, where we had a potato bash. There were many of our men who had varying degrees of frostbitten hands, feet and faces from walking in the bitter cold.

At Spremberg, I traded a cigarette to a German soldier in exchange for his skull and crossbones insignia, which I have to this day. He was in either a storm troop or a panzer unit, I have forgotten which. At Spremberg, we were crowded in boxcars on a long train ride and rode, standing up for the most part, the balance of the way to Moosburg. The only way one could sit down was between the legs of another man who also needed to rest. For the latter part of our stay in Moosburg, we slept in tents on the ground. It was further south, near Munich, and the snow was off the ground when we got there.

We were liberated by Patton's 14th armored force on April 29, 1945. After we were liberated, we had no food at all. We borrowed rifles, jackets and vehicles from American soldiers in the area and went out among the German population and obtained our food from them. While this may seem harsh, it was the only way we could get anything to eat. On May 1, 1945, we were flown to Camp Lucky Strike at Le Havre, France, where I obtained leave and had made arrangements to fly out to Rackheath to find out about my crew. But before I could leave, I became deathly ill with the flu and couldn't make the trip. After I felt better, I did write to the 467th group in England for information and when I arrived home in North Little Rock, I had a letter there from a Lt. Thomas Goodyear, advising me that I was the only survivor of our crew. The last sentence in his letter has often haunted me—"The Group has chalked up a good record *and life at Rackheath has continued just the same as before.*" Just the same as before. Nothing would ever be the same as before to those of us who didn't return to Rackheath from their missions—whether they managed to live through it or not.

There has been much soul-searching and considerable anguish in reliving these events. I will not belabor this account with further details. It is sufficient to say that air crew members had a special camaraderie for each other that is found only under circumstances where they routinely face danger together, time after time, and are dependent upon each other for their safety. To this day, I cannot watch a documentary of aircraft going down in battle without tears coming to my eyes for the gallant young men riding those machines of war to their deaths. I think of what might have been had the men of my crew been allowed to live and contribute their good minds, talents and enthusiasm to our world. I sometimes think that what we lost was greater than what we won.

My First Trip to Germany, And It Had to Be Berlin

Louis Loevsky, 466th

On March 22, 1944 the 466th Bomb Group and my crew flew their first mission to Berlin.

Our B-24, "Terry and the Pirates," was hit by flak over Berlin and we lost the #1 propeller. A mid-air collision then ensued, causing "Terry" to also lose props #2 and #3. The other B-24, the "Brand," lost its tail, causing it to go into a tight spin. Len Smith, our bombardier, was trapped in the "Terry" nose turret, and the electrical and manual systems had rendered it inoperable by the crash. The turret would not turn so that its doors could open to let Len out. Len had also sustained substantial injury.

Less than six hours into combat, and here I was, through as a navigator! I remembered when, less than four months before, I had heard the glorious words: "Lt. Louis Loevsky, you are now a navigator!" said my instructor as he pinned the coveted silver wings on me.

But now I had to extricate Len from his predicament, and

it was most difficult since he was in shock and kept removing his gloves (at -35F or below) and oxygen mask (at 23,500 feet). I repeatedly tried putting his mask and gloves back on while trying to spring the nose turret doors open; when I put an arm around his chest and pulled him out, that was quite an achievement. After I got Len out I released the bombs in train. Thirteen of twenty crew members were KIA, five from the "Terry" and eight from the "Brand."

After assisting Len in bailing out, our pilot, Bill Terry, yelled, "Hey, Lou, wait for me!" I waited until he left the control column, then bailed out through the bomb bay. While free falling I saw one parachute open above me, which had to be Terry's. Not trusting the Germans, I realized that with the "H" (Jewish) on my dog tags I risked being shot as a spy if I ripped them off and threw them away... and risked being shot as a Jew if I left them on and fell into the hands of the Gestapo or the SS! I left them on. Still free falling, I thought of the gross of condoms scattered in every pocket of my uniform... "My parents will think they raised a sex fiend!"

When I finally opened my parachute, I found I was being shot at from the ground. Slipping and spilling air, I became an instant expert in maneuvering the chute, despite admonitions to keep our "cotton-picking" hands off the shroud lines. I got away from a small camp where they were shooting at me, toward another small camp where they were not. Selecting a small tree in Berlin, I crossed my legs for posterity, crashed branches off one side of the tree, and with my chute caught on top, my feet whipped over my head and my back injured, I blacked out briefly and then came to with my toes touching the ground. A Home Guard (Volkssturm) had a gun in my ribs, repeating, "Pis-tole? Pis-tole?" Two Wehrmacht troops appeared and took over my custody. While I was getting out of the parachute harness, three SS arrived, apparently from the small camp where they had been shooting at me. The SS argued with the Wehrmacht; they wanted to take custody of me (and since my parents sometimes talked Yiddish, I could understand). Fortunately, the two Wehrmacht troops retained my custody.

As they marched me through the streets of Berlin to their headquarters, the angry civilian mob was yelling in perfect AMER-ICAN, "String him up!" "Hang him!" "Lynch him!" They wanted a necktie party. As they were closing in, the Wehrmacht troops had to draw their sidearm to keep the ugly lynching mob at bay. I believe Bill Terry was shot from the ground as he floated down in his parachute.

I became a POW at Stalag Luft III, Sagan, Germany until the Russians got close in January 1945. After that we were evacuated at 2 AM in a freezing blizzard. From there we reached Stalag VII A in Moosburg, by marching in sub-zero weather and being crammed into (40 & 8) boxcars. We were improperly clothed and improperly fed; our conditions were unsanitary and inhumane. Imagine hundreds of American officers and enlisted men lined up, evacuating their bowels when the train stopped at a station in full view of German women and children. We were treated like swine!

We were liberated by Gen. George Patton's troops on April 29, 1945. Joel Greenberg, flight engineer of "Terry and the Pirates," folded his wings in early 1993. Fifty-five years after the mid-air collision, the three survivors of both crews are: C. Wayne Beigel, of the "Brand" crew; Len Smith; and me, Louis Loevsky.

Are These the Final Details of Glenn Miller's Death?

Thomas E. O'Connel, 338th BG

Reprinted from the Torretta Flyer, Summer-Fall 1990

The mystery is solved. We now know quite certainly what happened to Glenn Miller. A Royal Air Force Lancaster Bomber was responsible for his disappearance on a flight from England to Paris in December 1944. The jettisoning of the Lank's bombs after an aborted mission to Germany accidentally caused a small plane flying below to spin into the English Channel. The small plane was carrying Miller, everybody's favorite World War II band leader.

Why in the world did it take forty years for the truth to emerge? The answer lies in the word "aborted." If that RAF bomber squadron had completed its bombing mission to Germany, the crews would have been debriefed after the flight was over. At that debriefing they would have been carefully quizzed by trained intelligence officers to find out everything that occurred during the mission. The Lancaster pilot and navigator who have now come forward to tell of the previously forgotten incident of their

1944 flight, would surely have informed authorities of seeing the small plane going into the Channel if that had been the case.

The particular crew in question took off in England, got in formation and headed for their target, the railway yards at Siegen, Germany. Then the weather deteriorated, and before the planes crossed into Germany they were ordered back to base. Under such circumstances, the procedure in both air forces was to jettison the bombs into the Channel. It would have been dangerous to land back in England with those heavy, volatile bombs aboard.

There was apparently one key procedural difference between the RAF and the USAF: in aborted missions the RAF bombs exploded and ours were dropped unarmed. Ours didn't explode; they dropped to the bottom of the Channel. I don't know why the RAF didn't do it this way.

I was a bombardier on the crew of a USAF bomber and flew missions from England similar to the one the "Lank" was on. I never armed our bombs until it was absolutely clear we were going to drop them on the target. In the event of jettisoning on an aborted mission, the impact on friendly craft below us would have been much less. Apparently, it was the shock waves from the exploding bombs which caused the little Norseman aircraft carrying Glenn Miller to fall into the sea. If the bombs had been from a USAF plane, Miller might be playing his lovely music even now.

Apparently, the weather was really terrible that day, December 15, 1944.

An early inquiry to the RAF about its possible inadvertent involvement in Miller's disappearance elicited the reply that "not even the pigeons were flying that day." But recently the RAF crew's navigator, who now lives in South Africa, caused an article about his suspicion of his plane's involvement in Miller's disappearance to be published in a South African newspaper. He thus set in motion a sequence of events which resulted in a further investigation of the RAF records. It turned out that, true, no RAF bombing missions were officially recorded for that date, but yes, there was one flight of 150 Lancasters which had been sent out but then ordered back.

What prompted the navigator to remember now that his fellow crew members had seen a Norseman D-64 crash in the Channel that day after their jettisoned bombs had exploded? He saw a rerun of the movie *The Glenn Miller Story* in South Africa. As a further irony, he had first seen the movie in 1954, and had realized that his crew's bombs might have been responsible for Miller's death. But when he approached newspaper reporters on the matter, they didn't pay any attention.

Of course, there were lots of airplane accidents over England and the English Channel during that period. Thousands of bomber crews were zipping all over the sky, going to continental Europe and coming back. Most of us had little training compared to today's airline crews, and air control systems were nothing like the sophisticated current ones. My crew got to England about six weeks after Glenn Miller's disappearance. By that time our planes were so numerous that there was more danger to young bomber crews in our chaotic daily pre-dawn rendezvous with planes from our own squadrons than there was from enemy action over Germany. Losing one small Norseman D-64 was no big deal.

What made it important, of course, was that Glenn Miller was on it, and he was everybody's darling. His sweet music stood for peace and for good times past and—if we all made it back—yet to come. I remember his death as a personal loss. It was so to millions of us, somewhat the way John Lennon's death was to my current students and their contemporaries.

Historical novelist Lillian de La Torre once advanced a theory that ran something like this: any historical mystery will eventually be solved if there is sufficient continuing interest in it and curious investigators are prompted to explore it for long enough. Glenn Miller's death was such a long-standing mystery. I'm glad it is solved after forty years.

"Crunch Landing" at
Seething
Oak Mackey, 448th BG

The date was January 10, 1945, a bad day for the Jack Clarke crew of the 392nd Bomb Group of the Second Air Division of the Eighth Air Force. I, Oak Mackey, was the copilot; Brad Eaton, navigator; Bob Lowe, bombardier; E.C. Brunnette, engineer; J.T. Brown, radio operator; Ralph Heilman, nose gunner; George Peer and John Heckman, waist gunners; and Kevin Killea, tail gunner; perhaps the best crew in the 8th AF.

We were awakened at 02:00 a.m. for briefing at 04:30 a.m. The target was Dasburg in the Bastogne area to support our ground troops there. The weather was absolutely atrocious—through the night there had been a combination of freezing rain, sleet, snow showers and fog. The runways and taxiways were covered with a sheet of slippery ice.

At briefing we learned that our usual B-24 was not available and we were assigned the squadron spare. We were a deputy lead crew and would be flying off the right wing of the lead plane of the leading squadron. Upon reaching our assigned airplane, we found it had not been warmed up, the engines were cold and very difficult to start. Only after much cranking, priming and cussing were we able to get them running. We were supposed to be two for take-off just after the Group lead airplane. By now most of the entire Group had departed.

We made our takeoff, climbed through the overcast to on top of the clouds and had the rest of the Group formation in sight. At this time the #3 engine propeller severely over-speeded, probably because of congealed oil trying to pass through the propeller governor. This is a serious problem—because of the engine over-speed the engine might turn to junk, or the propeller might come off the engine and pass through the fuselage or hit the other engine on that side. Jack told me to shut down the engine and feather the propeller. I reduced power to the engine and pushed the feathering button. It immediately popped out again, for it is its own circuit breaker. Brunnette was sitting between Jack and me on the cockpit jump seat, as all good engineers should. He pushed the feathering button in and held it there, which caused the secondary circuit breaker to pop open, which he immediately held down with his other hand, a risky procedure as it could cause the feathering oil pump motor or associated wiring to catch fire. Oh-so-slowly the prop blades turned to the feathered position and engine rotation stopped.

With one engine out and a loaded airplane there was no way we could stay with the Group. We were now in the vicinity of Great Yarmouth, so we flew out over the North Sea and dumped our bombs. We left the arming safety wires in place so the bombs could not explode.

As we turned to go back to our base, the #2 propeller ran away, compounding our numerous problems. We got the engine shut down and propeller feathered with less trouble than we had with #3. A B-24 cannot maintain airspeed and altitude with two engines out and full fuel tanks, and we gave careful consideration to bailing out but decided to stay with the airplane for a while and conserve altitude as best we could. The weather at our airfield near Wendling had not improved, but we had little choice but to try to return there.

We were about due south of Norwich ten miles or so when we spotted an airport through a hole in the clouds, our first good luck of the day. We descended through the hole in the clouds and had gone through the before-landing checklists, lowered wing flaps to the landing position, extended the landing gear, and were turning to line up with a runway from west of the airport when the thick bullet-resistant windshield and side windows iced up, a common occurrence when descending through a temperature inversion. We could not go around with the landing gear and flaps down with only two engines operating—we were committed to landing.

Jack and I could not see through the iced-up windshields and windows. We had to continue our descent to keep airspeed above stalling. Through a small clear place on my side window I saw men running at full speed, and I also saw that we were about to touch down. I assumed those men were running from a building of some sort and we were lined up to hit it. Without any thought and perhaps with instinct, I pushed full left rudder that caused the airplane to slew around to the left and we touched down in a sideways attitude. The landing gear snapped off, the two outside engine propellers broke off and went cart wheeling across the air-field. We slid sideways on the fuselage for a long way on the ice and snow; it seemed like forever. The fuselage was broken behind the cockpit area and the nose tilted up, which enlarged the window to my right a bit so that I was able to go through it with my backpack parachute on. Likewise, Jack went out the left cockpit window. I ran along the right side of the airplane, stopped at the waist window to look in to see if everyone was out, continued around the tail and there they were, all nine of them and no one had a scratch. We had landed at Seething Airfield, home of the 448th Bomb Group, and we had missed the control tower by only 100 feet or so.

An ambulance pulled up in a few minutes and took us to the base hospital where the doctor looked us over to be certain there were no injuries. For medicinal purposes, someone brought out a bottle of 100-proof rye whiskey. We took our medicine like real men. Someone called our base at Wendling and a truck came for us in an hour or so. So ended a bad day for the Clarke crew. It could have been much worse.

Dessau Was No Picnic!

Howard Boldt, Ray Lemons, Jack Knox and Jim Baynham, 445th

The following account occurred on our third mission, Dessau, Germany, August 16, 1944. Lt. Jimmy Baynham, and his Liberator crew somersaulted through flaming wrecks of two other planes high over Germany, and the Texarkana pilot brought 'em back alive.

"With nobody dead—just standing on our heads," that's the newest line of the wing and a prayer thing recently enacted by First Lieutenant James Baynham, of Texarkana and his Liberator crew many miles over flak-flipping Germany. He wrote the details, with military stuff excluded, in a letter to his dad, J. D. Baynham, advertising manager of the *Texarkana Gazette & Daily News*, and it's a thrilling story. Here's the way he tells it:

We got up at 0245 and headed for the mess hall to receive fresh eggs for a change—they really tasted good. Then to briefing where we were told about our mission for that day. It would be a rough one, with plenty of flak, and a good chance for fighters. So, we took off and assembled in our squadron, then group, then wing, then division and finally the whole Air Force, and headed for Germany.

As we looked ahead we could see hundreds of planes stretched for hundreds, it seemed, of miles ahead, and that many more behind us. Then we rumbled across the enemy coast, and we wondered what the people there thought, as day after day, they saw all the heavies slowly go in and then, hours later, come out again, undisturbed, the empty places filled by other ships. They should know that there must be something terrific happening far back in Germany.

As we test-fired our guns, we found we had only one gun working in the nose and one of the tail turret guns ran away, expending a quarter of its ammunition, an unpleasant situation, but not meriting an abort from the mission.

As we flew to the target, we skirted any flak areas that came up, so we didn't get any shots close to us on the way in.

As we hit the IP (initial point), and opened our bomb doors, we started getting flak. At first, it was inaccurate, and just as Hec (one of the gunners) said "They're just a bunch of farmers," they closed in on us and really got our number. We were riding through it, however, hearing the flak explode it was so close, and hearing the shrapnel hit the ship, when I looked up and saw a burning ship flying upside down about 100 feet above us. It was going very fast and diving. It looked like a derelict, burning fiercely. Charley, (the copilot) looked up and saw it too, and we both sat spellbound as it dived into the very center of the ship in front of us, not more than 100 feet away. Then we began to act. As I turned the ship to the left, the blast hit us. Both ships had exploded in a great ball of red fire, smoke and debris. As the blast hit us, the force sent us over on our backs, going down and passing through the wreckage.

Instantly Charley and I were on the controls with all we had. The amazing thing was that we were working exactly together, not fighting for the controls. I was sure we were on fire too after flying through that flame, and our only thought at the time was to right it long enough to give everyone a chance to jump.

So as we turned it back over and pulled it up, we looked, and amazingly enough, all our engines were turning. As we had turned over, the bombs had torn loose from their racks and battered the bomb bay roof and sides, then dribbled out as we righted the ship. The inside of our ship was really in a mess. Our equipment was strewn everywhere; some of it had fallen out.

Hec, in the nose turret, released the doors and came tumbling out of the turret backwards, as the explosion occurred. He was weak with the loss of oxygen, so Johnny (another crew member) applied oxygen to him. No injuries in the nose turret. Next, on the flight deck, Charley and I were not affected mentally as were the others because we were busy. Boldt, the engineer, was in the upper turret and was all right. Fields, the radioman, who was under the flight deck at the open bomb bays, was nearly thrown from the ship during the violent maneuvers, but suffered no injuries.

Next, in the waist, Lemons was thrown back towards the tail, with ammunition boxes, chaff and equipment all around him. Byrd, the other waist gunner, was in the same fix. Knox, in the tail turret, seeing the smoke and flames, thought it was our ship that had been hit, and came out of his turret, crawling through the escape hatch, the centrifugal force not permitting him to make much headway. All three were ready to bail out, but the escape hatch was jammed, and by the time they made their way to the waist windows, the plane was in an upright position again, so they realized they were okay. They were all weak from anoxia, so they sat down while regaining their strength, but there were no injuries in the waist.

Then we found we still had one bomb, and the bombardier came back and released it manually. Then we found that the bomb bay doors could not be closed, so we left them until we reached a low altitude. In the meantime, we saw that we had no brake pressure. So when we reached lower levels, I crawled out in the bomb bay and cranked the doors shut, filled the gas gauges at the same time and found we were low on gas.

When we reached the field, we proceeded to come in for a no-brake landing. We were happy when the gear came down, then the flaps also worked, and we put the flap handle down. I noticed that about 700 pounds had been built up on the brake pressure gauges. So when we hit the ground, Boldt hit the flap handle and held it down, giving us some brakes—not enough to use constantly but enough to stop us once we slowed down. So after we slowed down as much as possible, I jammed on the brakes, and as the plane skidded to the side, the throttles kept it straight, and we finally came to a stop, taxied off on the grass and got out to kiss the dear old terra firma.

Upon inspecting the ship, we found the leading edge of the wing between Nos. 1 and 2 engines had been mangled and some more wreckage had hit the right side of the fuselage, bending it. The top of the cockpit had been cracked by more wreckage. Anyway you take it, we were nine very lucky guys that day.

That's the story, Pop. I believe I left out all the censorable stuff—but it's a good story—like a bad dream, no more. I guess the reason it doesn't bother us is that it all happened so fast and was so impersonal when we thought of it afterwards. We find ourselves joking about it and wonder how the hell we do it. I guess we have to be that way.

It's A Small, Small World After All

Jack D. Pelton, 445th

It was August 16, 1944, over Dessau, Germany that some lucky flak gunner found the "Sweetest Rose of Texas" at about 20,000 feet, just after bombs away. This wasn't our regularly assigned B-24; our war weary old bird was hanger-bound back at Tibenham and we had been assigned Arnold Nass' "The Rose," as it was affectionately known by its crew. Whoever the gunner was, he really peppered our big-ass bird with 88mm shells until he got lucky and severely damaged our flight control system with a hit that affected our elevator trim tabs in such a way that the elevators were thrown into a full nose-up position. The result was a full hammer head stall out of formation. After dropping rapidly to about 15,000 feet before recovering control, we surveyed our situation. The plane looked like a flying sieve. It had about 150 flak holes, radio knocked out, and severe damage to the flight control system—so bad, in fact, that my copilot and I could only maintain level flight by bracing our knees against the wheel and "stiff-arming" it with both arms. Fortunately, we had all four fans running, although No. 3 had a flak hole in the reduction gear housing and had lost all of its oil. Thanks to Mr. Pratt & Mr. Whitney, who made a superb engine, it continued running, without oil, all the way back to England! We made it with an escort of P-51s, Jugs (Thunderbolts), and a covey of P-38s for top cover and set the old girl down on the crash landing strip at Manston (or was it called Woodbridge?) We were afraid we might have flat tires around the wheel wells, so I gently dropped her in from about 100 feet with a 30-degree crab. She rolled to a stop in about 1500 feet. My flight engineer, Ray Pytel, didn't even say "boo" about the heavy landing. He just got out and kissed the ground like the rest of us.

The scene now changes to Hawthorne Municipal Airport in the Los Angeles area. It's May of 1993 and I have gone to see the "All American" B-24 and that restored primary trainer, the 909 B-17. I was also responsible for the Second Air Division recruitment booth that day. I noticed a man and his wife carefully examining our display of 1944 Group locations and airfield layouts in England. I approached the couple and asked if they were interested in what they saw, and did they have any questions. He answered, "No, is was on the odder end." I asked what he meant. He replied, "I vass a flak gunner mit de Cherman ground forces in central Chermany." Not only was he a flak gunner, it turned out he was directing the fire over Dessau on August 16, 1944! He remembered knocking two or three Liberators out of the sky on that fateful day. I asked him how he could be so damn accurate with those 88s. He told me they had optics so superior that he would see the waist gunners firing. He was only fourteen years old and had been "recruited" into the Hitlerjugend Corps when there were no more mature men left to man the flak guns. We had an interesting conversation and came to the conclusion that it was likely he had been responsible for our near-demise.

It is, indeed, a small world after all!!

448th's Mission to an Underground Oil Storage Facility

Jeff Brett

On 25 March 1945, 448th BG crews were awakened early, 1:30, for the briefing. John Stanford was one of the many men listening to the briefing that morning. *"Gentlemen, your target for today is the underground oil storage depot at Buchen. The secondary target will be the marshalling yards at Osnabruck. You will carry twenty 300-pound General Purpose bombs."* Lt. Robinson was the briefing officer and he continued with details of the mission. He showed us areas where we could expect flak, and said we could come under attack by 100 to 200 single-engine prop fighters and 40 to 50 Me-262 jet fighters. He ran through the order of penetration and other miscellany—code word for the target was 'Hayride'; for the secondary 'Cornsilk'; the recall word 'Coke'; fighter call signs, 'Balance 21 and 22'; weather scout, 'Bootleg Rum'; code word for dropping chaff, 'Black Sheep'; time in the air, 6:40; and time on oxygen, 3:30.

Palm Sunday morning erupted with a roar as the propellers of the Liberators spun to life at Seething. After an uneventful assembly, the formation encountered trouble leaving the English coast. Clouds thickened as they neared the Zuider Zee, making formation flying difficult. The lead squadron elected to fly in a circle in an effort to climb above the clouds. Lt. Elmer Homelvig, flying OLD POP, struggled to stay with his formation as they entered the clouds. *"We did alright for a few seconds. Apparently they increased their turn rate, and it's like snapping a whip, the guy on the tail end always gets the message later, and of course they increase their rate of turn. I lost sight of Tod (Lt. Fred Tod), and the only thing I could do was gradually increase my turn, hoping I'd catch sight of him before I ran into him. It wasn't more than a few seconds later that I saw a plane coming at me in the opposite direction, coming right at me. After we got on top of the clouds, Stalland was calling out giving his position, and in a few minutes, we found and caught up with him. Stalland had only two airplanes with him; I assumed they were Ray and Wikander. Tod was not with him, or had taken a different position. Stalland kept flying in a circle, and we kept picking up additional airplanes. We finally ended up with eight airplanes."* The turn scattered the formation, leaving the 713th BS perilously out of position and lagging behind the remainder of the Group. Despite their scattered state the Group continued with the 713th vainly trying to make up time. By the time they reached the Wing Initial Point, they were still two minutes behind.

Just after 10:00 the sky filled with German fighters. A large force of Me-262s attacked the 448th with deadly results. Sgt. Clair Rowe, a gunner on SONIA, witnessed the jet attacks. He shot one of the attackers down before his aircraft was seriously damaged. *"When he began the attack, I began firing as soon as I thought he was in range. I saw two puffs of smoke when he fired his cannon, which was followed by a loud explosion, and I was blown out of my turret. I immediately got up and put on my chute and opened the* escape hatch. *We had no communication with anyone up front. Since the waist gunner was lying on the floor, I took over the waist gun. The explosion on the right side of the ship had knocked out our communication system and rudder controls. Our fighter escort then arrived, and we got home without further incident.*" When the cannon shell tore into SONIA, the plane dropped 1,500 feet, but the pilots were able to regain the formation. The shrapnel dug into Sgt. Rowe's left leg and foot as well as causing lacerations on his face. With several wounded crew members and a severely damaged plane, the crew of SONIA faced a daunting return trip.

Sgt. Ed Chu fought a raging battle in the tail turret of MY BUDDIE. "*Before the IP, Max, our copilot, called 'Bandits in the area.' I saw three planes approaching out of the sun at six o'clock level. When they got within range, I recognized them as Me-262s. I opened fire at approximately one thousand yards at the closer of the two, the third in trail. I continued firing until he broke away through the squadron toward two o'clock high. I observed no hits or damage to confirm hits, although my tracers appeared to go right into the jet. P-51s boxed one up in front of the squadron and he exploded. Out of the corner of my eye, I could see the plane on our left wing flying the left element, 'Purple Heart Corner,' peel off and in flames. No chutes were observed and the plane was later seen hitting the ground and exploding. We later were told that it was Steffan's crew. Another Me-262 appeared at six o'clock, and this time I opened fire at extreme range. My left gun jammed, the ammo locking up in the booster sprockets. P-51s kept this jet from the formation. 'Bombs were away' and they appeared to have landed in an open field. Four more planes approached from six o'clock level. They looked like jets and I opened fire at extreme range with my one remaining gun, but stopped firing when I recognized them as P-51s. There was a P-47 off to the right being shot at by some other gunners, but luckily they recognized it before it was hit. I recall swearing at those gunners under my breath not to shoot, as it was one of ours. P-51s and P-47s dove by our formation after the jets, one P-47 cutting real close to our tail. I saw a B-24 explode and another one spin down in flames, as jets hit a trailing squadron.*" It was the 713th BS still trying to catch the formation.

The first attacks hit the main part of the formation. Lt. Joseph Steffan and crew in TARFU II fell first at 10:17 after Me-262s hit them with cannon fire over Dömitz, Germany. The navigator, Lt. Gerald Gottlieb, bailed out of the burning bomber after the interphone was destroyed. *"I suspected the plane exploded after I left it because I was knocked unconscious for a short while and regained consciousness just before hitting the ground."* The last time Lt. Gottlieb heard from his crewmates was during an interphone check two minutes before the attack. Only he survived. The aircraft crashed near Langenhorst, Germany, and was totally destroyed.

After the initial pass, the fighters focused their attention on the straggling low left squadron. Cannon fire exploded in the flight deck of the lead aircraft, 42-50646 at 10:20, mortally wounding the pilot, Lt. Knute Stalland, and the copilot, Lt. Theodore Warner. F/O John Stanford watched from his nearby aircraft. *"The bursts moved up on Stalland's plane, and suddenly he is on fire—bright red-orange flames sweeping back from the left wing inboard fuel tanks. The plane dropped fifty feet or so, recovers, slides off out of formation to the right to about 200 feet, in a shallow climb. Then it pauses and starts to swing back towards the squadron. Someone jumps from the stricken bomber, his chute opening immediately, and boots flying off from the sudden jar. We are at 19,500 feet. It is 10:46."*

Suddenly, the right wing ripped off the fuselage and the plane exploded. The bombardier, Lt. John McHugh, bailed out through the nose wheel door escape hatch. Flames quickly engulfed the B-24 as it started its death spiral. The pilotage navigator, Lt. William Whitson, intended to follow Lt. McHugh but the plane exploded, blowing him clear. Although uninjured, he pulled the ripcord and was captured. The explosion also saved the radio operator, Sgt. Bobbie Glass. The force of the explosion rendered him unconscious just as he buckled his parachute. He fell ten to fifteen thousand feet before regaining consciousness. Amazingly, his parachute dangled from his chest harness by a single clip. He connected it and pulled the ripcord, only to be captured shortly after landing near Schneverdingen, Germany. These three men were the only survivors from the crew of twelve. A normal crew complement consisted of nine to ten men, but lead crews routinely carried twelve due to the specialized equipment.

DO BUNNY with Lt. Paul Jones and his crew went down next. On the first pass, Me-262s knocked out their number one engine with 20-millimeter cannon fire despite the curtain of lead from the B-24s fifty caliber machine guns. Subsequent passes by the Me-262 and a JG7 and flown by Luftwaffe ace Lt. Rudolf Rademacher further crippled Lt. Jones' Liberator. Two more engines ceased and numerous holes filled the aluminum skin of the plane. An exploding shell knocked the engineer out of the top turret and the plexiglass tail turret exploded in the face of the tail gunner. Somehow both escaped injury. Fuel and hydraulic fluid from the ruptured lines filled the inside of the aircraft, creating a potentially explosive situation. Also, the electrical system and intercom both failed. To the radio operator, Sgt. Chuck Blaney, the aircraft looked like a sieve from the inside.

"Lt. Jones ordered everyone to bail out, but with no intercom it was obvious that the word did not get out. Also, we were reluctant to jump because intelligence reports suggested that a crew's chances of survival were amplified if we were captured as a group. Single crewmen in the hands of angry German civilians were a poor risk in these times. Our navigator, Lt. Herman Engel, could see the heavy clouds of smoke caused by our heavy bombing in the Hamburg area. He was

able to set a course toward Wesel on the Rhine where British para-troopers had landed just the day before. I guess that we never really expected to make the Rhine, even as we threw everything out of the plane that was not nailed down.

Our copilot, Lt. Jim Mucha, kept his eye peeled on a safe place to set DO BUNNY in a soft landing. With minimum power and con-trollability, our candidate landing sites were always dead ahead. At 11:43 we were at 2,000 feet altitude and sinking fast. One sputter-ing engine does not provide much power to a B-24 even at minimum loading. The pilots had selected a perfect field to put DO BUNNY down. It was right on the edge of the town of Soltau. We came in wheels-up and all went smooth until one wing dipped and the plane broke up. It was now 11:48 and we had covered all of thirty-six miles of the 180 needed to reach the front lines and freedom. The pilot, copi-lot, tail and ball gunners were able to get out of the aircraft and were immediately greeted by angry town folks with pitchforks.

An SS officer appeared on the scene and arranged to have those crew members already outside of the aircraft run into the town square about 500 yards away. There they were all pinned to a wall across the street from the Mehr Hotel. I was trapped in the wreckage along with the navigator, flight engineer, and nose gunner. We had been pinned there by the top turret that broke away from the aircraft frame and lodged in the flight deck well. The navigator and engineer were unharmed and finally got out after German soldiers axed their way into the wreckage. The nose gunner and I were not so lucky. We were trapped by the top turret and each of us suffered a broken leg. The Soltau Chief of Police joined the German soldiers from the nearby riding academy and after much hard prying and much hack sawing we were freed from the wreckage. They put us on a horse-drawn cart and took us to the town hospital where our legs were set and put in soft casts. We then rejoined the other crew members who were not locked up at the riding academy."

Meanwhile, cannon fire from the four Me-262s tore into EAGER ONE, flown by Lt. Frederick Tod. The damage was severe: Right side flight control cables severed, right flap shot off, right rudder missing, four-foot hole in the left wing, generators out, amplifiers out, main fuel line leaking, upper and tail turrets inoperative, hydraulics gone, radio destroyed, and pilot's interphone not working. EAGER ONE immediately fell out of formation and started lagging behind. The B-24 vibrated and shuddered, testifying to the tremendous damage the Liberator endured. Despite the terrific pounding, Lt. Tod and the copilot, Lt. Warren Peterson, kept flying the aircraft. With some difficulty, the bombs were jettisoned and the engineer stopped the fuel leak. Shortly afterwards, a fire started in the number four engine but extinguished itself after they feathered the engine.

The navigator, Lt. Herman James, provided a heading and distance to the nearest emergency airfield, Malmo, Sweden. Lt. Tod ordered everyone to prepare to evacuate the aircraft, as continued flight was uncertain. He advised everyone they could bail out over Germany if they did not want to risk an over-water flight. Everyone remained. With control problems and an engine out, the crew threw all non-essential equipment overboard. Still, they descended while a German Ju-88 followed to witness their demise.

Approaching the southern coast of Sweden, the number three engine started running very erratically and another engine became uncontrollable. Lt. Peterson told everyone to prepare to bail out as soon as they reached the coast. From his position in the nose of the aircraft, Lt. Herman James noticed incredible physical strain on the pilots. Lt. Tod's right leg shook violently from fatigue. They kept the airplane in level flight by sheer strength.

The number three engine abruptly stopped and Lt. Tod issued the bail out order. After Lt. James exited the aircraft, he watched the plane turn away from the village of Falsterbo and head back toward the sea, a selfless act that undoubtedly saved many lives in the village. As the eighth man in the nine-man crew left the plane, the B-24 entered a spin and crashed into the Baltic Sea just off the coast. Obviously, fatigue caught up with the pilots and as Lt. Peterson attempted to bail out, Lt. Tod was not able to fly the crippled plane any longer.

On the ground, numerous people witnessed the life or death struggle. Mr. Herald Anderson and Mr. Lennart Ahlstrom were two men who rushed to the waterfront to help in the rescue. As the parachutes floated earthward, the pursuing German Ju-88 finally caught up with its intended victim, although too late to inflict more damage. Swedish anti-aircraft fire scared them away. The two Swedish men quickly located a boat and set out for the crash site to help anyone in need. Meanwhile, other locals rolled up their pants and waded into the water to help those who landed short of land. One, Sgt. Chester Labus, suffered shrapnel wounds in his leg but managed to make it safely ashore. The wind blew some of the men overland where local residents quickly aided them. Mr. Ahlstrom and Mr. Anderson recovered Lt. Peterson but despite their valiant efforts, Lt. Peterson drowned. Lt. Tod perished in the crash of the B-24. Due to their heroic actions, seven of the crew survived. These two gallant pilots were posthumously awarded the Silver Star for their heroic actions.

After the brutal attacks, the low left squadron fell further behind. However, they dropped their bombs on the target at 10:34, nine minutes after the rest of the 448th. Realizing they would not catch the formation, the decimated squadron took a more direct route back to Seething instead of the intended route flown by the rest of the bombers. With many damaged planes and wounded men, they needed the shortest route home.

While the crew of EAGER ONE fought for their lives, the crew of SONIA held their breath as their plane limped home. A thorough examination of their plane revealed extensive damage. Their hydraulic system was ruptured, rendering it inoperative. The pilot, Lt. William Holden, elected to land at the long emergency runway at Manston. They manually lowered the landing gear and prepared to land without brakes and flaps. Despite missing one rudder, they landed on the long runway without complications. Lt. Douglas Torrance landed short of home. He selected a forward airfield in Belgium to land his shot-up Liberator.

Lt. Ed Anderson struggled to keep his damaged aircraft 42-50590 airborne. With two engines shut down, the crew dumped everything overboard. They even resorted, although unsuccessfully, to using a crash axe in an attempt to jettison the ball turret. With four P-51s providing escort, they received headings from a homing station to a forward airfield. Using maximum braking they stopped the damaged Liberator on the short runway and followed a Jeep to a parking spot. As they parked, the two remaining engines sputtered and shut down as they ran out of fuel.

After taking the shorter route home, the battered remnants of the 713th BS arrived over Seething thirty minutes before the rest of the formation. Red flares indicating wounded on board shot skyward from numerous planes. It was the first indication to the ground crews of the severe beating the Liberators endured.

Damage from the jets was tremendous. Four crews were missing and their friends at Seething wondered about their fates. Thirteen B-24s endured damage but still brought their crews home. Still, numerous men suffered injuries ranging from small lacerations to more severe shrapnel injuries. After a long absence, the Luftwaffe struck back with a mighty blow. Only three other missions flown by the 448th during the entire war suffered more losses. All were early in the war except this one. The new jets attacked with near impunity, as the family escorts were unable to match their tremendous speed. They added a new dimension to the air war and reinstalled the fear of the Luftwaffe in the aircrews.

Half A Mission Gets You

W. A. Henderson, 392nd

A person flying combat always takes for granted that it won't happen to him. Then, the day of reckoning comes and you are listed as, "Missing in action." You always wondered what happens when a plane went down, and now you know. Our turn was Gotha—24 Feb. 1944. Our crew was on its 22nd mission.

Just as we turned on the bomb run, six FW 190's came in at 12:00 o'clock level; eight more 2:00 o'clock high. We were hit in #4 engine and the oil pressure zeroed out, so #4 was feathered. Another pass just after bombs away and they got #3 engine and set it on fire. Number 4 engine was un-feathered in hopes we could keep up with the Group, but since it had no oil, it promptly ran away. Johns put the airplane in a steep dive to try to blow out the fire; #4 tachometer had wound around beyond the numbers—screaming away. There was no question—get out and walk! He slowed the aircraft down for bail out—leveling off about 8000 ft.

The bail out was accomplished, but not without a bit of unintended humor. When we rang the bell, "prepare to bail out" the bombardier was locked in the nose turret. He called the navigator to let him out. And what was the navigator doing? Folding maps, putting things away neatly. He finally did open the nose turret door and out tumbled the bombardier. As the navigator was first of the two to bail out, he crouched over the open nose wheel doors, turned to the bombardier and said, "Push me." The #11 shoes did that—post haste.

I made a free fall from about 7500 ft. to about 2000 ft. because we had been told the German fighter pilots might shoot you in your parachute if it looked like you might get away. You never think of the chute not opening while free falling, and mine opened just as it was supposed to. As I was coming down in my chute, I counted the others. Two chutes were missing. We later learned after the war that the graves registration teams had found the graves of waist gunner, Felix Zerangue, and engineer, Jack Indahl. As I neared the ground, our B-24 had made a steep 360° diving spiral and was headed for me when a friendly came between us.

The search party sent out by the Germans had about eight people in it. They were coming on foot on a road that had a very elongated bend because of a long ridge covered with pine trees about a foot in diameter. I reasoned that it would take some time for them to reach that bend, so after burying my chute in the foot-deep snow, I hurried over the hill onto the same road and ran toward them—wanting to be in a position near to them so they would pass me before starting the search. At the bend I got off the road and into the timber and watched them pass by, about 100 ft. away. They had guns, pitch forks, and the like for weapons, not a very friendly reception committee. After they had gone past, I continued through the trees to the road on the far side of the bend; got on it and walked away as if I was one of the search party returning.

I walked across a field in foot deep snow to a railroad to head south, and home. A troop train went by. The soldiers waved and I waved back thinking, "You would be off that train in a hurry if you knew who I was." This gave me confidence in my lack of identity, so I walked down the railroad through a small town, acknowledging greetings with a raise of the hand or a nod of the head, but not speaking. Apparently this was customary of the German populace at the time.

The next town was larger. I could speak very little German, but I could understand it to some degree. I asked a German for a drink of water, but I could not say it like a native. He became suspicious. My ankle was swollen, either badly sprained or broken. He took me to the Mayor of the town, who in turn called the authorities.

Thus ended my missions with the 392nd Bomb Group, and the start of sixteen months of prisoner of war time. Next came the ride to the P.O.W. camp, the interrogations, and the delousing, but those events are another series of stories.

Mission with a

Surprise Ending

Robert W. "Bob" Lambert, 453rd

How many of you old-timers from the 453rd Bomb Group remember a B-24 plane named the "Lonesome Polecat?" As a replacement crew, we inherited this wonderful plane in May 1944. After many successful missions, with a number of close calls, we flew its last mission with Jimmy Woolley as our pilot and I was the radio man. Our crew picture with this plane and some formation missions are in the book *In Search of Peace.*

I am not sure, but I believe this mission was over Hamburg, Germany; if not it was another large city where the sky was black with flak. During our bombing run (bombs dropped) we were hit several times and lost an engine. As we pulled away from the formation, a second engine on the opposite wing began to cough and act up. A short time later, we lost the second engine and gradually began to lose altitude. We stayed aloft, continuing to lose altitude, but since we were over enemy territory our pilot felt it was best to see how far we could go.

After what seemed like an eternity, we finally could see the English Channel. I was immediately told to send an S.O.S., as we

317

probably could not make it across the Channel. I pressed so hard on the key (thinking the signal would go farther) that it broke off; I had to quickly jury-rig an alternative and kept on sending SOS signals until I received a response. Then I continued a signal so they could obtain a fix on our location.

While I was doing this, the crew was ordered to throw everything out of the plane into the Channel that was not fastened down. Out went the guns, ammunition, equipment, etc. In the excitement even a gunner's parachute was tossed out—what a shock—plans were quickly made that if we were to jump, Barney Feeney (a waist gunner) would take Jack Day with him and the two would go down together on one chute.

Even with the loss of weight, we were still losing altitude and getting closer to the water. Jump or ditch? As we got even closer to water we prepared to ditch. We then saw the coast of England in the distance and counted our blessings. Maybe we could reach shore and land somewhere on the beach area. However, we felt it would be safer to ditch and then swim ashore.

As we were thinking "ditch," our pilot saw a patch of grass he thought he could make and headed for that. We barely cleared the surrounding trees and our pilot was able to land our shot-up B-24 on the grassy area. We all climbed out and kissed the ground. When we looked up, we found we were surrounded by British troops with Tommy-guns and rifles pointed right at us. They stated in English and German that we were under arrest. Naturally we were surprised and spoke to them in English. They paid no attention; ordered us to put our hands behind our heads and marched us to a hidden building. As we did this, we saw many strange planes strategically placed under the umbrella of trees with camouflage netting over some of them. We were ushered into a room and then they asked for the commander of our aircraft. They took our pilot away while we were guarded by British troops.

After what seemed like hours, our pilot came in saying we had landed on a very secret British Royal Air Force experimental aircraft base. They thought we were German spies flying in on a captured American plane. Our 2nd Air Division Headquarters cleared us as Americans returning from a mission.

The British then became friendly and furnished us with tea and crumpets. Later we were led to a waiting bus that returned us to our base at Old Buckenham for debriefing, food and bed. We all *counted our blessings*, being very thankful we were all alive and "home."

Still To Come...

Because there was too much material to fit into one book. *BOMBS AWAY! Volume II* has an additional 73 war stories.

World War II Photos
and Maps from the
Author's Collection

Celebrating graduating from cadets, Santa Ana, California Air Base

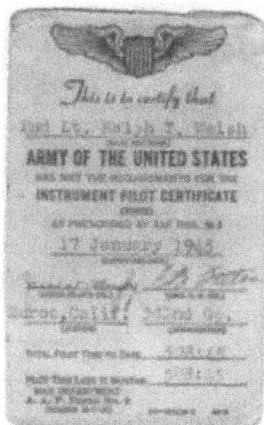

Pilot Certification for the author.

THE DEFINITIVE MAP OF VIII BOMBER COMMAND BASES

Smoke screens were put up by Germans to hide targets.

This thick flak glass is from my Mission #15 to Berlin. The angle of the flak would have come out of the middle of my chest (where there's a heart). So thankful for the thick flak glass this day!

448th BG B-24 dissected by German jet.

Bomber crews and ground crew personnel awaiting the return of bomber groups from a mission.

About the Author

Col. Judy presenting me with a DFC for completing 33 missions.

Experienced great depression, WWII pilot/commander 33 European bombing missions. College, stockbroker, manager, finder/intermediary sale of eleven companies to H.J. Heinz, Labatt, etc. Founder, owner of a graphic arts supply mail order company for 30 years, and retired at age 87. Married to Ann for 60 years. Three fine boys, one great girl...